W9-DGE-814

WITNESS TO WAR:

A Thematic Guide to Young Adult Literature on World War II, 1965-1981

by

CATHRYN J. WELLNER

The Scarecrow Press, Inc.
Metuchen, N.J., & London
1982

Permission to reprint the following is gratefully acknowledged:

Quotes on pages 106, 158, and 159 from Bright Candles: A Novel of the Danish Resistance by Nathaniel Benchley. Copyright © 1974 by Nathaniel Benchley. Reprinted by permission of Harper & Row, Publishers, Inc.

Quotes on pages 77-78, 97, and 172 from The Evil That Men Do: The Story of the Nazis by Arnold P. Rubin. Copyright © 1977 by Arnold P. Rubin. Reprinted by permission of Julian Messner, a Simon & Schuster division of Gulf & Western Corporation.

Quotes on pages 38-39 and 186-187 from Fly Away Home by Christine Nöstlinger. Translated by Anthea Bell. New York: Watts, 1975. Reprinted by permission of Blackie and Son Ltd.

Quotes on pages 79, 80, and 81 from Fragments of Isabella: A Memoir of Auschwitz by Isabella Leitner, edited by Irving A. Leitner (Thomas Y. Crowell, Publishers). Copyright © 1978 by Isabella Leitner and Irving A. Leitner. Reprinted by permission of Harper & Row, Publishers, Inc.

Quote on page 101 from Friedrich by Hans Peter Richter. Translated by Edite Kroll. Copyright © 1961 by Sebaldus-Verlag GmBH Nürnberg. Copyright © 1970 by Holt, Rinehart and Winston. Reprinted by permission of Holt, Rinehart and Winston, Publishers, and Penguin Books Ltd.

Quotes on pages 7-8, 22-23, 25, 59-60, 63-65, 104, 133-135, and 196-197 from Howl Like the Wolves: Growing Up in Nazi Germany by Max von der Grün. Translation copyright © 1980 by William Morrow and Company, Inc. Originally published in German under the title Wie war das eigentlich?--Kindheit und Jugend im Dritten Reich von Max von der Grün; © 1979 by Hermann Luchterhand Verlag, Darmstadt und Neuwied, West Germany. Reprinted by permission of William Morrow and Hermann Luchterhand Verlag.

Quotes on pages 3-4, 5-6, 10-11, and 36 from I Was There by Hans Peter Richter. Translated by Edite Kroll. Copyright © 1972 by Edite Kroll. Reprinted by permission of Holt, Rinehart and Winston, Publishers, and Penguin Books Ltd.

Quotes on pages 43, 53-56, and 71-72 from Mischling, Second Degree by Ilse Koehn. Copyright © 1977 by Ilse Koehn. Reprinted by permission of Greenwillow Books (a division of William Morrow & Co.) and Hamish Hamilton Ltd.

Quotes on pages 27, 83-84, and 199-200 from Playing for Time by Fania Fénelon. Translated by Judith Landry from Sursis pour l'orchestre. Copyright © 1977 by Michael Joseph, Ltd., and Atheneum Publishers (New York: Atheneum, 1977). Reprinted by permission of Michael Joseph, Ltd. and Atheneum Publishers.

Quotes on pages 92-93, 136-137, 192, and 193 from Time of the Young Soldiers by Hans Peter Richter. Translated by Anthea Bell. Harmondsworth, Middlesex, England: Kestral Books, 1976. Reprinted by permission of Penguin Books Ltd.

Library of Congress Cataloging in Publication Data

Wellner, Cathryn J., 1946-
  Witness to war.

  Bibliography: p.
  Includes index.
  1. World War, 1939-1945--Germany. 2. World War,
1939-1945--Germany--Bibliography. 3. Germany--History--
1933-1945. 4. Germany--History--1933-1945--Bibliography.
I. Title.
D757.W387   940.53'43   82-5600
ISBN 0-8108-1552-4   AACR2

Copyright © 1982 by Cathryn J. Wellner
Manufactured in the United States of America

To my husband and Uncle Alex

TABLE OF CONTENTS

PREFACE

Dozens of books have been written that can broaden young people's understanding of the human stories behind the political, economic, statistical, and military history of World War II. Until now no guide has been available to help those searching for novels or memoirs or other books which fall outside the scope of textbooks. This guide is intended to fill that gap. It is designed to be used by secondary school teachers, librarians, students, education and library school professors, and children's and young adult literature specialists.

The books cited here represent a rich resource. Many of them were written by people who were witnesses to the events they describe. They have an immediacy which no straight presentation of facts can have. It is difficult to grasp the meaning of something as monstrous as the destruction of 6,000,000 Jews, but anyone can empathize with a Jewish child who is tormented by a group of Hitler Youth (Hans Peter Richter, Friedrich) or a teenager who has to help prepare people for transport to concentration camps (Marietta Moskin, I Am Rosemarie). As Horst Burger wrote in Vier Fragen an meinen Vater:

> Today it is generally known what happened then.
> There are numbers and statistics to prove everything. But the way it really was, how people
> thought, what they felt, what they believed and
> hoped, and what they actually knew--that can only
> be learned from themselves. [p. 7]

About no other war are there so many books for young readers which reveal the dislocations suffered by people on all sides of a conflict. Few of the authors are historians. They sometimes make mistakes or twist events to fit their own philosophies. Their books are not intended to stand alone as a record of the period. What they do accomplish is something no textbook can. They put flesh and blood on the bare bones of history. Books glorifying war are absent here. Authors of the past fifteen years have concentrated more on war's savage effects, its power to destroy normal human ties. These are books to make young people think, to make them angry, to make them weep, to make them understand.

The books described in this guide were published in English, German, and/or French. Not only does this make the guide useful to readers in countries where those languages are spoken, but it also makes it a valuable resource for teachers of foreign languages, students whose mother tongue is not the language of instruction, and those who are interested in a comparative study not possible in any one language. The books were all issued or reprinted since 1965 and represent a wide range of viewpoints, from that of the victims of Nazi oppression to those who profited from it. The resurgence of interest in World War II in the last few years has brought many out-of-print titles back into circulation. Of the 178 books described, 101 have been published in English, 96 in German, and 53 in French.

The absence of books concerning the war in Japan and the Pacific does not imply a lack of importance. There are fewer such books, but they would be an appropriate subject for another guide. More translations need to be done to bring some of the titles published in Japan to Western audiences. The reason for the lack of books about Italian fascists must be sought in the silence of Italian authors.

The guide can be used in a variety of ways:

1. By librarians as a source of books to suggest to teachers and students, an aid in preparing bibliographies, and as a help in preparing booktalks. The last approach is strongly recommended. Taking the books into the classroom and presenting them personally is the most effective way of encouraging their use and reaching students with them.

2. By teachers wishing to expand their students' understanding of World War II. Students can be asked to read books about particular topics, to compare the experiences of people in the affected countries, to relate their own concerns and inter-

ests to those of teenagers during wartime, or to contrast the attitudes of Hitler Youth with opponents of Nazism. Teachers can also use particular books or passages as stimuli for classroom discussions, since many of them are provocative.

3. By foreign language and literature teachers working in conjunction with history teachers to provide an interdisciplinary approach.

4. By students on their own, pursuing a personal interest or looking for books to help them fulfill an assignment.

5. By those training future teachers and librarians. With the current emphasis on reading, new teachers and librarians need to be made aware of books that can help them spark their students' interest.

School and public librarians are key people to cultivate. They can gather those books which are available locally, prepare them for distribution, buy or borrow others, bring them into classrooms for group presentations, and deal with the personal requests and interests of students and teachers.

Witness to War is easy to use. Someone interested in how the Nazis molded schools as an instrument of indoctrination can turn to the section on "Schools" in Chapter 2 to find books in which the topic is treated and a summary of related episodes. A title in French, English, or German does not mean that the book is available in only that language. Translations are listed in the bibliography at the end of the guide. A brief description of every book, along with an indication of the country in which it is set, whether it is fiction or non-fiction, the reading level, and the relative importance of the book in terms of a study of World War II are included in the bibliography. Books which are relevant but not discussed in detail are listed as "Additional titles" at the end of many sections. The index provides a further point of access to related books which are discussed in other sections of the guide.

Page numbers following quotes in the text refer to the English-language edition whenever possible. For books available only in French or German, pages cited refer to the editions listed first in the bibliography. They are given when

ix

the episode described is an isolated passage but are omitted when it represents a major or oft-repeated thrust of the book. When quotations have been translated, the page numbers refer to the edition translated by the person cited in brackets. If no name appears after a translated passage, I have provided the English myself.

Following the bibliography is a list of curriculum sources to help teachers plan a course of study. Many of the items listed include teaching activities and suggestions for additional text and audio-visual resources. The address of the distributor is included with each entry.

Educators are recognizing more and more the value of enriching the study of history with novels and memoirs. This guide will help those who want to know what books to recommend to their students. In addition, these books have significance beyond the study of one war. They explore the minds and hearts of people who have experienced war and been scarred by it. Perhaps they can have an impact on the young people who will one day be called upon to make decisions concerning peace and war. Witness to War is a tool for caring educators, who know that our actions in the future are based in part on our understanding of the past.

In doing the research for this guide, I was able to work at the International Youth Library in Munich (Internationale Jugendbibliothek, Kaulbachstrasse 11a, D-8000 Müchen 22, West Germany), a unique institution which houses the only truly international collection of children's and young adult books in the world. With funding from government sources, books supplied by publishers, a small staff, and visiting scholars, the IYL provides access to books from around the globe. My thanks to all those staff members who provided materials, suggestions, and support during my stay in Munich. Special thanks go to Beatrix von Reiswitz, who believed in what I was doing and collected books, articles, and ideas for me from the library, publishers, newsstands, and even demonstrators.

Cathryn J. Wellner
Munich, Germany
August 1981

Chapter 1

HITLER AND HIS CREW

On the anniversary of Hitler's birthday in 1981, plain-clothes policemen kept watch at the Feldherrenhalle in Munich. The hall and the square in front of it were the site of countless rallies and speeches during World War II and came to symbolize National Socialism. As expected, a man approached the hall with a wreath that day in 1981, wanting to honor his dead hero. He was promptly whisked away. Elsewhere, in an inn in the Black Forest, a group of old comrades came together to commemorate the occasion. An eavesdropper overheard one of them bragging of having shot 500 Jews and 100 Russians. Old habits die slowly.

Parents, politicians, and educators in Germany talk about a disturbing increase in neo-Nazism among youth. Swastikas and other Nazi symbols appear on school walls. Students use Nazi terminology and make anti-Semitic jokes. Children on playgrounds greet each other with, "Heil Hitler!" Hundreds join extreme right and neo-Nazi organizations. I have witnessed incidents of the same morbid fascination for the trappings of the Third Reich among American junior high and high school students.

The generation of youth Hitler misused for his monstrous ends was the same age as the young people the books in this guide are intended to reach. The Third Reich needed them. They collected millions of marks that were supposedly for the poor but ended up in the war coffers. They were a ripe training ground. The boys were trained to be soldiers and the girls to be housewives and mothers. Childbearing was the highest goal for girls, for to bear a child for the Führer was to maintain the supply of warriors. Children were taught to report anyone not showing enthusiasm for the government or the war. Even their parents were afraid of

1

them. From the age of six, they became members of Hitler
Youth organizations, their training carefully planned so as to
make them tools in Nazi hands.

Children and adolescents are particularly vulnerable
to skillful manipulators. Studying the ways in which others
have been used is no assurance of immunization, but it is
surely more effective than ignorance. Youth need to be confronted with the question of how they themselves would have
reacted. How did Hitler and the myths surrounding him capture the imagination of so many? What was it like to live
in fear of a knock on the door? What sort of people joined
the Party, the SS, the Gestapo? These are some of the
questions the authors in this chapter address. Their youth-
ful protagonists make it easier for today's young to identify
with the victims and understand the profiteers.

THE FÜHRER'S CHARISMA

On the subject of Hitler himself there are hundreds
of books. The teacher looking for a biography written specifically for young people will find several listed in the Bibliography under the following authors: Peter Borowsky, John
Devaney, Alain Desroches, Frank Gervasi, Mina C. and H.
Arthur Klein, and Georges Renoy. For their analyses of why
Hitler succeeded, books by Milton Meltzer and Arnold P. Rubin are recommended. Dieter Bossman's startling book reporting on his 1976-77 survey of what German schoolchildren
had heard about Hitler points out the need for educators to
address the issues raised by his success.

More to the point of this guide are books that show
how people were drawn to Hitler. A recurring theme in
books for young people is the adulation of the Führer. Seen
by his loyal followers, he is larger than life, capable of anything. They would be willing to die for him. He works the
crowds like a hypnotist, a magician who brings his audience
to heights of ecstasy, who persuades them to place their lives,
their loyalty, their love, and their complete trust in his hands.

Several authors describe this phenomenon in nearly
identical terms. In Hans Peter Richter's I Was There, the
narrator's Hitler Youth group forms a human chain to keep
back the crowds when the Führer arrives. In spite of waiting four hours in the hot sun, the crowd surges with joy when
the convoy of black cars rolls toward the square.

Suddenly, totally unexpectedly, we heard it.

At first it was only a murmur, but then it grew, increased in volume. Quickly it spread, grew into a roar. Like a storm it swept closer, rushed up the street in a thunderous roar. The crowds of people began to sway back and forth, started to shove and press forward.

. . .

You could feel the excitement everywhere.

Already enthusiastic shouts of "Heil!" could be heard clearly.

Then I saw them. A long line of large black cars slowly pushing their way forward between the waving and cheering people. Thousands of small swastika flags made of paper were waving in the air.

The noise swelled.

Behind me a woman sobbed with excitement.

A few people began to scream: "Heil!"-- "Heil!"

. . .

The voices tumbled over each other, broke.

Ten thousand voices roared: "Heil!"

The large black car rolled onto the empty square.

The chain broke.

Impossible to restrain, the mass of people surged forward.

. . .

They pushed.

Stamped.

Raged.

"Heil!"--"Heil!"

. . .

As suddenly as it had begun, the pressure lessened, stopped. Slowly the masses retreated. A double chain of black uniforms drove them back into their allotted space.

"Heil!"--"Heil!" thundered across the square.

. . .

"Attention!" a voice boomed over the loudspeaker.

Even the old people stood straighter.

"I hereby introduce our Führer and Chancellor of the Reich, Adolf Hitler!" bounced back from the houses around the square. He stopped short before the largest car and raised his arm in the salute.

"My Führer! I wish to report party comrades, members of organizations and town inhabitants duly

assembled!" rang clearly and distinctly across the
square.
I looked at Heinz. "But that's...." I whispered.
"My father!" he finished proudly, without looking
at me. [Translation by Edite Kroll, pp. 34-36]

Wendelgard von Staden (Nacht über dem Tal) went with
her parents to a rally in Stuttgart in 1937. There she fell
under Hitler's spell.

> ... The excitement in the hall was palpable. Out-
> side, waves of jubilation rolled over the crowd.
> The trumpets began to blare: "Youth, youth, youth
> knows no danger...." ...I ducked my head around
> the arm of the SA man in front of me and could
> look down the aisle to the entrance. A group of
> men neared it. A couple of steps ahead of them,
> the Führer. Thundering jubilation, "Heil! Heil!"
> accompanied him, swelling from the ranks of people
> who stood on both sides cheering wildly and with
> arms outstretched....
> As our car turned into the yard late that night,
> I still could not speak a word. I didn't want to
> hear what my mother was saying. I was too agi-
> tated. I swore in my heart that I would die for the
> Führer if he asked it. And I dreamed of the slowly
> striding man with the eyes that were focused on
> something no one else could see. [pp. 28-29]

James Forman's description of a crowd's response to
Hitler in Horses of Anger strongly resembles von Staden's.
Parading past a Munich beer hall on April 20, 1939, Hitler
is greeted by thousands of zealous followers.

> The crowd became quieter, as though entering
> a church. In the distance a martial air, the Bad-
> enweiler march, throbbed like a hymn. Then
> through the press of flags and marching men Hans
> could see a stately car. "He's coming! Hitler's
> coming!" The crowd drew a collective breath.
> Slowly the car came on and with it the round-
> shouldered figure of a man. The jagged part in
> his hair, lit by the sun, gleamed like a scar.
> Hans couldn't believe it. Surely this wasn't Hitler.
> As the car approached, he saw a face, neither ugly
> nor beautiful, with a strong nose and a hard line of
> mouth. Then he felt the impact of those pale gray

eyes from which sparked a lifetime of fury and
naked power. The huge Mercedes paused for a
moment, and the figure became animated. The
right arm extended and was drawn back, the hand
placed over the heart. "You are mine, and I am
yours. You are Germany! We are Germany!"
And for Hans, standing in a crowd suddenly gone
mad, that figure against the sun loomed as large
as God.
    "Sieg Heil! Sieg Heil!" the sea roared. Hans's
mouth worked and his voice was already hoarse.
He felt cold, afraid, exultant, and touched somehow
with glory. Here was the greatest, finest, most
magnificent man who had ever lived, and Hans longed
to do something to show his devotion. He would die
for him. If Hitler asked it, he would lie down and
die. [pp. 19-20]

Cornelia Keller catches her parents' enthusiasm for
Hitler in Renate Finckh's Mit uns zieht die neue Zeit. In
1933 Nela hears her father speak of God for the first time.
Now He is a frequent topic of conversation because He sent
the Führer to save Germany. As a mediocre artist, Mr.
Keller thrives under the Hitler regime. He models countless
plaques and then whole busts of his hero. So imbued with
this spirit is Nela that everything she does for the next twelve
years is guided by her love for the Führer. She allows no
tales of spying, executions, torturing of the opposition, or
the annihilation of the Jews to penetrate the armor of her
belief.

In one chapter of I Was There, Hans Peter Richter
compares the attitudes of three fathers toward Hitler (pp. 83-
89). The three are symbols of the silent majority, the boost-
er, and the opponent. The narrator's father is a modest
party member, and adapter who accommodates himself to
the times. He is sorry that Hitler is persecuting the Jews,
but things are so much better for him and his family that he
cannot be too troubled about an eccentricity that will surely
pass. Now he has a job, a comfortable life, and can even
look forward to a family vacation. The family has Hitler to
thank for all of its material blessings.

Heinz's father, a wealthy party official, is proud to
be living in a land led by such a wonder of a man.

"... Who would have thought, five years ago, that

a simple corporal would lead Germany to such greatness? This man is not obsessed by ambition like
so many before him. What does he get out of life?
He doesn't smoke, he doesn't drink, he eats no
meat, he even does without a family. All that remains is work, work and worry about us. Think
of it, boys. All of us should try to become as
selfless as our Führer....

"...He will require a great deal from us still,
but we can also expect a lot from him. Germany
will grow larger, will become more beautiful if
only we will give our whole strength to the Führer
so he will be able to realize his great plans. The
Führer will not only help us Germans to power and
respect, he will also reorganize the world. Boys,
I envy you the future you will be privileged to experience. Everything that today costs us effort and
difficulties will come true for you and your children." [Translation by Edite Kroll, p. 86]

The third father is a Communist who has been hounded
for his beliefs ever since the Nazis took over. Now his son
Günther has been taken from him as well and turned into a
Hitler Youth. He curses the man who has made him an ex-
convict and turned his boy into a brown-shirted follower. He
warns the boys that Hitler is bringing war, not greatness.

Horst Burger tries to explain the success of Hitler
and the Nazis in Vier Fragen an meinen Vater. He attributes it to a particular mentality:

..."You won't get Germans to the barricades for
democracy and freedom. But when it's a question
of order, they have no sense of humor. Woe to
the one who doesn't wash his windows regularly or
dust his furniture. In this country he's already
seen as practically an enemy of the state. Hunger
and misery in the world, brutality and inhumanity
--all that is secondary. The main thing is that the
streets are swept, and the church bells ring on time.
We've cheated our way through history with this attitude, closed our eyes when anything important
cropped up, with the excuse that we had to paint
the rabbit hutch or spade the garden." [p. 164]

Additional Titles:

> Blume, Judy. Starring Sally J. Friedman as Herself
> Spiraux, Alain. Hitler, ta maman t'appelle!

HITLER YOUTH

Hitler had plans for his youth. They were to be
"fleet as greyhounds, tough as leather, and hard as Krupp
steel." This generation of youth was to be trained to change
the world. In his hands they would be molded to the perfect
instruments to carry out his nefarious plans. They would regard all who opposed Hitler as unworthy of life and would respond to orders without questioning. Not the cleverest or
brightest would be called to leadership but those most manip-
ulable. From the age of ten on they would be allowed no
free time to develop their own thoughts. Hitler's formula
for education was simple. His youth would be trained to en-
slave the world. In a speech in Reichenberg on December
2, 1938, he declared:

> These young people will learn nothing else but
> how to think German and act German. And when,
> at the age of ten, this boy and this girl enter our
> organizations and there, frequently for the first
> time in their lives, breathe and feel a breath of
> fresh air, then four years later they will leave the
> Jungvolk to enter the Hitler Youth, and once again
> we will keep them there for four years; and then,
> instead of returning them to the hands of those
> adults who created our old social classes and ranks,
> we will immediately admit them into the Party or
> put them in the National Socialist Labor Front, the
> SA or the SS, in the National Socialist Motor Corps,
> and so on. And if they remain there for two years
> or for a year and a half and have not yet become
> totally dedicated National Socialists, then they will
> be sent to work in the Labor Service and will be
> polished there for six or seven months, all by
> means of a single symbol, the German spade. And
> if any remnants of class consciousness or the ar-
> rogance of rank is left in them after six or seven
> months there, they will be turned over to the Armed
> Forces to undergo an additional two years' treat-
> ment. And when, after two or three or four years

they return home again, then, in order to prevent
them from slipping back into the old way, we will
immediately put them back in the SA, the SS, and
so on. And they will never be free again, not
their whole lives long. [Translation by Jan van
Huerck in Howl Like the Wolves, p. 118]

Hitler wanted his youth to become a new breed of men
and women. Max von der Grün in Howl Like the Wolves
quotes Hitler's plans for the education of these young people:

My theory of education is harsh. All weakness
must be hammered out. The youth who grow up
in my Ordensburgen [training schools for future
political leaders] will terrify the world. I want a
youth that is violent, masterful, intrepid, cruel.
Young people must be all these things. They must
endure pain. There must be nothing weak and tender about them. The magnificent, free predator
must once again flash in their eyes. I want my
young people strong and handsome. I will have
them taught all types of physical exercise. I want
athletic young people. This is first and most important. Thus I will wipe out the thousands of years
of human domestication. Thus will I see before me
the pure, noble raw material of nature. Thus can
I create something new.
I want no intellectual education. Knowledge would
ruin my young people for me. Rather I would have
them learn only what they acquire voluntarily as
they follow their play instincts. But they must
learn self-control. They shall learn to conquer
the fear of death in the course of the most difficult
trials. Then they will have attained the stage of
heroic youth. From this will grow the stage of the
free being, the human being, the god-man. In my
training schools the beautiful, self-governing god-
man will be enshrined as an image of worship and
will prepare the young for the coming stage of maturity and manhood.... [Translation by Jan van
Huerck, pp. 117-18]

The Hitler Youth started as an organ of the SA and
became a major branch of the Nazi party in 1935. By 1936
membership in the para-military organization was compulsory
and began while children were still most impressionable.
Boys became Pimpf at six, Jungvolk at ten, and Hitler Jugend

at fourteen. Girls in the Jungmädel became part of the Bund
Deutscher Mädel (BDM) at fourteen.

Many of the authors who are writing today about the
Hitler Youth were once members of these organizations.
Their books stand, with varying degrees of success, as cautionary tales. They were caught up in the excitement, stirred
by the songs, kept loyal by the outings and the sense of cam-
araderie. Some developed doubts. Others remained blindly
loyal to the end, dismissing as enemy propaganda rumors of
concentration camps and victims of the regime, turning their
backs as their neighbors disappeared.

One of the questions Walter Jendrich's son asks in
Vier Fragen an meinen Vater is how people allowed themselves to be so manipulated. Walter uses the Hitler Youth
as the best example of skillful manipulation. He explains to
his son how the system worked, with everyone indoctrinated
to follow orders from above and to order those below. They
were taught that the world was full of enemies and that they
as individuals were nothing, the folk everything. All exist-
ing youth groups were incorporated into the Hitler Youth.
Walter felt a part of something important as he and his group
marched through town:

> Walter loved to march through the streets.
> Marching in step in close contact with the others--
> he wasn't alone anymore, felt himself sheltered and
> in the middle of friends, a sporting group. Before
> them fluttered the red-white-red Hitler Youth flag
> with the black swastika in the middle. But it wasn't
> the flag. It could just as well have been red or
> black. It was the feeling of belonging. [p. 70]

Hans Peter Richter was one of the first to write about
the Hitler Youth in such a way that the next generation of
youth could understand. His books opened a new avenue of
discussion and have found a wide, international audience.

The narrator of Friedrich takes his Jewish friend,
Friedrich, to a Jungvolk meeting. Friedrich would like to
be a part of the excitement and marching and outings, but
his father is opposed. To eight-year-old boys, the refusal
is just another grown-up eccentricity, so Friedrich borrows
the narrator's black scarf, secures it with his own swastika
ring, and comes along to a meeting. There he is subjected
to painful humiliation (pp. 38-44).

Richter's second book, I Was There, is the story of
three young friends: Heinz, the son of a wealthy party functionary; Günther, child of a Communist; and the narrator,
whose father quietly adjusts to the new times. Heinz, 10,
joins the Jungvolk in time to help with the election of 1933.
He helps lead people to the gymnasium to vote and goes with
his father to bring in the electors. As the narrator and his
parents leave the gymnasium, where they have seen Günther's
father hustled away for protesting the sham, they see Heinz
and his father helping an old woman out of a car. Heinz is
explaining to her:

> ... "On the white form you must make an X in the
> circle next to the Nationalsozialistische Deutsche
> Arbeiter Partei and on the green form you must
> mark the yes-circle. Then you will have voted
> correctly. " [Translation by Edite Kroll, pp. 26-27]

In 1934 the Jungvolk are sent out to collect for the
Winterhilfswerk (Winter Relief Fund). They are each to sell
at least fifty badges. Otto (der Dicke in the original version) explains that he cannot help because he is going to visit
his dying grandmother. The man from the Winter Relief
Fund rails at him for thinking that a dying grandmother ex-
cuses him from his duty and dismisses the boys. Heinz
secretly does Otto's collecting for him. When the boys report back, Otto's collection box is the heaviest, but his grandmother is dead.

> "You did well, " the man stated after he had emp-
> tied the box.
> Otto said nothing.
> "Why all this now?" the man asked. He stood
> up. "If you hadn't collected for the fund, your
> grandmother would still have died. This way you
> learn how to grow hard, as the Führer wants you
> to. " [Translation by Edite Kroll, p. 42]

In 1939 the whole squad is inducted into the Hitler
Youth. Their new leader gives a welcoming speech which
makes Günther, Heinz, and the narrator dread the coming
years:

> ... "Quite a lot will change for you in the Hitler
> Youth, " he began without greeting. "First, you
> are no longer Pimpfs, but Hitler Youths: you bear
> the name of our Führer. Second, this obliges you

even more than before to demonstrate always and
everywhere why the Führer has chosen you. All
childish behavior stops forthwith. Third, I regard
it as the mission of the Hitler Youth to prepare
you for your upcoming military service. . . .   Fourth,
in order that we may fulfill the mission given us,
we need experienced leaders. Only trial in service
will prove whether former leaders among you can
be utilized further. Fifth, the Hitler Youth, con-
sisting as it does of young working men, apprentices, and school boys, requires different hours.
Duty in the Hitler Youth, therefore, falls primarily
on evenings and Sundays. Sixth, Sundays belong to
the Hitler Youth, not to going to church. You are
old enough now to discard bourgeois prejudices.
Seventh, I expect absolute loyalty to the Führer.
The enemies of the Führer are your enemies, too,
be they Jews, Bolsheviks, parsons, or whatever.
Eighth, I demand from you unwavering dedication
to the ideals of National Socialism. The Führer's
word is both command and revelation. Ninth, I
demand from you the readiness to sacrifice blood
and life for Führer, Folk and Fatherland. To be
a Hitler Youth is to be a hero. Tenth, hundredth,
and thousandth: I demand obedience, obedience,
unconditional obedience." [Translation by Edite
Kroll, pp. 99-100]

The boys' last shred of idealism disappears when in 1942
they are sent into battle.

       The narrator of Eugen Oker's ...und ich der Fahnen-
träger is already a member of a paramilitary group when
Hitler comes into power. Kornprobst, the leader of Adler
und Falken, is a fanatic militarist with a crippled left arm,
fat cheeks, and a thin body. He puts the boys through military exercises and inspires them with tales of Germany's
former glory and the perfidy of its enemies. When Adler
und Falken is taken over by the Hitler Youth, Kornprobst is
kicked out of his youth leadership position and into the SA
because of his crippled arm. He is humiliated and stomps
angrily away. His boys are upset at his treatment until their
leader points out that his behavior at the ceremony was an
inexcusable breach of discipline. With that the boys decide
to be hard and turn their backs on him.

       The narrator takes the arrest of his uncle, the humil-

iation of a Catholic priest, concentration camps, and the persecution of the Jews in stride. He is pleased that degenerate
art and poetry are being replaced with paintings and poems
so real and approachable that even the simplest can understand them. How proud he is to be living at the cutting edge
of a great new era. The Third Reich will last forever, or
so he believes as he ends his diary in 1936.

In the Berliner family of Melita Maschmann (Fazit),
mistrust of the Weimar Republic, shame over the outcome of
World War I, and anti-Semitism set the tone. When Hitler
is named chancellor in 1933, 15-year-old Melita is ripe to
follow him. She has rejected her family's middle-class val-
ues and longs for an overriding ideal and the chance to lead
others to a better world. She secretly joins the Hitler Youth,
feeling it to be a link with the poor, particularly with youths
who have chosen poverty as a means of rejecting the bourgeois
comfort of their parents. Unsure of her own identity and
worth, Melita finds comfort and affirmation in the associa-
tion.

Her fascination is less with politics than with being
part of an elite, the leaders of the Hitler Youth. To this
select group, anyone over thirty is suspect. They scorn
those in their charge. They lead them without concern for
the deep, terrifying effects of their leadership and are ready
to sacrifice the children for the supposed good of the Reich.
The individuals they lead are nothing, the group all. Songs,
slogans, poems, and the flag become a religion to be followed
without question.

Throughout her recital, Maschmann is self-excusatory,
explaining her loyalty to the cause almost as though Adolf
Hitler and National Socialism played only a minor role in a
glorious ideal. She identifies with abstract ideas of Folk,
Fatherland, and Reich rather than with the people behind those
ideas. She learns of ghettos and persecutions but rejects the
knowledge. She sees suffering and ignores it. As the war
nears its end she becomes fatalistic. Her young charges
mean nothing to her. Her whole being, never philosophically
probing, has become deformed by her complete identification
with corrupt ideals. Her account is almost nostalgic, as
though this period of her life remains the high point of her
memories.

Nela Keller is a perfect candidate for the Hitler Youth
(Renate Finckh, Mit uns zieht die neue Zeit). She is almost

totally lacking in empathy for her fellowman. When she
pushes a child down the stairs, she is glad he is hurt and
not she. When beggar women and children come to the door,
she is glad they are poor and not she. Still, never having
fared well in groups, she is not happy when at ten she has
to join the Jungmädel.

Her fears prove unnecessary. She loves hearing the
stories about the Führer and the organization and is stirred
by the ceremonies. She at last feels important. Few take
their leadership training as seriously as do Nela and her
leader, Friedl. The other girls secretly laugh at Friedl,
but to Nela she is someone older and wiser who is as alone
and special as she. If Nela feels any disillusionment at all,
it is only because of the other girls' lack of enthusiasm.

Nela is proud to be German and doesn't notice when
her classmates start avoiding her. At 13 she becomes the
leader of fifteen 10-year-old girls, mostly from poor families. Night and day she thinks of her duty to the girls and
makes visits to their families. She bores them with her
preaching for the sake of their futures. Eventually even
Nela's mother tires of her single-minded devotion.

At 16 Nela becomes a BDM group leader, and immediately two girls quit. Nela is too idealistic, too zealous for
them. She and a comrade make plans for revamping the
Hitler Youth for the Führer. They will rekindle the enthusiasm of their girls.

Nela is dismayed to learn that some former Hitler
Youth members in Munich have been caught circulating flyers
attacking Hitler. She is a little upset when her Jewish neighbors are taken away but blots out the knowledge with heroic
tales. She begins to think that not all that is happening is
right, but her soul is frozen. When any seed of doubt takes
root she rips it out.

As the enemy comes closer Nela is horrified to see
the loyalty of others faltering. Everything she has believed
in is crumbling around her. Even the end of the war does
not release her from her loyalty to the Nazis. She is determined to tell her story:

> I swore to myself to write everything down. I
> couldn't imagine that I would have another reason
> for doing so than that which impelled me then. I

wanted to tell our children of the fire that filled
our hearts, of the loyalty which meant more to us
than ourselves. Until then I wanted to preserve it
faithfully within me.... [p. 188]

As the years go by, Nela comes to realize:

In the search for security I had let myself be
trapped in a single, big lie. In it I had lost a
large part of myself. [p. 190]

Finckh's book is nearly as repellent as Maschmann's
yet somehow more convincing. It is difficult to feel anything
but loathing for the two young women so totally empty of
emotion, so without empathy for others. Yet the Third Reich
would not have functioned as a well-oiled machine without its
Melitas and Nelas and Shatterhands. Now matter how repulsive are such people, students need to read their confessions,
for they are crucial to an understanding of National Socialism.

Not all members of the Hitler Youth are portrayed as
being as zealous as those in the preceding examples. Some,
like Ilse Koehn struggle with ambiguity. Others, like the
Scholls and Liselotte, find their enthusiasm turning sour when
the true nature of the movement becomes clear. In contrast
to Finckh and Maschmann, Koehn does not claim she was a
victim of Hitler and the Nazis. She shows that the influence
of teachers and politicians had its limits and that children
were not just dupes.

Ilse Koehn does not learn that she is a Mischling (part
Jewish) until after the war (Koehn, Mischling, Second Degree).
She joins the Hitler Youth in 1940 at her grandmother's insistence but drops out after two meetings. In 1941 she and
79 classmates are evacuated from their Berlin school to
Czechoslovakia. Although their teachers are theoretically
in charge and are to continue classes, the Hitler Youth leaders are actually in control. They fill the girls' days with
forced marches, surprise inspections, and war games. The
girls become so bored that even the most reluctant students
miss their lessons. In September the camp is disbanded, and
Ilse returns to school. That fall she volunteers for a harvest
camp. She has visions of beaches and swimming, for the
camp is on an island. Instead they are virtual prisoners
surrounded by a 10-foot fence. Iron discipline is the rule
for all but the leaders.

In her third camp the Hitler Youth leaders are cruelly
rigorous. During their inspections, they shame the girls
over trivia, but here Frau Doctor Margarete Pfaffenburger
stands up to them and asserts her right to teach the girls.
The classes soon peter out, however, and homesickness and
boredom settle in. The winter and summer seem endless,
but in August a new leader arrives whose passion for music
gives the girls a new purpose. The camp leaders select Ilse
for a special training camp, an honor that both pleases and
shames her.

The new camp is different. It focuses on music, art,
and literature. There is no Nazi propaganda and no manual
labor. When Ilse privately confesses that she does not want
to be in the vanguard of the Hitler Youth, the leaders promise to postpone her leadership by arranging further training.
That proves unnecessary as the Russians march toward Germany. Koehn makes no attempt to hide the pleasure she felt
at being one of the best. Yet she was never a blind follower.
Her experience is typical of the many youth from 1933 to 1945
who were neither fanatical idealists nor willing to be martyrs.

Hans and Sophie Scholl, who were executed in 1943
for their resistance activities, were early members of the
Hitler Youth. Hermann Vinke describes their progression
from supporters to resisters in Das kurze Leben der Sophie
Scholl. Hans, Sophie, and Inge all had leadership positions
in their organizations. The annual Nürnberg rally in 1936
marked the beginning of Hans's skepticism. The violence
of the rhetoric and the uncritical adulation of the masses were
repulsive to him, and he dropped out of the Hitler Youth.
He joined an alternative group. The Gestapo suspected that
the group was subversive so the Scholl children were picked
up for questioning in November 1937. After this Hans and
Inge broke their ties completely with the Hitler Youth. By
1942 Sophie had become disillusioned to the point that she
felt she must act against the Nazis. She joined her brother
in printing and distributing flyers, and both paid the ultimate
price.

In Doris Orgel's The Devil in Vienna two girls cling
to their friendship though Inge is Jewish and Liselotte is the
daughter of a Nazi official. Writing to Inge from Munich,
Liselotte tells of the thrill of a Jungmädel outing (pp. 151-
160). The walk to Starnberger See is a joy to Liselotte, but
she feels even more excited when the troop leader, Irmgard,
invites her to walk at the head of the troop. Irmgard is a

perfect Aryan, blond, rosy-cheeked, trim, lovely. She belongs to Faith and Beauty and hopes that her boyfriend will
be admitted into the SS so that they will be allowed to marry
some day. She inspires Liselotte with her vision of the future. Then Liselotte asks Irmgard her opinion of the Jews,
and the beautiful facade crumbles. Irmgard's casually vicious answer reveals the perversion of the whole youth movement. Liselotte envisions a bleak future:

> ... Looking down at the path, seeing all those dark-
> skirted, wind-jacketed, brown-capped girls march-
> ing by, was like seeing my whole future. I'll have
> to march with them, do everything they make you
> do; there's no way out. It made me want to die.
> [p. 159]

The pressure to be a part of the Hitler Youth was so
great that not joining required a strong sense of personal
identity. Not to march in step at an age when peer acceptance is more important than the approval of adults takes a
heavy toll. It is lonely to be an outsider. Furthermore,
not joining the Hitler Youth was dangerous. It implied a
treasonous lack of enthusiasm.

One of these outsiders is Eve Radek in Und das war
erst der Anfang by Eva Marder. Eve has liberal parents and
a mind of her own so does not go along with the new wave
in 1933. Very rapidly two opposing camps form in Eve's
class, the Browns on one side and everyone else on the other.
A rash of dirty tricks by each side increases the tension but
is dropped after adult intervention in favor of scholastic competition. That, too, pales as the children tire of the hard
work.

By the time the Nazis have governed for a year, only
a few children have not joined the Browns, but these are
Eve's fast friends. She is contemplating her increasing isolation one day when she sees Peter sitting with a group of
Browns around a fire. Just the day before she made a bet
with him as to which of their classmates would let themselves
be caught by the Browns first. Now she feels betrayed to
learn that he has been a member for a week.

A new school year begins, and all youth groups are
to be absorbed by the Browns. Nazi ideology invades the
school and seeps out onto the playground. Eve's good friend,
Ursel, takes her aside and tells her that although her athletic

club is becoming Brown, she will always remain Eve's friend.
As a symbol of friendship she gives Eve a harmonica.   The
next day Fritz gives her a rusty pocket knife for the same
reason.   Only Helmut remains, and the next day he gives
Eve the same pledge of friendship to soften the news that he,
too, is joining the Browns.

Fritz, Ursel, and Helmut become so busy preparing
for their induction into the Browns that they have no time
for Eve.   She makes one last attempt to shake Helmut loose,
but he is already on the other side.   She tries to make Ursel see that the oath she will pledge can be broken if it is
not honorable, but Ursel has been convinced that an oath is
holy.

The night of November 30, 1933, Eve watches in horrified fascination as a torchlight parade nears the spot the
Nazis have declared consecrated.   The Browns march in a
half circle around the sacred stones.   Then one by one they
step forward.

> ..."I promise to always do my duty in the Hitler
> Youth, with love and faith to the Führer and our
> flag, so help me God."
> ...
> Eve sees the solemn faces, hears again and
> again the same words, and suddenly feels herself
> cast out.   Cut off from that which once was.   Now
> there really is a rift between her and the others,
> as wide as the circle of light from the torches.
> Her mouth is dry.   Her eyes burn.
> "Indians don't cry," she says softly and lays
> her forehead on the rails.   And cries.   [p. 115]

Another child who is forced to be an outsider is Achim
of Martin Selber's Geheimkurier A.   For as long as he can
remember, Achim has been spending summer vacations with
his grandparents in his children's paradise, Brennermühle.
There things are timeless.   Old friends give him the same
warm greeting year after year.   This year he is particularly
keen to return, as the shadow of Hitler has fallen over his
city, and his father has been hounded for his union activity.

Unfortunately, Brennermühle has changed.   There is
a new, harsh tone in his friend Michael's voice.   With a cold
glint in his eye, Michael puts Achim through a dangerous test
of his courage and then rejects him completely when he learns

that Achim is not in the Jungvolk.   Watching children fling
themselves in the mud at Michael's commands, Achim knows
that his paradise is gone.

> And suddenly I understood: Time had not stood
> still in the land of my childhood.   Even here were
> all of the things I knew from home--the arrogance
> of those in uniform toward civilians, the bawling
> of orders, rattling collection boxes, teachers who
> told of the battle of Verdun with shining eyes.
> Everybody up! Sing! "I had a friend, a better
> you'll never find..."   And voices like that of my
> grave-digging father had become faint.
> Time had not stayed still in paradise.   [p. 11]

The times are wrong for an outsider.   Achim becomes
the scapegoat first of the children and then of their parents.
He refuses to bow to their demands for conformity and is
locked out of their fellowship. Only the village idiot, Moschke,
saves him from being beaten up by Michael's troop.

People lose interest in Achim when a reward is posted
for an escaped political prisoner.   Achim recognizes a kin-
dred soul when he hears talk of another who is standing alone
against the times.   Retreating to his grass hut in the meadow,
he finds the stranger and arranges his rescue.   Through his
act of defiance, Achim reclaims his paradise, for the few
people he confides in give him the courage to stand tall.

Fascist youth organizations existed in countries other
than Germany, but few authors have tackled the subject.
Perhaps no one wants to admit that he or she shared an enthusiasm for Hitler.   Such an omission is a disservice to
young readers, for it implies that fascism was a National
Socialist aberration that no one but Germans succumbed to.
Other than Alki Zei's Wildcat Under Glass, in which a Greek
girl is flattered into joining a fascist league, and Evert Hartman's War Without Friends, I found no books about non-
German fascist youth groups.   War Without Friends is the
story of a Dutch boy who is a member of the hated Nazi minority.   It has been translated from the Dutch but is not yet
available.

Additional titles:

    Noack, Hans-Georg.   Die Webers.

Schönfeldt, Sybil Gräfin. Sonderappell.
Seiffert, Dietrich. Einer war Kisselbach.

RANK-AND-FILE NAZIS AND SA

The National Socialist party was one for bullies, for
small-minded people who gloried in the chance to get even
with the world for their own inadequacies. Petty brutality
was not only sanctioned but encouraged. Not every member
participated in the violence. The majority did not but they
remained silent as their comrades imposed their will on the
nation. This section is concerned with the ways young adult
authors present rank-and-file party members and the SA.
They try to convey the soul-deadening fear that reigned under
the Nazis.

From the start the Nazi Party was coarse and brutal.
The behavior of its members in the government was astonish-
ingly obscene to those accustomed to conducting politics in a
dignified manner. The party had its own police unit, the SA,
whose members wore brown shirts and swastika armbands.
Max von der Grün (Howl Like the Wolves) gives two examples
typical of the party's methods. Five men who had killed a
Communist in 1932 and been sentenced to prison were dec-
orated by Hitler for their heroism in 1933 (pp. 54-55). That
same year a cattle dealer who fell into SA hands during the
boycott of Jewish businesses was beaten with rubber trunch-
eons. The SA cut off his hair, carved a swastika on his
back, rubbed salt in it, laid the hair on top, and then sewed
up the wound (p. 80). The reign of terror had just begun.

The narrator of I Was There, by Hans Peter Richter,
gets a preview of Nazi justice in 1933. A Nazi is murdered,
and his SA comrades sweep through the neighborhood in
search of the assailant. The rumor that he is a Communist
justifies their anger. Near dark of the following day, policemen cordon off the area and search for the murderer. They
are just leaving empty-handed when a unit of SA marches up.
They present the police with a blood-encrusted, unconscious
man, claim he is the murderer, and march proudly on (pp.
11-18).

Eve Radek also learns that the Nazis have their own
system of justice in Eva Marder's Und das war erst der
Anfang. Someone starts laying animal traps. A child's dog
is the first victim. The town's policeman, Pahlke, is sure

he knows who is placing the traps, but the man is in the SA
and cannot be touched.   Someone slices the throat of a 14-
year-old Jewish girl, just enough to terrify her.   Then Eve
herself is nearly strangled.   Again Pahlke investigates.
Again he finds his man.   This time Pahlke is transferred,
for the attacker is Kruschke, and Kruschke belongs to the
SA.   Their reputation must remain unblemished.

Eve rashly hints to Kruschke that she knows what he
has been up to and then refuses to elaborate.   He begins
beating her with his belt.   His superior stops him and tries
to cover for him, but this time Kruschke has gone too far.
He simply disappears.   The SA encourage the rumor that he
was part of the Röhm Putsch.   Though a laughable fabrication,
it enables them to sweep their dirt under the rug.

As the town turns brown, Eve becomes more and
more isolated.   For a child of her intelligence and independence, the coming years look bleak indeed.

The unemployment and poverty of the pre- and early
Hitler years lead some members of a family of eight to opt
for Nazism and others to reject it in Peter Berger's Im roten
Hinterhaus.   Father is a rat catcher until laboratories stop
buying experimental animals.   Then he turns from one scheme
to another to try to keep the family fed and sheltered.   He
is largely apolitical but thinks the Communists have the best
answers.   They would see that workers had jobs and children
an education.

His son Erich, second oldest of the four boys, harbors
secret sympathies for the Nazis and painstakingly scrapes together money to buy an SA uniform, but the money has to go
to the family when the oldest son, Gustav, quarrels and moves
out.   Somehow Erich manages to acquire a uniform.   On January 30, 1933, he can take it out of hiding and wear it openly.
On April 1 Father sees Erich standing guard in front of a
Jewish store.   The shame of it is too much, and he orders
the family to throw Erich's things out of the apartment.
Erich's own conscience revolts at standing guard, and he
begins to have doubts about the Nazis.

Gustav, on the other hand, becomes a Nazi zealot for
the sake of his true love.   Six months after he marries Elli
he becomes a father and names his son Adolf.   Both Elli and
Gustav throw all of their energies into the Nazi cause, but
Erich is chased out of the party for refusing to take part in

actions against Socialists and for apologizing to the Jew whose
store he guarded. By the time the war begins the family,
once close, has become scattered.

The Nazis of Austria become bolder after Schuschnigg's
weekend with Hitler (Doris Orgel, The Devil in Vienna). Although still officially outlawed, they feel free to wear swastika badges and paint anti-Semitic slogans on walls. Schuschnigg bravely calls for his people to stand behind the Fatherland Front. Red-white-red bunting appears everywhere,
but the Nazis tear it down. When they are challenged by
members of the Fatherland Front, the police arrive to arrest the latter.

With Schuschnigg's announcement of a plebiscite, Austrians rejoice. The Nazis seem to disappear, but it is only
a part of their strategy. They soon reappear:

> The streets were like in newsreels I have seen
> of Berlin and other German cities. Traffic was
> slowed down and in some places stopped, so many
> Nazis were marching, in leather boots up to their
> knees and brown and black uniforms, with pistols
> in their holsters. [p. 116]

They demand Schuschnigg's resignation and unification with
Germany. The plebiscite is cancelled, Schuschnigg resigns,
a Nazi government takes over, and Austria belongs to Germany.

The very next day Inge learns what it will be like
for Jews now that the Nazis are in power. Three SA men
come for her father and grandfather. They and other Jews
who had contributed to the Plebiscite Committee are forced
to clean the streets, some of them with toothbrushes.

> ... O.O., Rabbi Taglicht, my father, and some
> others thought that as long as they were scrubbing,
> they might as well try to scrub away the JEWS,
> GO CROAK scrawls they had uncovered by stripping
> the posters away. So they started to. But the
> paint would not come off. And the SA men hit
> them and kicked them and ordered them back to
> scrubbing the street. The most shocking thing to
> my father was how many people, whole crowds,
> came to watch the spectacle and joked and jeered,
> and not one said a word against it.... [pp. 127-128]

Inge is to see many more signs of Nazi cruelty before her family leaves Vienna. A few days after the Anschluss (unification with Germany), seven SA or SS men smash everything in Evi's father's shop. There is no one he can call for help because one of the attackers is a policeman. Inge is with Evi when she learns what has happened. On her way home, Inge sees a man with a swastika armband making a little boy wearing a skullcap paint J E W on the window of a stationery store. The incidents are recorded in her journal and burned in her mind, an impression of the Nazis she will never forget.

THE GESTAPO

The modus operandi of the Gestapo (Geheime Staatspolizei) was fear. The organization which began as Reichsmarschall Göring's police force in 1933 evolved into the State's arm of terror under Himmler. For many, the mere threat of being picked up by the secret police was a sufficient deterrent to dissent. Max von der Grün characterizes the pervasiveness of this fear in Howl Like the Wolves:

> I had begun to notice that my parents were becoming increasingly nervous and that they were frightened whenever there was a knock at our door. Usually the people at the door turned out to be friends or someone who shared my father's faith. We were seldom visited by strangers, except perhaps some stray peddler or salesman.
> Many people were experiencing the same feelings as my parents. Their fear of the Gestapo never left them in peace.
> People used to disappear suddenly from our neighborhood just as they did from others. As a rule, the Gestapo arrested people at night. When we children asked our parents why this person or that person did not seem to be around anymore, we might be told that these people had gone on a trip. But usually we did not get any answer at all.
> [Translation by Jan van Huerck, p. 132]

Grün goes on further to say:

> It was a time in which a person could no longer trust his own brother or his school friends or-- incredible as it may seem--even his or her husband

or wife. Married people used to accuse each other
of being involved in "subversive" plots, and one
spouse would denounce the other to the Gestapo
simply because this was an easy way to get rid of
a burdensome partner. Throughout the Reich the
torture and murder continued behind prison walls
and barbed-wire fences. [Translation by Jan van
Huerck, p. 139]

   In Barbara Gehrts's Nie wieder ein Wort davon, Mr.
Singelmann insists his children, Hannes and Hanna, perform
their Hitler Youth service although he privately opposes Hitler. They find it distasteful but have no choice. They understand their father's insistence when the Gestapo come for
him in the night. They take him away and then systematically and thoroughly search the house, taking his journals,
files, newspaper clippings, photographs, and books. The
family is instructed to tell anyone who asks that Father is
on a business trip for an indefinite period of time.

   The arrest is on October 9, 1942. February 10, 1943,
he is executed. Two weeks later the family receives a letter
from the Gestapo (pp. 122-124). It is a bill for the punishment of Franz Singelmann for his undermining of military
discipline. Everything is included--cost of execution, legal
process, arrest, investigation, postage--for a total of 871
Marks.

   The Deutschkrons (Inge Deutschkron, Ich trug den
gelben Stern) are forbidden to use their own name because
Jews are not allowed to bear a name which has the word
"Deutsch" in it. Mr. Deutschkron is called in to the Gestapo, ordered to choose the maiden name of either of his
grandmothers, and then forced to sign a document stating
that the change is voluntary (pp. 52-53).

   Wave after wave of arrests decimate the Jewish population of Berlin but not fast enough. The Viennese Gestapo
are called in to make the city judenrein (free of Jews). Their
method is less refined but more efficient. They drive moving vans through the streets picking up Jews, separating families, and shipping people to concentration camps (pp. 102-108).

   The door bell rings one day when Mrs. Deutschkron
is home alone. At the door is a tall Gestapo man and his
driver. They push their way in, and the Gestapo agent begins to torment her while his driver sits with his nose buried

in a newspaper. He orders her to pack, but she insists that
she not be deported without her daughter and calmly picks up
her sewing. With cruel pleasure, the Gestapo man taunts her.
Then when he tires of his practical joke he calls to his driver
and leaves (pp. 111-113).

Paul Eichhorn is questioned by the Gestapo in autumn
1942 and ordered to inform on his father (James Forman,
The Traitors). When he is released he hears the sounds of
someone being tortured across the passageway. He retreats
in terror but is sent back along the same hall to confront his
interrogator once again before he is allowed to leave (pp. 119-
122).

The Gestapo are also active in Denmark in Elliott
Arnold's A Kind of Secret Weapon. The despised Major
Heinz Gruber, head of the Elsinore Gestapo, becomes the
butt of local jokes. Whenever he sets out to make an arrest people see his official car and telephone everyone who
might be in danger. He becomes so frustrated by his elu-
sive quarry that he begins taking taxi cabs instead. This
makes the Danes' task even easier, for the taxi drivers call
in their destinations, and their dispatchers call the victims
(pp. 19-21).

When one of his men shoots an innkeeper, Major Gruber explains to the horrified crowd that they should be grateful. The innkeeper was a traitor against the Germans and,
therefore, his own countrymen, for the Germans are only in
Denmark to protect it from its enemies. The innkeeper's
wounds are superficial, but the Gestapo question him with a
ruler, slicing his face until he dies (pp. 40-47).

The secret police have little tolerance for insults.
An agent offers the publisher of a Danish underground newspaper 100 crowns to consider becoming an informer and an
additional 900 crowns if he accepts. Needing money for his
paper, he accepts and prints a receipt for the full amount in
his newspaper. He thanks the Gestapo for their generous do-
nation and writes that in the future they need not contact him
personally but may leave their contributions at any newspaper
kiosk. The Gestapo fail to see the humor in the insult and
torture the man until the underground rescues him (pp. 82-91).

Lars Andersen gets posthumous revenge on Major
Gruber. Though he is killed by the Gestapo, his editorial
thanking the Gestapo chief for his tender-hearted treatment

of the Danes results in the Major's being transferred in dis-
grace.

In all of these books the very name Gestapo strikes
terror in those who hear it.   The secret police earn and
deserve a reputation for cold, perverted brutality.

Additional titles:

> Cernaut, Jean.   Comptes à rendre.
> Forman, James.   The Survivor, pp. 153-159.

THE SS

The Schützstaffel (Elite Guard) was formed in 1925 as
the select organization of the National Socialist Party and was
responsible for Hitler's security.   In 1929 it came under the
direction of Heinrich Himmler.   Originally part of the SA,
the SS became a separate organization whose candidates had
to be at least six feet tall and able to trace their ancestry
as far back as 1750.   After the Röhm Putsch they answered
only to Hitler.   Administration of the concentration camps
was added to the SS security functions.   Under Himmler's
direction the SS became noted for its terrorism.

Young Nazis were honored to be chosen for the SS.
They were trained in special SS schools.   Academic education was not considered important, but practical training in
a concentration camp was integral to the complete prepara-
tion of the young candidates.   Max von der Grün (Howl Like
the Wolves) says this about their training:

> In other words, young men were forced to guard
> and probably torture--perhaps even kill--dissidents
> in order to receive their diploma from the SS.   This
> example, more than any other, makes it clear how
> deluded young people can be abused to serve a po-
> litical goal.   Every day it used to be drummed into
> the heads of these youngsters that the inmates of
> concentration camps were enemies of the State,
> Jews, traitors--in short, "worthless human beings."
> [Translation by Jan van Huerck, p. 88]

In the novels and memoirs concerning concentration
camp victims, the character of the SS is made most vivid.

The authors describe the baseness, the perversions of which
human beings are capable. That members of the SS were
neither the first nor the last to have practiced such inhumanity does not diminish the horror. The SS organized butchery
on an unprecedented scale in a country justifiably proud of
its rich cultural life.

Isabella Leitner writes of the SS from personal experience in her Fragments of Isabella. She and her family
are living in a Hungarian ghetto when the SS arrive to take
over the job begun by the local police. The gendarmes have
already imprisoned the Jews in the ghetto. The SS have only
to deport them. The young man with dog, pistol, and whip
who comes for Isabella's family is probably no older than
sixteen.

Along with Jews from the neighboring villages, the
family is taken to Auschwitz. Because of the beatings, the
starvation diet, the unsanitary conditions, and the psychic
damage, Auschwitz produces its quota of Mussulmen, the
living dead. To look like a Mussulman is to invite death,
for the SS sweep through the barracks unexpectedly, select-
ing for the crematoria all those whose physical condition has
deteriorated to the point that they are no longer useful in the
industries of the death camp. On one particular day the SS
bolt both doors of the barracks when they make their selection. Isabella and two of her sisters immediately begin
screaming orders, pretending they are kapos aiding the SS
guards. They fight to stay in the block as others are mo-
tioned out, but this time the SS change procedures. Those
still in the building are those chosen for death. With sudden
strength the sisters charge the door and fight their way outside (pp. 35-40).

The beautiful, blond, bisexual SS guard Irma Grese
terrorizes the camp twice daily. During one of the endless
roll calls, she punishes Chica because her neighbor is sitting
down. For the remaining hours of the roll call Chica must
kneel with her arms high in the air. In each hand is a heavy
rock which she must not drop, nor must her arms waver.
The prisoners pray fervently for her, and once again an inmate cheats death, no matter how fleetingly (pp. 41-45).

Another Auschwitz survivor is perceptive about the
character of the SS in charge of the concentration camps.
In trying to explain how it is that inmates can agree to become kapos and blockowas, to be the instruments of brutality,

the arms which club, Fania Fénelon (<u>Playing for Time</u>) writes
that in order to survive one had to be stronger than others.
The SS make it impossible for all to survive, so the stronger
live at the expense of the weaker. The SS choose those who
are most like them, those who learn most quickly to please
their masters, to carry out their orders. She describes how
the SS operate:

> ... The Nazis obliterate all traces of humanity in
> the internees, they appeal to the lowest instincts,
> set prisoners against each other, arouse all pos-
> sible forms of savagery, crush the weak, protect
> those who become monstrous like themselves--and
> that's how they attain one of the aims of National
> Socialism: the destruction of human dignity. And
> of course with some underprivileged people born in
> a socially impoverished milieu, where there's no
> education of any kind, the ground is already pre-
> pared; all you need to do is alternately beat them
> and reward them for them to become torturers in
> their turn. [Translation by Judith Landry, p.144]

The maximum number of people in the camp has been
set at 100,000, so each arriving convoy is matched with a
selection. Because she is in the orchestra Fénelon is not
quite as vulnerable but hears the whistles and heavy boots
in the night. The SS act as if selections are completely
ordinary and laugh and joke as they lock the truck doors then
go have a drink, play the piano, kiss a girl, order the orchestra to play (pp.61-64).

Some of the SS try to be ingenious in their selections
for the gas chambers and crematoria. One has a thousand
women stand naked in the cold. Passing in front of each,
he lifts their breasts. Those whose breasts fall are sent
to their death. Those whose breasts are firm are saved for
the day, unless they die of the cold (p.173). The same guard
orders a roll call and chooses fifty women to dig a ditch wide
enough that it is possible but difficult to jump. When the
ditch is ready he makes his naked charges run across it.
Those who fall in are gassed (p.190).

When the orchestra's drummer develops typhus Fania
has to learn to play the drums. She practices constantly,
frantically. By the next Sunday concert everyone in the barracks is exhausted from the noise. In the corridor between
camps A and B the orchestra plays its concert, with the SS

seated before them.   Fania leaps madly from one percussion
instrument to another, out to sing, back to drum.   The SS
find her hilarious.   Then a woman throws herself on the
electric fence.   Another tries to pull off the jerking body
and is herself electrocuted.   A third uses a stool to extri-
cate the first two.   All the while the SS are laughing and
poking each other while the orchestra plays "The Merry
Widow" (pp. 208-211).

Before the Jews of the orchestra are transferred to
Bergen-Belsen, Fania orchestrates numerous pieces for the
motley group.   None of the SS ever realizes the insult being
delivered when the orchestra plays music by Jewish compos-
ers or Beethoven's Fifth (the first four notes of which pre-
ceded BBC's broadcasts to occupied countries).

Red Müller is the worst of the SS guards in Marietta
Moskin's novel, I Am Rosemarie.   One day he accuses the
women of stealing two needles and threatens the camp with
three days without food.   The women know that a three-day
fast would kill many of them so agree to pay a ransom in-
stead--ten of their precious needles (pp. 123-129).

On Yom Kippur the SS harass the inmates by making
them shower.   This is one of the few showers Rosemarie has
while she is in Westerbork, and it is meant to humiliate the
religious Jews on a most holy day.   Four to five women are
driven under each shower head, there to stand briefly under
a trickle of water.   As they shower the SS watch them from
a catwalk above, taunting the emaciated women (pp. 130-134).

Guy Lambert becomes familiar with SS atrocities as a
prisoner of war (René Antona, Les Evasions du brigadier
Lambert).   In the first camp the SS take canned goods from
the prisoners under the guise of a redistribution plan.   Random violence is common.   As Guy is standing with a group
of prisoners an SS guard suddenly opens fire and kills two
of them (pp. 33-34).

In another camp the SS decide to disinfect.   They
make the prisoners empty their barracks before breakfast
and then stand naked in the snow for three hours.   Afterward
they give them cold showers, a cursory medical examination,
and only then, already past noon, do they allow them to dress
(pp. 57-58).

One of the SS men likes to have the prisoners stand

at attention by their bunks. He insults and slaps them, hoping to provoke a response that will give him an excuse to
kill. After a week of this he finds a soup pot in a closet.
Thinking it empty, he jerks it out and spills its contents on
his uniform. Furious, he breaks the pot and slaps around
its owner. His chief is incensed and demotes him, not for
slapping around prisoners but for destroying Reich property
(pp. 58-61).

Gerald Green, writing in The Artists of Terezin, cites
an incident typical of the bizarre concern with order that
even these perpetrators of death displayed. Terezin had been
set up as a model Jewish ghetto, a false front to give concentration camps a better reputation. When the new commandant came he wanted to set his house in order:

> Burger ordered a census. It took place on a
> misty, drizzling day, November 17, 1943. All
> forty thousand prisoners were marched to a muddy
> field, a low meadow lying between mountains. There
> this great host stood all day, without food or water,
> with no toilets, bending, weeping, murmuring, faint-
> ing. ... From seven in the morning until midnight,
> the census went on, and it established nothing at
> all--merely that there were approximately forty
> thousand people in the camp. When, after midnight,
> the Jews were allowed to stagger back to the camp,
> over three hundred corpses remained on the muddy
> field. [p. 83]

Two Jewish women in Auguste Lazar's Die Brücke von
Weissensand experience something unique, a spark of humanity in an SS man. They are part of the women being driven
from Auschwitz to keep them out of Russian hands. Any of
the exhausted women who step out of line are beaten and
killed. The women call one of the SS guards "der Lange."
Once when he is peeling an apple, he casually throws the
peels to the women until at last he is left with nothing but
the core. The other SS seem to respect and fear him, but
he does not try to restrain their brutality. To the women
he is a puzzle. Franziska and Mirjam support each other
on the march until Franziska becomes too exhausted to go
on. She climbs up on the death wagon. "Der Lange" pulls
her off. Franziska never speaks of what she saw on the
wagon, but she puts all her reserve of strength into marching on. "Der Lange" remains an enigma to the women.

In M. E. Kerr's Gentlehands an ex-SS concentration
camp guard is living quietly and wealthily in Montauk, New
York.   Skye and Buddy learn about him just after they have
been swapping anti-Semitic jokes.   The Nazi-hunting journal-
ist who is looking for "Gentlehands" lost a cousin in Auschwitz.   He reads a poem his cousin wrote about the barbarous
guard.   Gentlehands threw his prisoners to vicious dogs and
would play "O dolci mani" from Tosca to taunt the Italian inmates.   To his horror, Buddy sees his grandfather, a refined and gentle animal lover, unmasked as the notorious
killer.

One incident of humanity appears in this litany of horrors.   Small gestures seem like kindness only because of
their context.   Lazar's "Der Lange" is the exception that
proves the rule.   The SS dehumanized their victims and in
so doing became monsters.

Chapter 2

THE HOME FRONT: CIVILIAN
VICTIMS OF WAR

There is no such thing as a neutral battleground.
"The field of battle" sounds like a giant game board on which
the strategists move their players, each seeking advantage.
According to the rules, only players are directly affected,
with the outcome determined by the cleverness of the strategists and the skill of the combatants.   But the neutral field
is a farmer's land.   The wall so hotly contested once housed
a family.   The fallen player leaves a widow and children behind.   The field no longer supports life.   The soldier no
longer plants grain.   The city's sidewalks become a gunner's
targets.   And as the machinery of war grinds up its players,
new contestants are needed.   Education for understanding and
peace is replaced with training for enmity and death.

The lives of the non-contestants are the subjects of
this chapter.   Under "Schools" are the experiences of those
Hitler sought to manipulate.   The authors show what can happen to schools when they are seen as means to a political
end.

With resources being poured into destruction, no
country involved in war can provide the same level of goods
and services to its people as it can in peace time.   In the
countries occupied by Germany during World War II, hunger
was common.   Food became another weapon in Hitler's arse-
nal.   Ration books reflected the relative importance or worth
of the people in occupied lands.   In 1941 the following numbers of calories per day were allowed: Poland, 800; Belgium,
950; Norway, 1500; France, 1600; Holland, 1900; Germany,
2500.   The grim competition for scarce goods produced black
markets, thieves, hoarders, prostitutes, and informers.
Even though some authors in the section below on rationing

31

treat the subject lightly and certainly not everyone reacted
selfishly, the fact remains that hunger and suffering were
widespread.

Traveling in Germany, one is continually reminded of
another occurrence that becomes routine in war: air raids.
Tour guides point out areas of cities which were leveled or,
as in such cities as Heidelberg and Goslar, speak with pride
of having been spared the devastation.   Tourists look at ca-
thedrals and ask if they were standing after the war.   They
are often disappointed to learn that a quaint row of houses
was a pile of rubble in 1945.   People who survived the terror
still look shaken when they recall the nights spent in bomb
shelters, the friends crushed by collapsing buildings, the
grotesque anomaly of a bathtub hanging from the one remaining wall of their home, the stench of rotting corpses.   Those
still alive when the all-clear sounded emerged to carry on
with work or school, wore paths through the wreckage, ad-
justed to an abnormal pattern of reality.   Whatever their na-
tionality, wherever they crouched beneath the bombs, their
experience was similar and has been recreated by the authors
cited in this chapter.

SCHOOL

School is one of the most important institutions in any
society.   Its effectiveness is difficult to measure.   Research-
ers disagree on what methods work.   Dictators worry more
about ideology than pedagogical tactics.   They begin with the
premise that children can be molded to their will and impose
a curriculum that will properly shape them.   Schools under
Hitler replaced history with National Socialist ideology and
biology with racial science.   The books in this section show
what German students experienced in the Third Reich.

Even before the Nazis come into power the school in
Eugen Oker's ...und ich der Fahnenträger is affected by the
new doctrine.   In 1932 the boys' music teacher teaches them
forbidden Nazi songs.   They do not take the bellicose lyrics
too seriously but use them to irritate Bavarian peasants (pp.
12-15).

In 1933 the new greeting is required.   In his journal
entry for June 30, the narrator tells how his religion teacher,
a favorite among the boys, copes.   He raises his hand but
with two fingers together as if making the sign of the cross

and says, "'Heil Hitler im Namen des Vaters und des Sohnes
und des Heiligen Geistes, Amen.'" ("Heil Hitler in the name
of the Father, the Son, and the Holy Ghost, Amen.") (pp. 99-
102).

  Rassen-Biologie replaces the normal science curriculum. The teacher explains the change:

> New times, new lesson plans, he said. So now
> we're having race biology.
> It's really exciting. First we're learning what
> we really are. Until now we've thought that who-
> ever lives in Germany and speaks German is Ger-
> man. But that's not so. The foundation is the
> Indo-Germanic race. These are the Aryans. They're
> the most worthy beings on earth.... The Nordic
> race is the purest. The height of Germanism is
> embodied in it. They're called to build a new
> image of humanity. They are blond, long-skulled,
> have a straight nose, a determined mouth, and a
> vigorous chin. They're tall, slim, and strongly
> built. They have a noble character. They are
> born leaders. Unfortunately, they have become
> rare because of long racial mixing. But National
> Socialism will see to it that this race comes into
> its own once again. [pp. 124-125]

  Professor Eisberg, the biology teacher, makes a race
chart on which to display photographs of boys who represent
each type. Though the boys mock it, those who are desig-
nated racially superior scorn inferior types. The last box
on the chart is for Semites. Only one boy in the school is
Jewish, a quiet boy with no enemies. Now that the boys
have studied race biology they recognize that he is inferior.
Siegfried's father refuses to allow him to be photographed
for the race table. Soon afterward Siegfried stops coming
to school. In the last spot on the chart Professor Eisberg
fastens a picture of a repulsive boy cut from a Nazi publication and entitles it, "Siegfried Friedmann, ehem. 4a"
("Siegfried Friedmann, formerly of class 4a") (pp. 128-132).

  Not all teachers present the new biology as enthusiastically as Professor Eisberg. Fräulein Rosius in Irina
Korschunow's Er hiess Jan thinks it is nonsense. When she
should be teaching race ethnology Fräulein Rosius dismisses
it with an offhand comment:

/

"So it's been bandied about that there are different
races. East, west, Dinarish. Yes, and, of course,
the Nordic race. That's the top dog in the whole
menagerie. " [p. 50]

A new student from Berlin is offended and denounces Fräulein
Rosius to the authorities. Shortly thereafter she is taken
away (pp. 49-53).

Until Austria is taken over by Germany, school continues as usual, but in 1937 Inge gets a foretaste of days to
come (Doris Orgel, The Devil in Vienna). She is Jewish,
but her best friend, Liselotte, is the Jungmädel daughter of
an SA officer. Liselotte moves with her family to Munich
where her father can openly be a part of the National Socialist movement. From there Liselotte writes about her new
school:

This school is quite a change after Herrengasse
Gymnasium. For instance, here we don't have
Latin, Geography, or Natural Science. We do have
five hours of physical training a day: two and a
half of calisthenics, two and a half of games....
We also don't have French or English or Ancient
History. On the other hand, we have Housewifely
Arts--to learn to wield the ladle! And we have
Racial Science with a Herr Professor Wandke, who,
except for being bald, looks more like a hedgehog
than any human I ever saw. Today we measured
one another's heads from tops to chins and mem-
orized the names of different "Germanic racial fa-
cial types. " [34-35]

When Austria capitulates Inge's teachers are frightened.
Fräulein Pappenheim refuses to comment. The English
teacher disappears. The Latin teacher cries over the sentence in Cicero's letters to Atticus, " 'As yet I have encoun-
tered no man who would not rather yield to Caesar's demands
than fight. '" School is dismissed until further notice (pp. 114-
116).

Liselotte's family returns to Vienna, and the two
friends meet secretly. School reopens on March 21 after
a restructuring of the curriculum. The director has been
replaced by someone from Berlin. Nazi flags and propaganda
are everywhere. English, Latin, and Home Lore have been
eliminated for National Socialist ideology. Physical education

classes are doubled so that the girls can learn military
marching. The school splits into pro- and anti-Nazi factions. On March 25, the day that all Jewish girls are expelled from the school, Inge is at home grieving because she
knows her friendship with Liselotte has become too dangerous
for her family (pp. 197-215).

Hiltgunt Zassenhaus's father is the principal of a girls'
high school when Hitler becomes chancellor but is soon fired
(Zassenhaus, Walls). On January 30, 1933, Hiltgunt awakens
to find her bedroom window papered with thick, yellow paper
printed with black swastikas. Her school changes immediately.
Her favorite teacher and her classmates are intimidated. Their
book club can no longer read the same books. Being accustomed to thinking and acting freely, Hiltgunt defies the order
to greet everyone with "Heil Hitler." Her teacher reports
her, and the principal threatens her with expulsion. The
next day both the principal and teacher are watching for her
response. She desperately throws her left arm in the air,
breaks a window, and is rushed to the hospital. After this
no one looks her way when the "Heil Hitlers" resound. Hers
is a small refusal but the beginning of resistance (pp. 11-14).

Two opposing groups develop among the children in
Eve Radek's class (Eva Marder, Und das war erst der Anfang), the Browns on one side and every one else on the other.
The battle begins with a harmless street game which turns
into a serious struggle between the Browns (for Flag and Fatherland) and the others (for Honor). The Browns lose the
game and vow revenge. The tricks on each side become increasingly dirty until the Browns' leader puts a stop to them
by loftily refusing to believe that his troops would stoop so
low: "Unsere Jugend kämpft nicht mit Schmutz ... Unsere
Jugend hat Ideale" (pp. 53). ("Our youth does not fight with
filth ... Our youth has ideals") (pp. 44-55).

With the new school year all the town's youth groups
are to be absorbed by the Browns. Their first day back, the
children learn that their teacher is gone. Dr. Reisig takes
over the class and informs them that, by order of the local
Nazi leader, every day will begin with the national anthem
and the Horst Wessel song. So upset is he by the new order
that he is carelessly frank with the class. Watching Anna,
the most zealous of the Browns, the class knows that Dr.
Reisig has made a dangerous enemy (pp. 95-100).

In 1935 the Saar is returned to the homeland, and the

school in Hans Peter Richter's I Was There holds a special
celebration.   The narrator's teacher is visibly disturbed to
see his class appear in brown shirts and asks the narrator
to tell the principal he will not be at the ceremony, "for personal reasons."   In one class only the narrator's friend,
Günther, the child of a Communist, breaks the brown pattern
with his green suit.   The principal gives a chauvinistic speech
about the perfidy of the French and the overwhelming vote of
the Germans of the Saar (91 percent) to come home to the
Reich.   He thanks the Führer and then turns to his restless
audience:

> "It saddens me," the principal was saying, "when
> I see how little gratitude we show our great leader
> who is in the process of raising the German Reich
> to its true glory and heroic greatness.   I will feel
> no real pleasure until only Brown Shirts surround
> me, until all the opponents of the Führer have been
> wiped out!"   He pointed to Günther's class and went
> on.   "Look how the uniform picture of one whole
> class is destroyed by one boy, the only one who has
> not found himself willing to join our supreme leader.
> It is a disgrace for our school.   I feel ashamed
> each time I remember that there are still boys in
> my school who do not unreservedly proclaim their
> loyalty to the Führer, boys who do not belong to
> Jungvolk or the Hitler Youth.   I feel ashamed!" he
> shouted in a plaintive voice. [Translation by Edite
> Kroll, p. 47]

Suddenly Günther finds himself isolated, and when the principal declares the rest of the day a holiday, he has to walk
home alone (pp. 36-39).

In 1936 everyone has Olympic fever.   The narrator's
town schedules a contest in which the best athletes from each
school are to compete.   Although Günther is the fastest run-
ner in his school, he is not allowed to participate because he
does not belong to the Jungvolk (pp. 48-50).

Until Jonas Partell brings home a frightened Jewish
girl he does not question what he learns in school (Werner
Toporski, Mädchen mit Stern).   Since the Socialists and Communists stabbed their own troops in the back by forcing the
Kaiser to capitulate in World War I, it is only right that they
be hounded out of the country now.   The teacher tells them
how the party of Adolf Hitler is saving Germany:

And then he told how it went after the capitulation. How great was the suffering of the German people because of the reparation payments, particularly to France. How the Social Democratic government ("those unpatriotic hacks") showed itself incompetent to help the people. And how the Jews had stolen the last penny out of the pockets of the poverty-stricken folk. But then came the National Socialists, the party of Adolf Hitler, and restored order step by step!

Jonas found German history interesting. He hated Social Democrats ("Sozis"), Communists, and Jews. What did they have against Germany anyway? After all, they were Germans too! Why did they have to oppose everything? He didn't understand it. If he ever got one in his hands he'd show him! [p. 19]

Jonas begins to see through the lies once he takes in Agnes but continues to go along with them so as not to endanger her.

Were the lies and deceit effective? Certainly not every child became a zealous Hitler Youth, but enough did to make them a mighty force for National Socialism. Successful products of the new ideology became desensitized to the humanity of all those classed as inferior or enemies and provided a huge pool from which the Nazis could draw.

Additional titles:

Finckh, Renate. Mit uns zieht die neue Zeit, pp. 100, 155-156, 163-164.
Grün, Max von der. Wie war das eigentlich?, pp. 68-69, 71-73.
Hautzig, Esther. The Endless Steppe, pp. 95-107 (Jews exiled in Siberia).
Moskin, Marietta. I Am Rosemarie, pp. 27-31 (Jewish girl in Holland).
Sachs, Marilyn. A Pocket Full of Seeds, pp. 87-89 (France under Pétain).

RATIONING

Not only war's violence damages ties between human

beings. The struggle for inadequate supplies of food, clothing, and shelter shrivels the soul and makes people regard
each other with jealous wariness, as is seen in the books in
this section.

Austria

Two books give a picture of food shortages in Austria
at the end of the war. In the first, eight-year-old Christine
is living with her grandparents in Vienna until she and her
mother are offered the villa of a fleeing Nazi woman (Christine Nöstlinger, Fly Away Home). They have little more than
potatoes to eat, but Grandmother is quite firm about sticking
to a schedule. Monday they eat them with dill, Tuesday baked,
Wednesday as potato pancakes with turnips, Thursday mashed,
Friday as goulash, Saturday as potato cakes. Only once does
she deviate by mistake from the fixed plan:

> ... Grandmother only once went wrong, when she
> made potato cakes on a Tuesday, and on that oc-
> casion she was all excited because she had won
> thirty marks in the lottery. Directly afterwards
> she got very angry because she found that there
> was nothing she could buy with her thirty marks.
> Grandmother ran back to the lottery ticket office
> and flung her thirty marks down on the table in
> front of the woman there, shouting, "Here you are!
> You can put that silly bit of paper in your pipe and
> smoke it! I can't get anything for it! So much
> for your stupid money! Why don't you give meat
> coupons for prizes instead--at least they'd be worth
> something!" [Translation by Anthea Bell, p. 7]

One of Christine's favorite stops when she goes with
her grandfather on his deliveries is to a clock dealer who is
now a black market businessman. He always has a piece of
lemon candy for her. Christine's mother, however, cannot
stand the man, and Christine tells why:

> My mother could not stand the man who owned
> the Clock Studio. The reason for this was that
> once my mother came by a lot of money, a legacy
> from an old aunt who died. In the evening, when
> the shops were closed, my mother went to see the
> antique clock man. She gave him all the money,
> and in return he got her three kilos of bacon and
> four kilos of sugar. My mother had expected to

> get half a pig, at least, for all that money, but the
> antique clock man just laughed at her and said that
> money was worth nothing in times like these.   Half
> a pig! She'd need to give a piano or five winter
> coats, for half a pig, he said.... [Translation by
> Anthea Bell, p. 9]

Nöstlinger has further memories of finding hoarded food in
an empty house, of looting an abandoned Nazi home, of helping her old neighbor to sort the noodles and beans he has
shoveled from its floor, of being given food by the Russians.
The second book is well written but lacks Nöstlinger's sensitive acceptance of people no matter under what flag lie their
loyalties.

    In the last days of the war a peaceful Tirolean valley
fills with refugees (Maria Klingler, Nimm den Diktator und
geh).   They flock to Uncle Felix, who does his best to find
them shelter.   One day Teta, the housekeeper, decides to
make blood sausage.   She is furious that the refugees, who
live in the best rooms, eat their last bread, spread lice and
dirt, and take over the kitchen, have had the gall to give her
nothing more than a bucket of blood and casings from the sow
they slaughtered.   Still it's not to be wasted.   She prepares
the sausages and fills the casings.   Bibi's job is to cut the
strings.   She aims carefully with the knife but cuts the wrong
end.   The bloody filling sprays the kitchen (pp. 46-50).   The
blood on the walls nearly gets Uncle Felix in trouble.   When
the Americans come one of the refugees tells them that he
killed a soldier in the kitchen (pp. 67-71).

    The arrival of the Americans does not end the food
shortages, but Bibi learns from a friend how to make the
best of the situation.   Each day they sit alongside the road
eating sorrel.   The Americans think they are eating grass
and give them chocolate, gum, sour drops, and chicken.
Bibi refuses to accept alms from the enemy, but Anger Sepp
has no such scruples and shares what he gets with Bibi (pp.
80-81).

Belgium

    Gil Lacq remembers the deprivations brought on by the
occupation in Belgium with the light-hearted acceptance of a
happy child (Les enfants de la guerre).   During the bitterly
cold second winter, people gather anything combustible.   The
only thing being sold is "schlam," a combination of coal dust

and nonflammable residues. Before it can be used it has to
be dampened and broken up, a muddy job Gil adores. Wheat
is scarce, so bread is a grey, heavy mass enriched with
livestock fodder, straw, and dead insects (pp. 22-25).

        To supplement their food supply, Gil's family starts
raising chickens and a few rabbits. The feed grain attracts
rats, so the boys raise guinea pigs to scare them away. The
scheme works well until the population expands so dramati-
cally that the guinea pigs are eating more grain than the rats
ever did. Before they solve that problem, Gil and his brother
have incurred the wrath of dozens of angry parents, whose
offspring have become proud owners of the fertile brood (pp.
30-43).

        The neighbors buy a pig to raise on their 1 x 2 meter
balcony. The whole neighborhood supplies scraps and watches
Adolf's growth with anticipation. On the day of Adolf's slaughter no volunteer steps forward to help, so the totally inexper-
ienced owner swallows his horror and starts the chase. Gil
and his brother watch the spectacle with mixed hilarity and
revulsion, but it is too much for Emile's father. He takes
to his bed, and a neighbor calls his brother, a butcher, to
carve the pig. When the butcher declares the uncastrated
male pig's meat fit only for dog food, the neighbors alternate
between calling Emile's father an imbecile for raising an uncastrated male pig and for falling for the butcher's story.
Gil is sure he smells lard and roast blood sausage through
the windows of the butcher's brother (pp. 58-70).

        Not all of Lacq's memories are lighthearted. He
remembers peasants as being greedy and crafty. Belgian
civilians were hired to prevent people from making black
market purchases from them. Lacq considers those civilians
to have been traitors and good-for-nothings who probably ate
or sold most of what they found during their inspections (pp.
76-78).

France

        Ruses to supplement rations were sometimes comic
though their intent was serious. French authors give two
such examples. In Ouf de la forêt by Minou Drouet the
peasants of Ille-et-Villaine stop bringing their produce into
the weekly market, and the villagers start making direct
black market deals with them. When the police crack down,
people hide food in their clothing. The notary's wife crochets

a fine new hat with room inside for six eggs. Normally,
after her forays to the country, she tips Victor, a young
scamp, so that he will not give her away, but one day she
forgets. A policeman stops her. Victor looks at him and
then, meaningfully, at her hat. The policeman's umbrella
accidentally strikes the hat, and two ribbons of yellow roll
down her cheeks. When he pulls off her hat, four more eggs
tumble to the ground. From then on the proud woman is
called "la mère Omelette" (pp. 79-82).

In spite of the general scarcity of food, the Marquess of Hélène Ray's Ionel, la musique et la guerre often
has delicacies to share with her friends. Curious about the
source of the food, Ionel accompanies her one day and learns
of her audacious scheme. From churches she finds out who
is marrying and from shops, where and when the receptions
are to be. On the proper day she presents herself to the
bride's parents as the Marquess of so and so. Puzzled but
not wanting to offend nobility, they say nothing as she stuffs
herself and her purse. Then after giving her best wishes,
the Marquess makes a dignified exit (pp. 162-166).

Germany

Hiltgunt Zassenhaus first experiences rationing in Hamburg as soon as war is declared (Zassenhaus, Walls). On
September 1, 1939, the Nazi government issues food and gasoline coupons and orders a general blackout. By the time
she reaches the store, Hiltgunt is too late to buy blackout
material, so she starts home. Passing the family's regular
grocery store, she sees a long line. Anxiety and panic sweep
over her, and she joins the line. After hours of waiting she
finds only scouring powder left in the store. She buys ten
pounds and feels quite proud of herself. The author claims
that even today she has trouble buying one of anything (pp. 48-
49).

From the beginning of rationing, Jews receive less.
On August 27, 1939, the Deutschkrons receive rationing cards
marked with "J" (Inge Deutschkron, Ich trug den gelben Stern).
They are allowed no extra allotments and cannot buy nonra-
tioned items. By 1942 they are issued no coupons for meat,
sugar, vegetables or fruit. Anyone lucky enough to acquire
special rations by any means cooks them late at night, running the risk of being turned in by an envious neighbor. Even
housing is rationed to Jews. Inge and her mother have to
move into a Jewish house. Eleven people are crowded into

five and a half rooms with one bath and one kitchen. Each
morning the bath is the center of contention, for to be late
to work means certain deportation (pp. 98-101).

Another family, the Singelmanns, feels the pinch of
shortages in spite of their being outward supporters of the
regime (Barbara Gehrts, Nie wieder ein wort davon?). Mr.
Singelmann works evenings writing radio broadcasts to earn
enough money to buy black market butter from Holland. They
and their close friends lease a plot and dream of raising
enough vegetables on it to feed them well. Their first problem is that the field is a sewage plot and lies under a layer
of feces. Even when it soaks in, no one is eager to start
digging. With cigarettes and schnapps they persuade a farmer
to turn it over, and with "Vitamin B" (the author's term for
acquiring things through extra-legal means), they get seed
potatoes. During the harvest of 1942, the narrator's father
is arrested. As the two children push home the cart with
four sacks of potatoes, they are caught in an air raid. When
they emerge from shelter, two of the sacks are gone.

Nothing can be wasted. When an enemy plane is shot
down in Evelyn Hardey's ... damals war ich fünfzehn, people
cut up the dead pilot's parachute for cloth. Evelyn's mother
carefully winds up the cords and uses them to knit a jacket
(pp. 48-49). Blankets become coats, with the border bands
falling like a decorative stripe beneath the arms (p. 66).

Medicine is in short supply. In December 1944 Evelyn
gets chilblains on her knees and has to use an old folk rem-
edy:

> Crap! I have chilblains on both knees. Grandma's
> salve is all gone, and now I have to use an unbe-
> lievably old home remedy: urinate on it. We're
> already living like cavemen, and now I'm supposed
> to pee on my knee! [124]

The Dereks are grimly determined that their daughter
and granddaughter will suffer no want during the war (Ilse
Koehn, Mischling, Second Degree). They persuade their
daughter to divorce her half-Jewish husband and to move with
Ilse to their farm outside Berlin. One Saturday in the fall
of 1942 they rouse Mutti and Ilse at 4:30 a.m. to pick wild
raspberries and gather mushrooms. All day and into the
night they clean berries and make jam. Two air raid alarms
send Mutti and Ilse cowering to the basement, but the grandparents go right on working (pp. 96-98).

Day after day people spend hours standing in lines.
As she waits in a line at the Kulewski's bakery in October
1942, Ilse watches a familiar scene:

> ... I am standing in line at Kulewski's bakery.
> The line moves slowly. The woman behind me
> knits a sock for her son in Stalingrad. ... She
> mumbles to herself and keeps knitting while her
> feet move automatically as the line advances.
> Among the eighty or so people waiting here there
> are few young women. Most are children or old
> people. ... Everyone looks gray, weary. We are
> all resigned to standing here for some time. Three
> or four women seem to be squatting strangely. They
> have brought folding chairs, but these become vis-
> ible only when the line moves. Then hands reach
> under broad behinds, drag the chairs a yard for-
> ward, and the women sink back, hiding the chairs
> again. The one in front of me reads, doesn't look
> up. The one who knits uses her needles to scratch
> her head occasionally and mumbles something about
> her son. ...
> Talk is scarce: last night's raid, the expected
> sugar delivery at the grocery. Yawns and excla-
> mations. "I'm so tired. Wish they'd let us sleep
> one night. Just one night. But no. Alarms every
> goddamn night." All the usual topics. ... It has
> all been talked over, discussed from every possible
> angle. ... [pp. 101-102]

By January 1945 ration cards are nearly worthless.
Only 25 grams of sugar and 50 of butter are allowed per
week and then only when supplies are available. People
stand in line for hours only to be told that nothing is left.
Because of the farm the Dereks have enough to eat, but they
do not have coal. When Grossmutter hears of a coal delivery,
she asks Ilse to come with her to help with the cart. People arrive with every possible sort of container. Through
the line run rumors and complaints. Grandmother has just
decided to give up and return home when Farmer Neuendorff's
head appears over the gate. "Go home!" he tells the crowd.
"There is no coal! I don't know where you got the idea that
I have coal. Go home. I don't have any" (pp. 183-185).

Additional titles:

Richter, Hans Peter. Die Zeit der Jungen Soldaten,
    pp. 46-47.

Toporski, Werner.   Mädchen mit Stern, pp. 46-47.

Greece

The suffering of the Greeks in World War II receives
scant attention in books for young people, but Alki Zei makes
up for the lack in the quality of her books.   In Petros' War
she describes the cruel winter of November 1941, when snow
fell in Athens.   The only fire Petros' family has is for cook-
ing, their fuel just sawdust in a can with a twist of newspaper
as a wick.   Grandfather plods through the house with a blanket tied around his waist, and Petros' hands are blue and
swollen.   People collapse in the street and sell everything
of value for a few crumbs.   Only the baker's three daughters
stay plump.   Each Sunday they sit in the window of the bakery, flaunting the dolls and jewelry and finery sold to their
father by people desperate for bread.   The daily bread ration
is 30 grams of a soggy, yellow mass.   It sticks to the paper
it is baked on, so people eat that as well (pp. 80-88).

Petros is ashamed to catch Grandfather shaving thin
slices off everyone else's bread ration.   Then he sees the
old man turn Theodore on his back.   With knife in hand,
Grandfather eyes the turtle.   As he rescues his pet, Petros
sorrows to see the once-proud man brought so low (pp. 100-
101).

Holland

In Gertie Evenhuis's What About Me?, Dirk is skep-
tical of his brother's tales of pre-war plenty.   Sebastian's
stories are outlandish.   Dirk cannot imagine having as much
chocolate, fruit, white bread, soap, toys, and clothes as he
wants, and without having to use ration books or coupons or
stand in lines.   Lighted streets and fireworks are just fairy
tales in 1943.   Eleven-year-old Dirk's coat is fourth hand;
his socks are made from his father's underwear; his raincoat
was once a sheet (pp. 11-14).

The situation becomes worse as the war drags on.
Els Pelgrom writes in The Winter When Time Was Frozen
of Germans looking for shelter one night and mistreating their
sick horse.   The horse dies in the night, and they bury it.
A day later the grave is empty.   Hungry villagers have dug
up the horse and divided it (pp. 154-156).

Poland

Rations for the ghettos of Eastern Europe were just enough that people died slowly. Hershel in Yuri Suhl's On the Other Side of the Gate uses his ingenuity and his skilled worker's certificate to smuggle food into the ghetto. Even when he works at ordinary jobs, he is allowed to carry his tool box so he builds into it small compartments for hiding bits of food. After having to forego buying an egg because he has nowhere to hide it, he fashions a copper tool whose hollow length can hide two eggs, an apple, a potato, or an onion. His decision to smuggle a herring, a rare delicacy in the ghetto, nearly gives him away:

> One day he had the opportunity to buy a herring. A commonplace item before the war but a real delicacy now in the ghetto. He couldn't resist the temptation. By rolling the herring tightly into a ball he was able to squeeze it into the copper receptacle. It was not until he'd opened the tool box for inspection that he realized his mistake. He hadn't counted on the smell. The herring had been in there since lunchtime and in the ensuing hours had filled the box with its distinctive aroma. The guard sniffed, crinkled his nose, then dumped the tools on the ground. It was a tense and anxious moment for Hershel as he watched the guard separate the tools with the toe of his boot. "All right. Pick 'em up!" he finally barked. Then he gave Hershel a thorough going over, passing his hands up and down his trousers, his sleeves, and turning his pockets inside out. Finally, still looking baffled, he let him go. [pp. 56-57]

Among the most audacious of those who smuggled food into the Warsaw ghetto was Martin Gray. Au nom de tous les miens is his autobiography. He is not yet sixteen when he organizes a successful contraband route. He hires street punks outside the ghetto to be his bodyguards and violent types within to act as porters. He makes direct contacts with peasants to arrange for grain shipments. In spite of his forged identity cards and perfect mastery of German, Polish, and German-accented Polish, he is in and out of the hands of the police. When the trams stop running through the ghetto, he loses transportation for his supplies and has to switch to caskets and burial carts and then to garbage trucks. Before the Gestapo pick him up and torture him,

Gray has become so frantic that he is operating openly, driving loads directly through the ghetto gate and paying everyone along the line. Gray's desperate courage brings hope to many, but the odds he challenges are overwhelming.

Hunger was the constant companion of millions of people during World War II. Its effects are incalculable. No accurate count records all of the deaths. No survey numbers the people who even now keep their larders filled not out of foresight but because they fear the memories of the terrible years.

AIR RAIDS

The accounts in this section are some of the most terrifyingly real in young adult literature. The authors have succeeded in recreating the horror and fascination of the fireworks that wrought destruction.

Animals

Animals as well as people were caught in the hell of raids and had no chance of comprehending. A Stuka swoops out of the sky, guns blazing, and kills two gypsies in Sheila Burnford's Bel Ria. Their little dog is cut adrift from his familiar world and starts on a sad, strange journey during which he will touch many lives.

Bel Ria has already made a deep impact on two men when he is caught in the hellish bombing of Plymouth. He had grown accustomed to the sounds of battle while he was on a ship at sea but had never been alone. This time he is trapped in a strange house.

> When the first stick of bombs screamed down, each earthshaking crump landing inexorably nearer, almost as though they searched him out, Ria started to his feet, and cowered against the back door; then as the last bomb began its shrieking pursuit, he bolted under the table. The bomb landed squarely between the next two adjoining houses of the terrace, slicing a path between them as cleanly as a knife through bread. The kitchen rocked and shuddered to the blast, then settled, sagging. [p. 132]

The house collapses. Bel Ria drifts across the rubble and

out into the courtyard, then bolts into the street as the door
crashes down behind him.

> Now he smelled fear, death, and terrible human
> excitement, an evil blend that sent him, eyes glazed
> and wild, skittering and slithering across the rubble
> and glass-strewn streets, shying away from the
> running boots of wardens and firemen, leaping over
> obstructions, until he reached the open spaces of
> the Hoe. And here he ran madly again, up the con-
> crete paths, across the grass, from crater to cra-
> ter, then down to the sea, his claws scrabbling
> wildly on the slimy steps as he turned away from
> it again. Each flare, each bomb, each salvo from
> the guns galvanized the desperate aimless running
> in the red glare of this world gone mad. [p. 134]

Three days later the little dog finds Alice Tremorne, a 76-
year-old semi-invalid who is trapped beneath the rubble of
her garage. The dog's soft concern helps give her strength,
and once again Bel Ria fills a human being with joy (pp. 131-
146).

> Käthe Recheis' friend Willi teaches his dog to run from
the sound of shooting (Käthe Recheis, "Unser Hund und der
Krieg," Damals war ich vierzehn, pp. 27-35). When everyone's pet dog is tested for usefulness in combat, his dog fails.
Unfortunately, Käthe's Donar is too dumb to learn such tricks,
so she kicks him with a nail when the shooting starts. His
startled escape disqualifies him.

> Though he is not bright enough to master tricks, Donar
learns quickly that air raid sirens mean danger. He is always
first into the cellar during raids. A stranger tells Käthe's
parents that dogs can go mad when they panic. Next time
the siren blares they lock Donar in the hen house. He howls,
bombs drop, explosions rend the night. The terrified animal
breaks free and runs to the basement. Never again do they
lock him out, but long after the war Donar remembers. Each
Saturday when the factory siren blows, he runs to hide in the
basement.

Additional title:

> Ruck-Pauquet, Gina.   Kralle.

Belgium

One of Gil Lacq's greatest pleasures during the war
is drawing airplanes (Lacq, Les enfants de la guerre). When
the Allies begin bombing Germany, the nightly squadrons passing overhead are a sign to Belgians that someone is fighting
on their side. They rejoice in the flights without thinking of
the civilians caught below the bombs:

> We listened, laughing and rubbing our hands in
> satisfaction. The bastards--they started it; now it
> was their turn!
> We didn't tell ourselves that each one of these
> bombardments meant thousands of women, children,
> and old people killed, burned, crushed, mangled.
> We didn't think about the life of these other people,
> their terror and their panic as, night after night,
> for weeks on end, during 55 minutes as in Berlin,
> the deafening noise over their cities announced death
> and destruction, never allowing them respite or
> sleep.
> No, we didn't think about it. We cheered. We
> rejoiced.
> When men fight, even civilians and spectators
> quickly become vicious. [p. 92]

The author gives one of the most graphic descriptions
of the bombings of Hamburg and Dresden (pp. 93-96). The
bombing of Hamburg is timed carefully to catch people at
home. The first wave of bombing is followed by the dropping
of incendiaries. The city burns for days:

> What also burned during these days was people.
> Covered with sticky, gummy phosphorous, they ran,
> rolled in the earth, threw buckets of water on each
> other. None of that helped. The only way to ex-
> tinguish phosphorous is to smother it by depriving
> it of air, of oxygen. The only solution--to cover
> themselves with sand or jump in the water. Hun-
> dreds of them plunged into the Elbe. Those whose
> wounds or burns were not serious enough to kill
> them stayed in the water, only their faces or noses
> protruding. As soon as they tried to emerge, the
> phosphorous with which they were covered would
> burst into flames. All this in the middle of the
> ruins and fires of a destroyed city.
> Their families, or doctors and emergency work-

ers, fed them, gave them to drink, tried to encourage the poor unfortunates, who were burned, suffo-
cating, freezing in the cold water. Sometimes, unable to stand it any longer, one of them would let
go of the rope, the boat, or the quay to which they
had been clinging for days and drown.

How to help them? How to rescue them? Go
underwater to undress them, scrape their skin, cut
away the wounds impregnated with phosphorous?

After several days and when the most urgent
problem, the fires, had been taken care of, the
authorities realized what was happening and particularly the horrible effect, depressing and deplorable,
that these hundreds of unfortunates, neither dead nor
alive, were having on their families and the rest of
the population. A regiment of SS arrived at the
spot, pushed everyone back, took the situation in
hand. Not to worry; everything would be taken care
of.

Everything was taken care of all right--the SS
slaughtered all of the victims and carried away
their corpses.

Such was the first major experiment in the sci-
entific bombardment of a civilian population. [pp.
94-95]

Three of the bombardments of Brussels remain in
Lacq's mind. The first raid kills a classmate of his brother's
who has gone back into his school to retrieve his new pen.
The second kills nearly everyone on a streetcar in which
Gil is riding. Smaller than the others on the tram, Gil survives because of the cushion of their bodies. He extricates
himself from the corpses and walks home, a little shaken
but proud of himself. The third time, he remembers being
in the school shelter, standing by a little girl to watch the
bombers fly overhead. A bomb drops in the schoolyard.
Gil awakes in the rubble, a little decapitated girl in his arms
(pp. 103-108).

Great Britain

Instead of being bowed by the bombing that levels
whole sections of their city and kills and mutilates many,
the Exeter folk raise themselves from the rubble and get about
the task of resuming normal life, feeling proud and defiant
(David Rees, The Exeter Blitz). Through the activities of
one family, the author relives the destruction of the town.

Mr. Lockwood and his daughter, June, are at home when they
hear the crack of explosions, and the house disintegrates
around them.   Mrs. Lockwood is assisting at a fashion show.
She is among the last to head for shelter and, when the elec-
tricity shuts off, is trapped in an elevator between floors.
Though those in the elevator are imprisoned by tons of ma-
sonry, they are the only ones in the building to survive.
Colin watches the bombing from the church tower.   Mary
waits it out in a shelter, then reports for work at the hospital.
She is dazed by what she sees is left of her town:

> Several churches had been destroyed.   The top
> of the tower of one of them had been sliced off,
> horizontally, exposing the bells to the wind and
> the weather, and St. Sidwell's had lost its west
> front: looking into it was like staring into the
> throat of a giant fish.   The books in the public
> library were still burning.   The probate registry
> had received a direct hit; six hundred years of
> private and public history lay in ashes.   In places
> where the rubble had not yet been cleared, steel
> girders wound and bent as if they were made of
> plasticine; a few walls stood, their windows just
> gaping squares, around them a desert of stone and
> plaster.   Electric light wires and telephone lines
> were tangled in grotesque knots, their poles totter-
> ing at weird angles, missing insulators like empty
> sockets in rows of teeth.   Half-damaged buildings
> curiously reminded her of people.   One whose roof
> had fallen in looked squashed, its windows flattened
> and crooked, like a man who has been hit on the
> head, so brutally that his eyes bulged out.   Any
> broken window was a face with a shattered eye, a
> blown-off door a mouth open with shock.   One house
> had tilted sideways into another; it was a woman
> fainting on a man's shoulder.   Everywhere missing
> arms, sagging jaws, men on crutches, lunatics:
> that was what whole streets resembled.   Screams
> of agony, frozen in stone. [pp. 111-112]

While Mr. Lockwood looks for a new home and Mrs.
Lockwood lies in a hospital bed, Colin and a friend revel in
their freedom.   They set up a fish-and-chips business, frying
fish that would spoil otherwise, roasting potatoes, and passing
them out free.

For Colin, the bombing has opened a new era in his

life, more free and exciting. In a complicated way he feels
almost grateful to Hitler. Best of all, his beloved cathedral
is still standing, its two towers giving the victory sign.

Air raids bring Bill and Julie together in Jill Walsh
Paton's Fireweed. Bill's aunt sends him to Wales after his
father enters the military. The family he stays with is kind
enough, but when he learns his father is to be home on leave,
the homesick boy returns to London. Julie's parents send
her on a ship to Canada. The boat is torpedoed, and the
children are returned to England in lifeboats. Most return
to their families to wait for the next ship, but Julie's wealthy
father does not want the fuss of another goodbye so leaves
her in the hostel. Both young people end up lonely and alone
in the city. Bill spots Julie in an air raid shelter and follows
her out.

The two join forces. In spite of the incessant air
raids, they experience a glorious sense of freedom from
adult constraints. One night they are caught outside in an
air raid when they run from a young man who wants to en-
roll them in school. The force of a nearby explosion nearly
pins them to the girders of a bridge. Bill is the first to recover:

> Very cautiously I got up and put my head over
> the parapet. I remember hearing my own voice
> saying very slowly and clearly, "God ... in heaven
> ... look at that!"
> She moved. She looked too. Below us, the
> water of the river was a sheet of orange and gold.
> The eastern sky, as in a monstrous sunrise, was
> an expanse of limpid golden light, as though the
> sky itself were a wall of fire. Against it we could
> see the slender spires of Wren's churches and the
> great dome of St. Paul's. They were not mere
> silhouettes; the corners, the columns, the curve
> of the dome had been traced in lines of reflected
> light, as though they had been drawn with a pencil
> of flame. London was burning. It was all on fire.
> The immensity of it quenched my own fear in a
> wave of awe; it seemed like the end of the world.
> [p. 64]

Bill and Julie establish a cozy hideaway in the still-
intact basement of her aunt's house but lose their precious
independence when they take in a little lost boy. Food be-

comes a problem. Julie can no longer help forage because
Dickie panics if she is out of his sight. Bill returns from
one of his food hunts to find that the house has collapsed
around Julie and Dickie.

Searchers find Julie completely buried, Dickie sleeping
peacefully. At the last minute someone thinks to tell Bill
that Julie is alive. Reunited with her family, Julie is no
longer accessible to Bill. She is remote, a protected child,
and Bill feels betrayed. Too late he realizes that she may
have been hiding the nature of their relationship from her
family so that they would allow him to see her again.

As with many authors for young people, Walsh keeps
her focus narrow. It is not her intent to give an overall
view of the war or of England's participation in it. The novel
focuses on two young people thrust into maturity before they
are prepared.

Additional titles:

> Allan, Mabel Esther.   Time to Go Back.
> Burton, Hester.   In Spite of All Terror, pp. 178-195.
> Cooper, Susan.   Dawn of Fear.

Germany

Human beings are remarkably adaptable. One night
150 planes bomb Berlin, and the glass in the balcony door
of Evelyn's house is blown out (Evelyn Hardey, ... damals
war ich fünfzehn). What impresses Evelyn most is that she
gets to stand by Axel, the boy she admires, in the bucket
brigade. As the two start home Axel hunts for bomb fragments to add to his collection. He finds the largest he has
ever seen and gives it to Evelyn (pp. 42-45).

Ironically, an air raid saves her mother's life. The
night of November 24, 1943, her labor pains start. During
a break in the bombing, Evelyn defies the block warden and
runs for the doctor. Next day she learns that had her mother's pains started before the alarm, her mother and her new
sister would have been buried in the rubble of the clinic (pp.
76-78).

The shelter in which Walter Jendrich's family waits
through air raid warnings is a dugout in a cliff, formerly

used as a beer storehouse (Horst Burger, Vier Fragen an
meinen Vater). One night there Walter falls in love with
frank, open Marianne Bork. He remembers when mothers
used to warn their children not to play with her. The poor
child was always dirty, her nose running, probably lice rid-
den. This night Walter puts aside any distaste he might have
had. He has never been so close to a girl before, and here
is Marianne beside him, talking freely about school and marriage and movies. While Marianne is questioning Walter and
he is falling in love, a drunk in the shelter starts grumbling
about the war and final victory. When the all-clear sounds
the man is arrested. That makes little impression on Walter,
who spends a sleepless night worrying about what Marianne
thinks about him (pp. 54-62).

Next day he buys flowers and leaves them on Marianne's doorstep. For days he finds reasons to pass by her
house. He never sees her and longs for an air raid to bring
them together again. Then comes an alarm at midnight.
Never before has his small, non-industrial, non-military town
been bombed. This night it is, ferociously. Walter searches
the shelter in vain for Marianne. At the all-clear signal, he
is the first out the door, first to see the flaming hell where
houses had stood, first to see where once he left a potted
plant on a girl's doorstep. Inflamed by the death of Marianne, Walter's hatred for the enemy grows (pp. 63-68).

On February 3, 1945, Ilse's grandfather sends her to
Tegel, near Berlin, for a pail of pig fodder (Ilse Koehn, Mischling, Second Degree). It is one of her mother's rare days
off, and mother and daughter have been looking forward to
baking a cake. That makes no difference to grandfather. Nor
does it matter that they do not need the fodder. He has made
arrangements with two old friends, who hope for part of his
pig, and Ilse must go. Ilse is near Tegel when the sirens
sound:

> Sirens! A drill? An alert? Probably one or
> two reconnaissance planes. But I look for a shelter
> just in case. The tiny houses of old Tegel village
> look far from safe, and, anyway, all the garden
> gates I try are locked. I keep on walking, hoping
> to reach the shelter before there's a full alarm.
> The sirens blare, howl. Full alarm! Oh my God,
> where is everyone? The only being in sight is a
> little girl pushing a doll carriage. She can't be
> more than six years old. I run, catch up with her
> and see that there's a live baby in the carriage.

"Where do you go? Where's your shelter during
air raids?"

"The bunker." She points to the other side of
the bridge.

Thank God, a bunker. Bunkers are safe. God,
how slow she is! "Come on, come on, hurry up!"
I carry the baby, with my pail banging against my
side. She has only to pull the empty carriage, but
it's slow going up the steps to the bridge. Steps,
more steps, damn these steps! Finally, the top.
We race onto the bridge, stop for breath in the
middle of the hundred-yard span. What's that noise?
A swarm of hornets? Where? And then we see
them, and for one long moment we stand frozen.

"Oh, my God!" What a sight! Hundreds, thousands of airplanes are coming toward us! The whole
sky is aglitter with planes. Planes flying undis-
turbed in perfect V formation, their metal bodies
sparkling in the sun. And no anti-aircraft guns.
Only the terrifying, quickly intensifying hum of
engines, thousands of engines. The air vibrates,
seems to shiver; the water, the ground and the
bridge under us begin to tremble. It's unearthly,
a tremendously beautiful sight! A whole blue sky
full of silver planes.

We run. The first formation is already overhead. All hell breaks loose. The anti-aircraft
guns shoot and bombs fall like rain. Millions of
long, rounded shapes come tumbling down around
us. The sky turns gray, black, the earth erupts.
The detonations begin to sound like continuous thun-
der.

A house! Shelter from this nightmare. We
reach it, though I don't know how. I collide with
the old lady who is standing in the door. She tries
to take the baby away from me. We stand in the
doorway, entangled by the pail, and I see the bomb,
watch it hit the roof, and see the house cave in
behind her.

"God in heaven!" she screams. "God in heaven!"

"Grandma! Grandma!" wails the little girl,
pulling at her skirt. "Grandma, let's go to the
bunker, please, please, Grandma!"

I'm flat on the ground. Bombs, bombs, bombs
fall all around me. It can't be. It's a dream.
There aren't that many bombs in the whole world.
Maybe I'm dead? I get up, drag pail, old woman

and girl with me toward a porch, a concrete porch
with space underneath.   Above the detonations, flak
fire, shattering glass rises the old woman's high-
pitched voice: "God in Heaven!   God in Heaven!"
And now the baby is wailing too.

Hang on to the earth.   It heaves as if we are on
a trampoline, but I cling to it, dig my nails into it.

Why is it so dark?   The old woman crouches
over the baby.   She shakes a fist at the little girl,
then screams:

"God in Heaven forgive her.   Forgive her her
ugliness, her sin. . . .   O Lord, I know she didn't
say her prayers!"   Her fist comes down on the
little girl's head.

A sizzling piece of shrapnel embeds itself in the
concrete of the porch.   The little girl grabs me,
her nails dig into my neck.   Her voice, as if in
excruciating pain, pierces my eardrums:

"Mama!   Mama!   Where are you, Mama?"

A clod of soil hits me in the face.   I'm still
alive.   Alive with fear and ready to promise any
powers that be that I'll become a better person if
only my life is spared.

Warrooom.   Warrrooomwarroomwaroom.   My
whole body is lifted off the ground, dropped again,
up and down again.   This is beginning to be fun,
if only the earth wasn't so cold.   Woweeee!   But
this sets the old lady off again.

. . .

Suddenly, it's quiet.   Dead quiet.   A spine-chilling,
eerie quiet.   I'm breathing.   We're all breathing.
Strange to hear our breaths.   What's that?   Oh,
only a fire engine.   Sirens.   Sirens again?   All
Clear.   That means I can leave.

"I'm sorry, but I have to go.   I have to collect
some pig fodder," I say.

"Of course, my dear," the old lady replies.
"I'm sorry you have to leave so soon.   You must
come again.   Come visit us.   We'll have tea.   It's
very nice to have met you."   We shake hands very
formally.

Pig fodder, shelter.   Where's the shelter?   Where
am I?   I walk, stumble, get up, feel nothing, no
legs.   Funny to walk and not feel your legs.   They
look all right, I just don't feel them.   Bomb crat-
ers everywhere.   Amazingly, there are still some
houses standing.   What's this?   A bomb.   Interesting

I must take a look. Ah, it's probably only the
twenty-kilo type. Relatively harmless. No wonder
there were so many of them.

...

"You must be Ilse!" two old men in steel hel-
mets say to me. One takes my pail, disappears
with it into the shelter. Oh, that's where it is.
He comes back, hands me the pail full of something
gray and slimy. Did he have to make it so full?
Step carefully, Ilse. Your grandfather will be
mad if you lose any of it. Why did they have to
throw all that junk on the road? A whole kitchen
range. Glass, pieces of furniture, parts of houses....
...A thought occurs to me. I forgot to say
thank you. I should have said thank you for the
pig fodder. Maybe Grossvater can tell them. He
can say that I had to catch a bus or something.

...

When I pass the large housing development, I
walk in the middle of the street. All the houses
are burning. Flames crackle; there is a terrible
smell. People are running in all directions. Fire
engines, ambulances, police. I barely avoid a
police car, step in a hole, trip, but somehow manage to keep the pail upright. I only lose a little
bit of the slop. Grossvater won't even notice it.
[pp. 188-192]

Ilse hears a policeman screaming at her and looks
down to see that she is standing on an unexploded serial
mine. She passes a movie theater in which two hundred
people are trapped. She walks, runs, stumbles. Not until
she reaches home, pail in hand, does she break down (pp.
186-193).

Additional title:

Borkowski, Dieter. Wer weiss, ob wir uns wiedersehen, pp. 77-80, 83-86, 168-170.

Italy

Twelve-year-old Guido is one of the "little fishes,"
the beggar children of Naples (Erik Haugaard, The Little
Fishes), but with an inner strength that sets him apart. He
survives by doing odd jobs. After a major bombardment in

the spring of 1943, he goes with old "sack of bones" to clear
rubble from the harbor.   The old man knows that the children laugh about him and have given him his nickname, but
he is shyly open with Guido.   He worries that the work is
too hard for his horse and laments the evil in men that causes
such suffering.   Near noon the harbor is attacked.   Everyone
hides behind a wall.   Guido misses the old man and runs out
to find him.   "Sack of bones" is standing beside his mare,
caressing her neck.   Then Guido forgets all about the old
man as the planes strike their target, a German ship lying
in the basin.   Three of the planes fly off, but the fourth
turns to strafe the harbor with its machine guns.   As it flies
away Guido and the men laugh in their relief at being alive.
Guido turns to look at the old man and sees the horse lying
beside the cart.   "Sack of bones" lies beside him, shot in
the back.   The old man could have run for shelter and lived,
but he remained by his horse.   He would not desert his faithful companion and co-worker, even in death (pp. 50-59).

Chapter 3

CONTROLLING OPPOSITION

The National Socialists were the sole arbiters of what was acceptable under the Third Reich. All forms of mass media were closely censored. The Propaganda Ministry decided what books would be published, films produced, music composed, art created, and news disseminated. Anyone who protested, complained, or showed a noticeable lack of enthusiasm was an enemy of the state. Concentration camps were built to supply laborers for munitions factories and to organize the killing of Jews, Gypsies, Jehovah's Witnesses, and political opponents.

In an article which appeared in the March 12, 1981, issue of Stern, Arnŏst Lustig, himself a survivor of Auschwitz, had this to say about what happened in Germany in World War II:

> In the 200 years of the existence of Germany in Europe, during which barbarians evolved into civilized human beings, Germans stamped their indelible imprint on the map and the history of Europe. They brought the spirit of their magnificent culture to us all, like a bee that pollinates a flower out of which fruit and trees grow. The twelve years of the Nazi dominance eclipsed their past so thoroughly that it will be at least 2000 years before the balance returns to where it was before the Germans chose Hitler, before Hitler became Germany and Germany --Auschwitz-Birkenau. [p. 63]

The four sections of this chapter present books which describe for youth the imposition of censorship, the dissemination of propaganda, the ubiquitousness of informers, and the incomprehensible horror of the concentration camps.

CENSORSHIP

The Nazis quickly took measures to assure that only approved ideas would reach people. The books in the following section describe some of their methods.

Germany

Max von der Grün writes in Howl Like the Wolves of the censorship which sweeps over the land after Hitler's take-over. The propaganda office compiles a list of forbidden works, including 12,400 titles by authors known and respected in Germany and throughout the world. In the spring of 1933 students steal books on the list from lending libraries, reading rooms, and book stores. Rather than being punished they are lauded for their patriotism. On May 10 funeral pyres are erected in university towns, and students burn the works of 149 authors. As the flames destroy the flower of German thought and belles-lettres, Erich Kästner looks on, perhaps the only author to watch his own books burned (pp. 67-75).

Joseph Goebbels becomes the judge of appropriate literature, art, music, and news. Of his work Grün writes:

> Of course, the Nazis' propaganda machine was not without its effect. After all, there was nowhere one could read different accounts of events or where one could hear another opinion. Everything conformed to the party line; no opposition was expressed either in the provincial legislatures or in the press, not to mention on the radio, of which the Nazis had taken firm control on the very first day. Joseph Goebbels alone decided what could appear in print or be broadcast. He issued to the editors-in-chief of all the newspapers orders that specified everything down to the last detail. Goebbels said verbatim: "We make no secret of it. We and we alone control the radio, and we will use radio in the service of our own ideas and ensure that no other ideas are expressed." Censorship was absolute. [p. 76]
> . . .
> On October 15, the Chamber of Culture was founded and placed under the control of Goebbels. This position enabled him to supervise and direct German literature. However, most of the members of this Chamber of Culture did not need his "super-

vision," for they were in any case writing just the
kind of thing the Party wanted them to write--that
is, they conformed. [Translation by Jan van Huerck,
p. 77]

On the day the Nazis burn the books, Wilhelm Weber
watches in disbelief (Hans-Georg Noack, Die Webers). A
long-unemployed worker, Wilhelm takes great pleasure in
books and reading. An old man standing near him is rubbing
his glasses. Quietly, Wilhelm remarks that it is not the
smoke that is making his eyes water. The old man agrees
and compares the fire to those which burned witches as late
as 1727. Wilhelm counters:

> "Today it's only books anyway."
> "No, no, don't you believe it! What the young
> people there are flinging into the flames is not just
> bundles of paper with printer's ink. It is more.
> People only burn that which they fear, and no one
> is afraid of paper. They are throwing into the
> fire the spirit that lives in the books. That is
> brutal--but it is also stupid. No one can burn the
> spirit." [p. 24]

A twenty-year-old comes by with a pile of books. He
admits that he doesn't really understand why they are burning
them. He is just following orders. Wilhelm and the old man
leave together to talk and share a glass of wine. It is Wilhelm's first contact with the professor whose literature circle
he joins and who later falls victim to the Nazis (pp. 22-26).

Eve Radek and her grandmother see the burning in a
movie newsreel (Eva Marder, Und das war erst der Anfang,
pp. 15-26). The scene is frightening:

> It is night on the screen, and a fire burns. A
> sort of funeral pyre. Men in uniform with swastika
> armbands and young faces are standing around it.
> Next to them lie piles of books. What are books
> doing by a funeral pyre?
> "Against class struggle and materialism, for
> solidarity and idealism, I give to the flame the
> writings of Marx and Kautsky!" cries a Brown Shirt
> and throws books into the fire. "Against decadence
> and moral decay," he shouts, "for discipline and
> ethics in family and state, I give to the flame the
> writings of Heinrich Mann and Erich Kästner!"

Erich Kästner, who wrote <u>Emil and the Detectives</u>
and Pünktchen und Anton?
More names follow. More books burn on the
pyre.
"Against insolence and arrogance, for respect and
reverence for the undying spirit of the people, con-
sume, oh flame, the writings of Tucholsky and Os-
sietzsky!" he cries, and more books fly through the
night.
. . .
She pays no attention to the rest of the newsreel.
She sees only the burning books, the showers of
sparks, the ashes. As the lights go on in the cin-
ema, she rubs her eyes. "Ashes flew into them,"
she says and, after a pause, "Why are they burning
books? Why?"
"Because those are books they reject."
"There are lots of things that don't suit me.
Should we burn everything that rubs us wrong?"
"That is just the beginning," says Granny lightly.
"He who burns books will one day burn people."
[pp. 18-19]

Someone else is watching the newsreel, an unbalanced
SA member who becomes inspired to build his own pyre.
Later that night Eve looks out her window and down onto the
town square and sees Kruschke throwing books onto a fire.
The man can hardly read, so Eve is curious and sneaks down
to watch from behind a statue:

What lies next to the fire looks like torn-up
school books and magazines. Kruschke has planted
his foot on top of them as though on an enemy.
For a while he stands in the light of the fire like
a second statue. Kruschke, the Great. Kruschke,
the hero, of whom they will sing around campfires
in the future. Then he takes his foot away and
throws a pile of books onto his private funeral pyre.
"Against lies and unfair grades, for honor and
truth in the SA," he cries, "I give to the flame
the school books of the establishment!" A bundle
of magazines flies after. "Against falsehood and
indecency, for purity toward our wives, daughters,
and mothers," he shouts, "I give all books to the
flame!"
He says that even though Adolf Hitler has written
a thick book. But maybe Kruschke doesn't know

that.   And again he hurls into the fire all the
printed paper he has gathered from his apartment.
School books and magazines burn.   [pp. 22-23]

Two of his SA comrades appear and ask what he is doing.
They remind him that the book burning is only taking place
in university cities and is supposed to be spontaneous, but
Kruschke has been so moved by the film that they help him
burn the books.   Only later, when the drunken oaf returns
to put out the last of the last of the fire, does one person lean
out his window to protest and then only because of the fire.

Hiltgunt Zassenhaus finds a way of skirting censorship,
as she explains in her autobiography, Walls.   She finishes
her degree in Scandinavian languages and then takes a job in
Postal Censorship.   Her task is to censor letters from Jews
in Polish ghettos to friends and relatives in Scandinavia.   Although she is instructed to destroy all requests for food, Hiltgunt smuggles many away from work and arranges their delivery.   Fortunately, she is preoccupied on the day the Gestapo check her purse and has forgotten to put any letters in
it (pp. 56-60).

Her next assignment is to censor the mail of Norwegian political prisoners.   She amasses a file of their names
and addresses and as much personal information about them
as she can glean from the fifteen lines they are allowed.
This assignment leads her to direct contact with the prisoners, a position she uses to better their lot and help to arrange
their release near the end of the war.

Additional titles:

Deutschkron, Inge.   Ich trug den gelben Stern, pp. 11-
    14.
Haugaard, Erik.   Chase Me, Catch Nobody!, pp. 57-63.

Greece

The fascists of Greece impose censorship years before
Italy invades.   In Wildcat Under Glass Alki Zei writes of a
book burning in 1936.   Myrto and Melia's school is dismissed
for the day so that the children can take part.   In the middle
of the square a huge bonfire is erected.   On a platform above
the crowd stand the Mayor, the Dutch Consul, and the Bishop.
As the children watch, men bring sackloads of books to throw

on the fire.   The school director preaches against harmful
books which poison the soul, and the children leap over the
fire as though it were a May Day celebration.   The book-
shelves of Melia's grandfather now look strange and incom-
plete.   For the first time, the old man looks bent and tells
his granddaughter to leave the spots on the shelves empty
after he dies, reminders of this terrible day (pp. 138-143).

Switzerland

In 1933 the Nazis forbid Anna's father to publish his
writings (Judith Kerr, When Hitler Stole Pink Rabbit).   He
leaves Germany immediately, and his family soon joins him
in Switzerland.   A few months later Onkel Julius makes a
secret visit, it now being unwise to associate openly with an
outlawed author, and reports that Papa's books were among
those burned.   Even the Swiss are afraid to publish his works
for fear of endangering their neutrality.   Unable to continue
writing in Switzerland, he moves the family to France (pp.
52-67).

PROPAGANDA

Examples of the pervasiveness of Nazi propaganda are
found throughout books for young people.   They consist primarily of a sentence here and there, but in the books in this
section, the examples are enough in the foreground to give
readers a feel for the ways in which the Nazis manipulated
reality to suit their political ends.

Max von der Grün shows Hitler as a master of propaganda (Howl Like the Wolves).   Under his control the daily
news promotes National Socialism.   Thus the Reichstag fire
becomes the act of the "Red Mob" and justification for rounding up dissidents.   The burning of books is an outpouring of
spontaneous anger on the part of patriotic students.   He relentlessly wears down opposition to war:

> All the activities of everyday life were given a
> military orientation.   This military aura extended
> even into the realm of language.   Henceforth one
> heard only:
> instead of "employment office"--"labor mobiliza-
> tion"
> instead of "job procurement"--"labor battle"
> instead of "worker"--"soldier of labor"

> instead of "work"--"service to Führer and folk"
> instead of "entrepreneur"--"factory leader"
> instead of "staff" (or "personnel")--"subordinates"
> (or "followers")
> instead of "factory meeting"--"factory roll-call"
> instead of "industrial agreement"--"the industrial
> order"
> instead of "equal partners in society"--"the labor
> front"
> instead of "production"--"the production battle"
> It is easy to understand that if, for whatever
> reasons, these words are hammered into a person's
> brain every day, they soon become a part of his
> language, and he does not necessarily stop and think
> about where they came from and why they were
> coined in the first place. [Translation by Jan van
> Huerck, pp. 76-77]

Cheap, mass-produced radios give the government access to every ear. So pervasive is the propaganda of Hitler and Goebbels that:

> Every day one saw, read, and heard them every-
> where: in the press, which always conformed to the
> party line, on the radio, in films, and in the news-
> reels, which in those days were as popular as the
> daily television news programs are today. We saw
> Hitler at banquets and parades, both of which events
> took place somewhere every day. The Nazis were
> master practitioners of the ancient Roman formula
> that all the people needed were bread and circuses.
> Hypnotized by flags, banners, speeches, and march-
> ing feet, the German people did not awaken from
> their organized delirium. They were left no time
> to think about why the whole production was being
> staged.... [Translation by Jan van Huerck, p. 89]

Grün's last chapter illustrates the success of the propaganda. He is taken prisoner by the Americans and sent to a camp in the United States. There he and his fellow prisoners are exposed to the hideous crimes of the Nazis and forced to watch films taken in the concentration camps:

> Many of my fellow-prisoners used to start crying
> and leave. But others, after they had seen the
> film, left the theater and laughed in the faces of the
> American soldiers, for they thought that all these

pictures were horror stories invented by the enemy,
just as Goebbels, with his cunning propaganda, had
for years been teaching them to believe. In discussions that went on all day long, they attempted to
grasp the inconceivable fact that even German soldiers were capable of performing acts of inhuman
atrocity. [Translation by Jan van Huerck, p. 266]

Nela of Renate Finckh's Mit uns zieht die neue Zeit
is an easy target for propaganda. She is totally without empathy for the suffering of others. The pro-Nazism and anti-
Semitism of her parents help make her ripe for the new ideology.

Telling her story in retrospect, the first-person narrator writes:

1933 to 1937. Four years during which our lives
change radically. The effects of the economic crisis ease. There is work once again. The little
man doesn't ask about the goal of his work. He
doesn't see that that which gives him bread will
reap destruction. Even the Autobahn. He only
knows that he will be able to buy a Volkswagen for
this highway. They will cost only 900 marks. He
is happy that he can already start making small
payments toward one.
Thanks to the Führer, we have work and bread.
Thanks to the Führer, law and order reign.
Thanks to the Führer, a firm bond links heart
and hand, town and land.
Thanks to the Führer, mothers of large families
are honored instead of scorned. Instead of subsi-
dies they receive the Mother's Cross.
Thanks to the Führer's splendid military parades,
even people in other lands take off their hats to the
losers of the war. Ambassadors, diplomats, everyone travels to bask in the glory of the olympiad.
The little man listens to the radio. He hears:
Thanks to the Führer, we are once again some-
body!
The propaganda machine works its wiles with
words.
The Germans, the people of poets and philoso-
phers, have a weakness for words. Many have forgotten how to think. [p. 65]

In the Hitler Youth Nela learns unquestioning loyalty
to the Führer. From her father she learns the new National
Socialist view of Christianity. The Bible, in particular the
Old Testament, is a book of Jewish fairy tales. Jesus hyp-
notized his followers, and his teachings are no longer relevant. Instead of the Bible the German people now have the
Edda, a collection of Norse poetry and myths (pp. 76-87).

Nela rises quickly through the ranks of the Hitler
Youth. Every chink in the armor of her belief she fills frantically, not allowing doubts to take hold until long after the
war ends.

Dieter Borkowski begins the reconstruction of his diary,
Wer weiss, ob wir uns wiedersehen, with an entry dated November 2, 1942. He records Hitler's stirring speech, assuring his audience of final victory, and feels proud that Germany has occupied most of Europe. So thoroughly has he
accepted the teaching of racial superiority that he is horrified
when on December 18 he sees Propaganda Minister Goebbels
opening the Christmas Market in Berlin. This small, crippled man with five sickly daughters is far from his ideal image of Aryan manhood (pp. 10-15).

The top actors of the day, those still allowed to per-
form, are making propaganda films. Dieter delights in them.
On March 2, 1943, he sees Ohm Krüger, a film about the
Boer War. Watching the British fighting the smaller folk and
putting women and children in concentration camps, he learns
to hate for the first time. He leaves the theater vowing
never to forget the treachery of the British (pp. 25-26). In
May his hatred of the Jews solidifies when he sees Jud Süss
(Sweet Jew), which shows how a Jew takes advantage of an
Aryan, opening his land to an influx of Jews and raping a
blond Schwabisch girl. He has never understood why the
Jews have to answer for the killing of Christ 2000 years ago,
as his mother says, but figures if they are as bad as those
in the film, in the Kremlin, on the London Stock Exchange,
and on Wall Street, they deserve to be put in work camps
(pp. 42-44).

Walter Jendrich and his friend Max also see Jud Süss
by sneaking in with the brother of a girl who works in the
theater (Horst Burger, Vier Fragen an meinen Vater). When
the boys leave the theater, Max is filled with righteous anger
against the Jews. Walter points out that films exaggerate in
order to draw in customers, but Max is not to be dissuaded.

Everyone knows that Jews drink human blood. They catch
runaway children, slit their throats, and bleed them into
buckets, then drink the blood in an attempt to destroy the
German race. Max is sure of his facts, for he has them
from a reliable source, an SS newspaper (pp. 34-36).

Until she falls in love with Jan, Regine believes all
that she has heard from her parents, the newspaper, in school,
and in the Hitler Youth (Irina Korschunow, Er hiess Jan). Jan
opens her eyes to the rotten core of it all. He is a young
Pole forced to work for the Germans and is a gentle pacifist.
An informer ends their affair, but Regine is able to escape
from the Gestapo. To the sympathetic farm family that hides
her, she tells her story and the credo by which she has lived:

> The Jews are our affliction.
> Germans are better than others.
> The Führer knows everything.
> The Führer will lead us to victory.
> You are nothing, your folk is everything.
> One folk, one Reich, one Führer. [p. 53]

Regine's mother had found nothing disturbing about concentration camps. When Regine wondered about them, her mother
told her:

> "Naturally," said my mother. "That's where
> they put Jews and Communists so they can learn
> to work. It's really necessary." [p. 55]

Regine was not convinced and pushed her for more information:

> "Be still," she snapped when I tried to talk to her
> about it. "The Führer knows what he is doing."
> [p. 55]

That attitude and the contrary notion that not Hitler
but his aids were responsible for the abuses of power carried
many through the dark years. So effective was the propaganda
that even after the war people clung to their beliefs.

Additional titles:

> Oker, Eugen. ...und ich der Fahnenträger.
> Orgel, Doris. The Devil in Vienna.

Schönfeldt Sybil Gräfin. <u>Sonderappell.</u>
Seiffert, Dietrich. <u>Einer war Kisselbach.</u>

INFORMERS

Spies were everywhere in the Third Reich. Children
informed on parents, neighbors on neighbors, collaborators
on resisters, customers on shop keepers, husbands on wives.
How often the denunciations stemmed from misguided loyalties
or how often from personal jealousies is unknown, but that
the system worked to stifle dissent is sure. An unguarded
moment, a misplaced confidence could lead to imprisonment
and death. Examples of informers are found throughout young
adult literature on World War II.

Austria

Doris Orgel demonstrates the success of the Nazis in
destroying normal ties of loyalty in her autobiographical novel,
<u>The Devil in Vienna.</u> The Dornewald family is trying to make
arrangements to leave the country. Mrs. Dornewald's father
has already gone, as has Mr. Dornewald's mother. The latter's servant, Usch, feels bereft. She has given her life to
the family. Now she intends to collect her reward.

She tries to blackmail the Dornewalds, demanding that
they pay her 10,500 schillings. She has seen Mr. Dornewald,
a Jew, toasting his Aryan servant's wedding. Insisting that
he made a pass at the girl, Usch threatens to report him to
the block warden. Just one day before she carries out her
threat, the Dornewald family acquires the necessary papers
and leaves for Yugoslavia.

Brigitte Peter ("Denk lieber an den Nikolaus," <u>Damals</u>
<u>war ich vierzehn,</u> pp. 7-23) remembers vividly that her mo-
ther's moment of glory was spoiled by an informer. Coming
out of the air raid shelter, she sees the city burning. She
rushes into a burning house to save some children. For her
heroism she is honored at an awards assembly. When she
returns home she flushes the award down the toilet, for at
the same ceremony an informer received a higher honor. He
had denounced a young boy, whose brothers had all been killed
in the war. The boy's crime had been assembling a secret
radio.

An old railroad conductor, friend of all the neighborhood boys, trains and befriends a younger man in "Der rote Eisenbahner," Damals war ich vierzehn, pp. 40-44. He holds his peace about the war until the disaster of Stalingrad, when just once he complains. The young man turns him in, and the old conductor spends the rest of the war in a concentration camp.

Belgium

In her autobiography about the women's orchestra in Auschwitz, Fania Fénelon tells a story that demonstrates what cruel use people made of the Germans' eagerness to pursue any opposition or unwanted people (Playing for Time). Irène falls madly in love with the 22-year-old scion of a wealthy Brussels family. Both families oppose the marriage, but Jean-Louis persuades hers that with him she will be protected. Though his family disowns him for marrying a Jew, they are happy together the first year. Then it becomes obvious that the Germans still consider her a Jew, so they move with her little brother to the country. One day the Belgian police pick up Irène and her brother while Jean-Louis is at work. The police are sympathetic in spite of their grim task and tell her that she has been denounced by her mother-in-law. In the concentration camp Irène lives for the day she will be reunited with Jean-Louis. She doesn't know until after the war that Jean-Louis's suffering was short-lived. Two months after her arrest he remarried (pp. 119-124. This episode is omitted in the English translation.)

Denmark

In Dorte Larsen-Ledet's Zwei Kaffee und ein Berliner, an informer shadows a friendship long after the war. A girl learns that her father, as a young factory owner, was part of the German minority. He was from a Nazi family so considered it his patriotic duty to manufacture products for the Wehrmacht. A resistance group bombed the factory, and he recognized one of the conspirators. As a good citizen, he called the authorities. The resister died in a concentration camp. Years later the factory owner's daughter and the resister's grandson meet. They are astonished by their parents' reaction until they learn the story and then must decide if their friendship is worth their families' pain.

Additional title:

Benchley, Nathaniel. Bright Candles, pp. 34-37, 189-196.

Eastern Europe

If the lives of all those suspected of opposing the Germans were endangered by the pervasiveness of informers, the
lives of the informers themselves were made as precarious
as possible by organized resistance movements such as Uncle
Misha's Partisans (Yuri Suhl).   From their Ukrainian contact
the partisans learn that the village elder is planning to denounce a peasant who is hiding Jews.   Dressing as Germans,
they call on the village elder.   One of them knows enough
German to pass as one among Ukrainians.   The elder is delighted with their visit and orders his wife to prepare them
a feast while he leads them to the peasant.   He proudly points
out the house and then returns home to await his guests.
The partisans rescue the peasants and the two Jewish girls
they are hiding and return for the feast.

The village elder is obsequious and assures them that
his village is cooperative.   After playing cat and mouse with
him, the German-speaking partisan reads the death warrant
drawn up by Uncle Misha's Partisans and carries out the
sentence (pp. 43-51).

Twelve-year-old Olin has never understood why his
parents forbid his friendship with Zyrill Vitlich (Jan Procházka, Long Live the Republic).   The strange, grumpy old
man has been a faithful friend to Olin, whose keen sense of
justice separates him from the other village boys.

The Russians take over the village and are greeted as
conquering heroes.   Jubilant crowds hang Czech and Russian
flags everywhere.   In the middle of the cheering, an angry
mob forms around Zyrill.   They begin throwing stones at the
exhausted, already beaten man, denouncing him as a collaborator.   They follow him to his home, encircle him, and
order him to beg.   Instead, he jumps to his death in a well.
Suddenly all are ashamed and afraid and trying to save him.
Olin turns away in sorrow and disgust.   Over it all float the
sounds of the village band.

Additional titles:

Däs, Nelly.   Der Zug in die Freiheit, pp. 8-12.
Suhl, Yuri.   On the Other Side of the Gate, pp. 108-
    117, 140.

France

In France, where the resistance movement was widespread, collaborators were still responsible for the deaths of
many of their countrymen.   In Paul-Jacques Bonzon's Mon
Vercors en feu, Adrien Meffre profits handsomely from the
occupation.   When the debacle first breaks out he stocks up
on goods, which he then sells at huge profits. He urges com-
pliance with the Germans and entertains their officers. Through
persistent snooping, he learns that the baker is hiding a Canadian
aviator and turns him in to the authorities. They shoot the
baker without process. For this and for the deaths of other
resisters which can be traced to his hands, Adrien Meffre is
executed after the liberation.

The informer in Claude Stokis's Réseau clandestin is
responsible for his own undoing.   The resistance network
assigns a radio expert to relay messages from the member
Roland is hiding to contacts in London. When the operator
is arrested he is replaced by someone Roland mistrusts instinctively.   His fears prove justified.   Someone is tipping
off the Germans whenever a bombing target is assigned.   Roland suspects the new radio operator.   They go swimming together, and Roland pretends that the last message he sent
was in a code designed to trap the traitor.   The technician
senses his own doom and tries to force Roland to tell him
where the bombardment will take place.   When Roland refuses to say, the technician tries to drown him and ends up
drowning himself (pp. 171-180).

Germany

The threat of informers was not an idle one, but it
alone was enough to make people afraid to oppose publicly
the regime.   Ilse Koehn (Mischling, Second Degree) relates
an episode which serves as an example.   Block wardens are
assigned in 1938.   Their job is in theory to make a thorough
inventory of their neighborhoods in case of fire or other
emergency.   In reality they serve as a widespread and convenient means of keeping people under control and making
them fear their neighbors.   One day Ilse's grandmother sends
her to a grocery store, where she hears the following exchange:

There's talk about the latest nuisance, this business of having house wardens, block wardens and so
on.

"They have to know where you are in case of
fire," says one woman, whom I call "Red Hand."
Since I don't know their names, I invent names for
them.   "Fire? Don't make me laugh," says "Rabbit." "They just want to know about every nook and
cranny.   When they have it all written down, there
won't be a place left to hide.   Not that we have any
reason to hide," she adds quickly, casting a furtive
glance at her audience.   "That superintendent of
mine," she continues. "Well, I won't say it here.
He has been dying to have a good look at my apartment. I've never let him in, but now I have to.
Now he is the house warden! Can't fix a leaky
faucet, that one.   Only thing he can do is look important.   You should have seen how he ogled my
closet! God knows what he thinks I keep in it.
But I know how his wife, that dirty slut, would
like to get her filthy paws on my furniture.   Those
two would surely like to settle themselves in my
nest.   Can't say I blame them, considering the
hole they live in."

I look at her and find it hard to believe that this
woman has anything of beauty, anything anyone
would envy her for.

Rabbit continues without pause.   "I know all
about them, and he knows I know.   But not a chance.
I won't give him a chance to have us conveniently
'disappear'! I 'Heil Hitler' him right out of the
door.   Give him his own medicine.   Yes, sir! I
love our Führer ... and Heil Hitler to you all!"
The last is said almost triumphantly.

There is some uneasy laughter and, to judge by
the faces around me, no one is quite sure whether
she is joking or really means it.

Rabbit has left with her groceries.   Now a quiet,
whining voice takes over: "My husband has just
been named house warden.   He doesn't like it, but
what can he do? He has to report about the people
in our house, the space they occupy and everything.
But he wouldn't denounce anyone! Not my husband,
he wouldn't hurt a fly."

"Shut up! Why don't you shut up!" says Red
Hand.   "No one has accused your husband of anything.   Who's talking about him? [pp. 27-28]

Not only open opposition but lack of enthusiasm was
dangerous.   Twelve-year-old Evelyn in Evelyn Hardey's

... damals war ich fünfzehn hates the Jungmädel so skips a meeting. Her leader complains to her mother. Fearful that the local Nazi leader will learn of it, Evelyn's mother gives her a scolding. Evelyn frets:

> It's getting to be just like with the grown-ups. You can't trust anyone anymore. If you say out loud that you don't like the Führer or are fed up with war, the Gestapo hear about it right away. And then they take you away in the night. That's no exaggeration. They take people away, lock them in a camp, and don't let them out again.
> In our class a girl suddenly stopped coming to school. The whole family had disappeared. The rumor went around that they'd been traitors. Miss Ganse agreed and said, "Enemies of the people have no business among us in these troubled times!" But our geography teacher rolled up the map and whispered, "That's shocking! Where will it lead?" [p. 8]

As part of her German homework, Evelyn has to compile a list of all the books in her home. Fortunately, her father is home on leave and sees the list before she turns it in. In place of forbidden titles he substitutes such safe ones as, Die nordische Seele, Rassenkunde des deutschen Volkes, and Germanische Heiligtumer (The Nordic Soul, Ethnology of the German People, and Germanic Shrines) (pp. 21-22).

The normal play and strife between children takes on sinister aspects. While Evelyn's friends are playing together in her house one day, the son of a Party official makes a crack about homosexuals and gets into a fight with another boy. Her mother sends them all home and then cries.

> ...She said Kilian's father is an important man in the local Party leadership. We shouldn't make Kilian angry or he would turn us in. [p. 25]

In September 1944, 17-year-old Regine falls in love with a Polish forced laborer (Irina Korschunow, Er hiess Jan). Until she meets Jan, Regine believes in the Führer and Final Victory and the superiority of Germany. Under his influence she learns how blind she has been. Their relationship is short. Someone informs on them. When the Gestapo come they beat Jan, and while witnesses watch with perverse cur-

iosity, they hack off Regine's hair. She never learns what
happened to Jan, but she is freed from the Gestapo by a
bomb and a sympathetic warden. From her hiding place,
she speculates on who turned them in. She thinks it might
have been the lame messenger everyone laughed at but feared.

> ...I'm almost certain he was the one who turned
> me in, but I'm not positive. Maybe it was someone
> entirely different, one of the nice ones in the house,
> who had smiled at me the day before and who I
> can't imagine is guilty. [p. 15]

She remembers that another woman was arrested for bemoan-
ing the death of her son.

> But it's true there were spies everywhere. Right
> in Steinbergen a woman who owned a dairy store was
> arrested. One morning when her shop was full of
> people she received the news of the death of her
> son. With the letter in hand, she stumbled into the
> shop. "He's dead!" she screamed. "He's dead!
> This damned war! This damned Hitler! He killed
> him!"
> A couple of women rushed her out of the shop
> and closed the door behind her. You could still
> hear her screaming. That afternoon she was picked
> up. Taken away. [p. 123]

Inge Deutschkron's father recognizes the danger for
Jews in time to flee to England (Deutschkron, Ich trug den
gelben Stern). Unfortunately, war breaks out between Germany and England before he is able to bring Inge and her
mother to safety. During the years of hiding places, false
identities, and fear that follow, Inge and her mother come
to know the best and the worst of mankind and the ubiquitousness of informers.

A married couple invites the two to live with them.
Before long a neighbor inquires about the family's visitors.
Suspicious when the two women stay longer than visitors
normally do, the neighbor comes again to check on them.
They find a new hiding place and again have to leave because
of a nosey neighbor (pp. 121-136).

A Jew working in Otto Weidt's workshop for the blind
tells a friend about the workshop and of Weidt's hiding of
Jews. The friend denounces Weidt to the Gestapo (p. 141).

Another Jew, who is surviving by selling on the black market, is denounced by an informer posing as a customer (pp. 153-154). Jenny Rieck turns in her own husband to the Gestapo because she is afraid of losing him to an actress. Fortunately, the Gestapo do not take her seriously (pp. 163-168).

Inge is not free of informers even after the war. As a Socialist working in the Russian sector of Berlin, she ruffles someone's ideology and is marked for arrest by the Soviets. She is able to travel to safety in England but cannot escape the shadow of Nazism. Even there she receives hate mail and threats because of her outspokenness concerning the Third Reich.

Holland

The informer in Jan Terlouw's <u>Michel</u> turns out to be an old friend of the family rather than the man Michel has thought. Michel has plenty of reason to suspect Schafter, who spends a lot of time with Germans. The day of Michel's first act of resistance Schafter is there to hamper him in delivering an important message. When Michel delivers two Jews to the liberated sector, Schafter is there on the road as he drives his passengers toward the river. Michel needs proof that Schafter is the informer. His Uncle Ben suggests he plant an accusatory letter in Schafter's mailbox. The scheme backfires, and Michel still has no proof.

When he needs false papers for the English flyer he has been hiding, Michel confides in Uncle Ben. Ben prepares the papers and leaves with Michel's sister for a rendezvous with the fugitive. By chance, Michel overhears a conversation that convinces him that he has made a mistake. He rushes to the rendezvous point in time to keep Jack from falling into Ben's hands.

Ben escapes but is killed by a fighter plane before he can denounce anyone. When Holland is liberated Michel learns that Schafter has been hiding three Jews and showing favor to the Germans to protect them.

CONCENTRATION CAMPS

Only someone who survived the abyss of a concentration camp can grasp the full implication of organized, authorized sadism, of its toll on the spirit. The camps required

thousands of bureaucrats to maintain them, from the brutal
SS guards to the clerks and accountants who sat in comfortable offices and maintained detailed records. In reading
about concentration camps, we grapple with the unspeakable.

For explaining the phenomenon of concentration camps
and the complex question of what people knew about them
during the war, the following three books are valuable. All
are written for young readers. Through both straight reporting and numerous examples of personal experiences, they make
clear the magnitude of the Nazis' crimes against humanity.
The passages cited here can stand alone in classroom discussions. The section which follows is arranged by camp. The
chapter ends with books showing the reactions of people when
confronted with victims.

Milton Meltzer in Never to Forget writes that 50 concentration camps had been erected in Germany by the end of
1933. They were reputedly for protective custody but were
used by the Gestapo to silence opposition. In 1934 the SS
took over the administration of the camps and organized them
to hold three kinds of prisoners: political opponents, asocials
(criminals, sex offenders), and inferior races (Jews and Gypsies). Through senseless work and senseless punishments,
the SS robbed the inmates of their dignity (pp. 27-30).

In 1941 the Nazis began to make plans for the Final
Solution to the Jewish problem, the annihilation of all Jews
in occupied lands. All the technical ingenuity of German
manufacturers was tapped to devise better and faster ways of
killing human beings. Extermination camps were set up. To
make the task easier, the Germans began to relocate Jews
nearer to the death camps. A majority of the deportees were
shot or gassed. The Allies were informed by such people as
Jan Karski of what was happening but did nothing (pp. 104-
115).

Meltzer describes the efficiency with which the mass
murders were planned:

> ... All told, more than 47,000 people staffed the
> extermination industry. It took time to train them.
> It took careful planning to design the killing proc-
> ess and collect the tools and materials for it. It
> took inventiveness to perfect the proper gas for
> the mass production of corpses and the capacious
> furnaces needed to consume them. Think of the

> bookkeeping alone--the millions of Jews processed
> through each camp, each assigned a number, each
> number entered in the record, then tattooed on the
> left arm. [p. 117]

Nothing was wasted in this system. Gold teeth and
fillings were melted into ingots. Hair was made into industrial felt and then slippers for German sailors. Germans
wore second-hand clothing with labels from all over Europe,
never asking its source (pp. 118-126).

The list of the Nazis' uses for the end product of their
perverse deeds is continued in Arnold P. Rubin's The Evil
That Men Do:

> ... [Before the bodies were burned], the Nazis re-
> moved gold teeth, jewelry, and eyeglasses. These
> filled warehouses, along with clothing and shoes.
> The Nazis left nothing for waste. Human beings
> became resources for production. Human fat was
> used for soap, ashes for fertilizer, skulls for pa-
> perweights, skin for lampshades, hair and bones for
> industry. [pp. 74-75]

An SS officer, Kurt Gerstein, who handled the payments
for Zyklon B, witnessed the mass extermination of Polish
Jews and wrote an account of it. The papal legate in Berlin
refused to see him, so he delivered his account to the Arch-
bishop in 1942, requesting that it be sent to the Pope. Then
he told the story to a Swedish diplomat, who sent a report
to his government. The Dutch resistance also learned of it.
No one reacted. His horrifying account of watching people
driven into gas chambers, their corpses being thrown about
like so much cordwood, is repeated in all three of the books
mentioned in this section.

The question continues to nag. Did the German people
realize what was going on? Rubin responds to this by quot-
ing Sigrid Schultz, a former foreign correspondent:

> As far as the death camps themselves are con-
> cerned, the question remains how much the German
> people knew, and if they could have done anything
> about them if they did know.
> Sigrid Schultz had this reaction to claims that
> Germans didn't know what was going on.
> "That's ridiculous," she said. "Because after

all, they knew where the drugstore owner--who was
Jewish--had gone to, where he had disappeared to.
They knew that. After all, they employed them in
their homes in Weimar. When we liberated Buchenwald, near Weimar, [U.S. General George] Patton
forced the population of Weimar to march out to the
concentration camp and to view the concentration
camp. And there were all these emaciated prisoners, who were just skin and bones."

The citizens of the town, Miss Schultz added,
who were then mostly women, "turned to the American soldiers and to us--we were in uniform, too--
and said, Oh, they had never known about that. And
then, we had a little group of prisoners who stepped
down from the wall and went to them, kind of threat-
eningly, and said, 'Look. You forced us to work
in your homes. We were taken to Weimar to do
your plumbing and your other things, and when any
of us dared to tell you that we were hungry, you
reported us. You know how many dead you have
on your conscience?'"

"Some people," Miss Schultz said, "say they saw
the Germans cry when they went around Buchenwald.
I didn't see any cry. You know, they closed their
minds to the horrible things they were ... forced
to see." [pp. 170-171]

Max von der Grün relates another incident concerning
people's knowledge of the camps in Howl Like the Wolves.
On July 1, 1937, Pastor Martin Niemöller was arrested.
Although according to the court he should have been set free,
he was sent to a concentration camp. Once sentence was
passed, a proclamation was read from the pulpits of all Protestant churches, protesting his incarceration in Sachsenhausen.
Certainly anyone attending church that day heard about the
existence of concentration camps (pp. 123-125). Grün gives
further evidence throughout his book as well as eyewitness
accounts of some of the horrors that took place in them.

When the Allies marched through territory that had
been occupied by the Germans, they made ghastly discoveries
which hardened their resolve to show the enemy no mercy.
Although the Germans had tried to hide the traces, had gassed
and machine-gunned thousands of prisoners to keep them from
talking, they had extended their crimes over too large an
area. The evidence was in every concentration camp liberated by the Allied troops.

Auschwitz

Auschwitz was built to be a model of German efficiency. Its gas chambers, ovens, and poison gas were all manufactured by major companies. Twenty thousand people could be disposed of in a day. In his trial at the end of the war, Rudolf Höss estimated that 3,000,000 died in Auschwitz: 2,500,000 by extermination and execution and 500,000 through starvation and disease. The 20 to 30 percent of camp inmates who survived were forced to labor for the Nazi death machine in the camp industries.

One of the most moving personal accounts of Auschwitz is Fragments of Isabella by Isabella Leitner. It is a series of scenes, poetic and evocative while at the same time searing.

Isabella's father goes to America to try to prepare a place for his family. He procures immigration papers for all of them, but the papers arrive too late, after Hungary has declared war on the United States. In desperation, he arranges permission for them to emigrate to Israel. Again the papers come too late, this time four weeks after Hitler occupies Hungary.

In May 1944 Isabella, four sisters, her brother and mother are deported to Auschwitz with the Jews of the Kisvárda, Hungary, ghetto. Dr. Mengele meets their train, motioning her mother and youngest sister to immediate death. The remaining members of the family vow to survive. Even as they become so tired that death would be a blessing, the four sisters force each other to stay alive. When a baby is born to one of the women in camp, her fellow inmates keep it from the mother so that the mother will not share her baby's fate. Isabella writes:

> And now that you are born, your mother begs to see you, to hold you. But we know that if we give you to her, there will be a struggle to take you away again, so we cannot let her see you because you don't belong to her. You belong to the gas chamber. Your mother has no rights. She only brought forth fodder for the gas chamber. She is not a mother. She is just a dirty Jew who has soiled the Aryan landscape with another dirty Jew. How dare she think of you in human terms? [pp. 31-32]

By October the sisters weigh 40 to 60 pounds apiece.
In November the Germans are frantic to destroy Auschwitz.
Half of the inmates are cremated.   The sisters are serene
waiting for death because at least they are still together, but
after a night outside the crematorium, they and other inmates
are put on an icy train and transported to other camps.

Isabella and her sister are taken to Birnbaumel.   Of
the new camp she writes:

> The camp was at one end of the forest.   The tank
> traps we dug were at the other end.   To go from
> one to the other, we had to march through the town,
> twice a day, coming and going.   In the morning, we
> were marched through the town, every day--a thou-
> sand wretched young women.   The pity of that sight
> could make a beast weep.   But not the Germans.
> ... Germany was one giant concentration camp,
> with Jews marching the length and breadth of the
> country, but these refined, sensitive Germans never
> saw us.   Find me a German who ever saw me.
> Find me one who ever harmed us.   [pp. 52-53]

Isabella refuses to cooperate with her captors by doing the
backbreaking work even when they are not watching.

> I was a one-woman sabotage team.   As soon as
> the Germans walked away, I would put down my
> shovel and stop digging.   Digging to me symbolized
> digging my own grave.   In reality, that was what
> it was.   And even in that place, I had self-respect
> to preserve.   My emaciated body still housed a
> soul to be tended and cared for, and when I could
> nourish it, I did.   [p. 54]

On the march to Bergen-Belsen the four sisters steal
away from the group, knowing the Germans will not have
time to look for them, but the Germans are diabolically
clever.   They start boiling pots of soup.   The smell draws
out the starving girls, although by the time they reach the
pot it is empty.   Even today Isabella feels shame at having
been so dehumanized that she could be lured out of hiding by
an aroma.

As the column struggles on, all but one of the sisters
escapes.   So emaciated are they that they appear more dead
than alive.   Isabella describes the way they looked when the
Allies arrived:

> Was it only a year ago? Or a century? ... Our
> heads are shaved. We look like neither boys nor
> girls. We haven't menstruated for a long time.
> We have diarrhea. No, not diarrhea--typhus. Sum-
> mer and winter we have but one type of clothing.
> Its name is "rag." Not an inch of it without a
> hole. Our shoulders are exposed. The rain is
> pouring on our skeletal bodies. The lice are hav-
> ing an orgy in our armpits, their favorite spots.
> [p. 2]

The Americans send the three sisters to the United
States immediately, but no passage of time, no material com-
forts, no amount of love can erase the nightmares.

A spare little book which is inspiring in the simple
humanity of those who hold out a hand to two young escapees
and frightening in the perversity of those who imprisoned
them is Auguste Lazar's Die Brücke von Weissensand. As
in Fragments of Isabella, a column of women is evacuated
from Auschwitz in the winter of 1945. They are sheltered
in barns while the SS leader rests. When the column moves
on, two foreign laborers and a German woman, Frau Kupferschmidt, hide two of the women. Little by little, Franziska
and Mirjam tell their story as they remember it.

The head Nazi of their Polish ghetto promised that all
those who volunteered to labor in Germany would receive good
pay, plenty of food, and good care. Of course, the promises
were accompanied by threats. Those not agreeing to go would
receive no rations, and anyone helping them would be killed.
No food reached the volunteers during their 36 hours in the
cattle cars. One bucket served their sanitary needs, and the
floor soon became mired in filth.

Finally the train arrives in Auschwitz. Dr. Mengele
sends Franziska's mother to the gas, the girls to living
death. Those selected to live are quick-marched into the
camp, where the humiliation begins immediately. The men
and women are separated. Driven into a large room, the
women are forced to undress in front of the SS guards:

> ... Some of them complain, but what do the SS
> care? They are all young men. Undress! Un-
> dress! We can't undress in front of these men.
> You can't? We'll show you what you can do. Down
> with that thing. You Jewish sows! There are many

young women here and very young girls.   At first
they remain standing as though frozen.   Then the
first blows fall, the first clubs whistle through the
air.   The SS men laugh scornfully.   [p. 114]

All of their hair is shaved and thrown onto piles.
Clothing is tossed onto one heap, shoes onto another.   Then
numbers are painted on their forearms.   The tattooers are
out of ink.   This shortage saves the girls later.   They have
no permanent numbers to betray them when they escape.

Mirjam and Franziska and many others with them
understand only gradually what is going on in the
camp.   They have no idea how close the gas chambers are, the biggest gas chambers anywhere.   The
gas chambers of Auschwitz-Birkenau are always in
operation.   The ovens in which the dead are burned
continually send their stinking smoke into the air.
They fit into the landscape.   There are countless
factories in and around Auschwitz, giant operations
of German industry in which hundreds of thousands
of prisoners work, starve, grind themselves to
death, or end up in the gas chambers when they
can be driven no more.
And yet work is the only chance for deliverance.
Work, until the Red Army comes to free the slaves.
[p. 115]

Mirjam and Franziska are only in Auschwitz for a few
weeks, but it is long enough to mark their lives forever.   As
with Isabella Leitner and her sisters, they are able to escape
as the Nazis try desperately to eliminate the evidence of their
brutality.

Fania Fénelon's memoir of Auschwitz is unique, for
she was a member of the women's orchestra, the strange
group which played for executions, marches, and SS pleasure.
Fania had been a political prisoner at Drancy for nine months
when in January 1944 she was deported to Auschwitz.   There
she would have joined the other victims of gas, labor, hunger,
and disease had someone not recognized her as a well-known
Paris cabaret singer and suggested she be used in the orchestra.   From that privileged (by camp standards) position, she
recorded everything she saw and heard so that someday she
could tell the world.

The orchestra is a hodgepodge.   Few of its members

are professional musicians. They play an assortment of instruments never intended to be combined. Of their bizarre
daily performances, Fénelon writes:

> Our parody of a band went on parade, playing a
> march of the cheeriest Tyrolean type, evocative of
> picnics in the Black Forest washed down with cool
> beer. Our barracks was about three hundred yards
> from the place where we gave our strange concerts
> morning and evening. The road was bordered with
> other barracks, and in front of each of them the
> deportees awaited the order of departure, which
> would not be given until we were in our place....
> Our platform, at the intersection of camps A
> and B, had four steps and lines of chairs: a band-
> stand! We took our places. Alma turned her head
> towards her audience as though sizing it up, turned
> back to her players, raised her baton and, while
> officers and kapos bellowed assorted Achtungs that
> echoed along the roads of the camp, an Arbeits-
> marsch burst out, martial, exhilarating, almost
> joyful.
> It was only now that I began to grasp the insan-
> ity of the place I was in. In the quarantine block,
> shattered by the shower, the tattooing and the shav-
> ing, starving, dazed, beaten, I hadn't been aware
> of what was happening to me, to me. Here, in
> the icy air of this winter morning, in this geometri-
> cal landscape of squat, stumpy sheds with barbed
> wire above them, the watchtowers, without a single
> tree on the horizon, I became aware of the exter-
> mination camp of Birkenau, and of the farcical na-
> ture of this orchestra conducted by this elegant
> woman, these comfortably dressed girls sitting on
> chairs playing to these virtual skeletons, shadows
> showing us faces which were faces no longer.
> [Translation by Judith Landry, pp. 48-49]

The question of whether or not the German people
knew what was happening in such camps as Auschwitz has
been argued since the war. Fénelon's opinion is clear. She
writes of being taken with another inmate into the town of
Auschwitz. As they walk through the quiet, orderly little
town, no one sees them. Fénelon writes:

> These people, doing normal things, going in and
> out of their houses, these women doing their shop-

ping, holding young children with apple-red cheeks,
did they know that they were happy? Did they know
that it was marvellous to see them, that for us they
represented life? Why did they begrudge us a look?
They couldn't fail to notice us, to know where we
came from; our striped garb, the scarfs hiding our
shaven heads, our thinness betrayed our origins.
When they went out walking, they were not forbidden to pass by the camp of Birkenau, whose sinister appearance hardly concealed its function. Did
they think that those five chimneys, with their sick-
ening smoke, were for the central heating? What
exactly was I asking for? That that little town of
five or six thousand inhabitants should revolt, that
its Germanic population, resettled there since the
German victory, should rise up and liberate the
camp? Why should they have felt responsible for
us? A sudden surge of violence sent the blood
into my head: they were all responsible! All men
were. The indifference of a single one was our
death sentence.

I stared at them intensely. I didn't want to forget their ratlike faces. They didn't see us. How
convenient! They didn't see our striped clothes
any more than they saw the detachments of "mos-
lems" who wandered haggard through their peaceful
little town, surrounded by SS and dogs. I was sure
that later, after the war, those people would say
that they "didn't know," and they would be believed.
[Translation by Judith Landry, pp. 79-80]

Additional title:

Forman, James. The Survivor, pp. 160-217.

Bergen-Belsen

When the Germans sweep through Holland, the Brenner
family is in a double bind (Marietta Moskin, I Am Rosemarie).
They are Austrians who came to Holland many years earlier
for business reasons. Now they are suspected by the Dutch
of being enemy aliens and hounded by the Germans because
they are Jews. In August 1942 the Gestapo send them to the
transit camp of Westerbork.

Life in the camp is stiflingly public for Rosemarie.

It is impossible not to know all of the intimate details of the lives of the people around her.   She rejects the camp and avoids making contacts until another young inmate, Ruthie, persuades her to take a messenger job.   The new task gives her a sustaining sense of purpose.

Rosemarie helps settle newcomers and aids those who are packing for the Monday night transports.   It is this part of the job which is most difficult.   Gradually she learns to handle the job without seeing the people in transit as individuals.   Rosemarie copes by telling herself, "We're in the shipping business, I thought, a terribly efficient, well-run business concerned with the orderly processing and transfer of a product from Holland to points east.   Except that our product happens to be people--ordinary people of all ages, sizes, and shapes" (p. 73).

Before the Brenners are transported themselves, they manage to acquire South American passports.   This puts them in line to be exchanged for German prisoners.   They are shipped to Bergen-Belsen to a special camp for those with foreign passports.   Although the chance of transfer seems slight, Mrs. Brenner clings to this hope, fighting fiercely for the survival of her family.

Bergen-Belsen is a step closer to hell.   Mr. Brenner is repeatedly beaten by the guards.   Roll calls last hours.   Typhus sweeps through the camp.   Lice and bedbugs feed on the prisoners.   Both Mr. Brenner and Rosemarie fall ill.   Only Mrs. Brenner's zeal keeps them alive.   When she hears that an Exchange Commission is in the camp and will interview people with South American passports, she forces her husband and daughter to appear with her.   The Commission puts the family on the list for the next day's transport.   Mrs. Brenner's intuition saves the family.   Another family who had hoped to go is turned down when two of its members are too ill to show up for the interview.

There are too few Germans waiting to be exchanged, so the Brenners end the war in a Red Cross-supervised camp.   The Allies liberate the camp, and although the Brenners cannot be repatriated to Holland (because they are Austrian citizens), Rosemarie feels reborn, like a butterfly fresh out of a cocoon.

Terezin

Terezin (Theresienstadt, in German) was to be a

model ghetto. Built originally to house 15,000 troops, it
became a prison for 70,000 Jews. Although theoretically
not a concentration camp, Terezin served as a way-station
to the death camps. As many as 33,430 internees died there;
another 78,000 died after being transported. Two books
evoke the spiritual strength of its inmates. The first is an
account of the "artists' incident," the second a novel.

In addition to telling of the Terezin artists, Gerald
Green recounts the establishment of Terezin and the inexplic-
able mentality of the Nazis, who want a ghetto showplace
(The Artists of Terezin). In spite of their might, the Nazis
are frightened by a small group of artists who dare to paint
and sketch the truth.

Terezin is changed from a military installation to a
ghetto by the Jews of Prague, who have been ordered by the
Gestapo to design it as a new Jewish town. Of this group,
the artists are the elite. They are the ones who can design
the charts that appeal to the Germans' sense of order. Their
creative works are tolerated, almost encouraged, by the Germans until they turn their talents against their tormentors.

The usual ghetto rules apply in Terezin: no smoking,
no letters, strict curfews, hard labor, short rations. The
only transportation in the camp is a hearse, a grim example
of Nazi humor which often appears in surviving examples of
camp art. Until early 1942 the prisoners remain optimistic.
Then 16 are executed for such bizarre offenses as an illegal
conversation with one's wife.

An astonishing cultural life develops, with theater,
opera, concerts, cabarets, and lectures. To prepare for a
major Red Cross visit, the Austrian SS Captain Karl Rahm
begins a beautification program. Troublesome inmates (such
as those with tuberculosis and a group of emaciated orphans)
are shipped away; certain buildings are refurbished and
screened off from the rest of the camp. When the Red Cross
officials arrive on June 23, 1944, Rahm puts on a show worthy of an Oscar. As Green describes it:

> It was a memorable day, that warm June 23. The
> band played in the square. Children in clean cloth-
> ing rode a merry-go-round. Judenältester Eppstein
> wore a pressed black suit and was chauffered around
> by an SS man who, the day before, had kicked and
> beaten him. Today he opened the door of Eppstein's
> car, and bowed.

> . . .
> After a relaxing day, the men from the Red
> Cross departed. As far as is known, they were
> satisfied with what they saw. Conceivably some
> of them went to Terezin predisposed to believe
> everything. It should not surprise us. [pp. 89-90]

A few weeks after the Red Cross visit four artists,
an architect, and an elderly merchant are called into the SS
office. The merchant, František Strass, has contacts in
Prague whose gifts have allowed him to build up a collection
of ghetto art. Some of his drawings reached Red Cross hands
during the visit. Revealing the true nature of Terezin, they
have infuriated the SS. Eichmann himself starts the process
against the artists by playing the part of the aggrieved victim
of ingratitude and presses them for names of others involved
in the "Communist plot." The artists and their families are
transferred to punishment cells. One dies from the beatings.
Five are transported to Auschwitz. Only a few of them are
alive at the end of the war, but some of their work survives
to tell their story.

In examining the question of whether or not the victims were guilty of complicity for developing a cultural life
in Terezin, Green writes, ". . . I suspect that the Jews of
Terezin did what they did naturally. What was more natural
than a library, concerts, schools, lectures, and exhibitions
of paintings?" (p. 152). Green considers the artistic expres-
sions of the Terezin inmates as true acts of resistance to
and condemnation of the Third Reich. Through his selection
of the work of the Terezin artists, Green pays tribute to
their noble spirit.

A novel by Michael Jacot, The Last Butterfly, is also
set in Terezin. The emaciated orphans mentioned in Green's
book take center stage. Antonin, a clown who is no longer
funny, whose proud days are gone, is commissioned to entertain the Jewish children of Terezin. It will make a good
impression on the Red Cross visitors.

The rumor that a clown is in camp spreads quickly,
making the children forget for a moment that their parents
have been or will be transported away or that the girls are
misused by the guards in exchange for small favors. Antonin
is to plan the entertainment for the Red Cross visit with the
help of Vera Lydrakova, a lovely young Jewish woman who
secretly teaches the girls in her charge and tries to give

them hope.   There are 120 tough, wily, suspicious, bruised
boys also to be a part of the entertainment, though Antonin
has no illusions that he will be able to reach them.

As the camp commandant prepares for the Red Cross
visit, he receives two pieces of bad news: He is to receive
a shipment of Polish children who are to be kept isolated,
and the visit has been postponed indefinitely.   The children
arrive at night.   They are in such terrible condition that the
SS officer who unloads them hangs himself.   Antonin, Vera,
and Dr. Weinberg are assigned to the children.   The commandant has no intention of letting them or the children leave
Terezin alive.

The children are so malnourished and abused that
some can barely move.   Antonin tells them in Polish that
they will be fed soon, and then suddenly, naturally, he is
performing, and the children are laughing.   No longer is
he a failure.   He is needed.

The camp commandant receives a cable giving him
three days to prepare for the Red Cross visit.   In a flurry
of activity he ships out all those who might blemish Terezin's image.   The destination chalked on the car into which
the children are loaded is Auschwitz.   With the camp cleared
of undesirables, the commandant can relax with his guests
and bask in the success of his fictional model Jewish town.

The train rolls toward Auschwitz.   It is bombed by
the Americans, and the prisoners revolt.   Antonin leads his
children toward the woods and then falls back to divert the
guards.   Villagers join the fight, but power is on the side
of the guards.   The revolt is squelched, villagers and prisoners executed.   Of the original 3716 prisoners, 2489 remain, 864 are dead, and 363 are still missing.   Antonin
wants to be killed, but the SS have a special plan for him.
He is to return to Terezin to entertain children destined for
the gas chambers of Auschwitz.

Other Camps

Without being devoted entirely to the experience of
concentration camp victims, a number of other books for
young people include passages which vividly portray the horror of the victims and the depravity of their persecutors.

A concentration camp survivor opens Walter Jenrich's

eyes to the true character of Hitler and his regime in Horst
Burger's Vier Fragen an meinen Vater (pp. 164-171). Karl
Lademann tells Walter what he has witnessed in the camp.

One SS guard has a fit of frenzy any time he sees a
crooked blanket or an open button. One day two of the criminal prisoners jump a Jew, this being the quickest way to
earn favors with the guards. Against all expectations, the
Jew wins the fight. Veske, the SS guard, holds back his
colleagues when they start to jump the Jew. The little man
has won the fight fairly. From then on Veske treats the
Jew like a human being. Then one day the Jew shows up
for roll call with dusty shoes. That he has just emptied the
ash can means nothing to Veske. The Jew has dared to upset the order of things, and Veske is furious. He orders a
prisoner to take the man's shoes, hang them in the latrine,
and then bring them back. Then he gives the Jew two minutes to lick them clean. The Jew silently refuses. Veske
attacks him in a mad rage. Long after the man is dead,
Veske continues to savagely attack the body, only stopping when
he is led away.

Another time Veske lets a barrack burn down because
he refuses to be distracted from his task of organizing the
prisoners in straight lines. So concerned is he with order
that he has the electric fence turned off and commands the
prisoners to straighten the barbed wire. He becomes con-
sumed with the task, working long after the prisoners are
returned to their barracks for the night. One night Veske
works too late, forgetting that the current is turned back on
at dark. In the morning he is found by the fence. He has
died for order, his highest value.

In 1944 the SS expropriate certain valleys for war
purposes. In one of them lives Wendelgard von Staden (Nacht
über dem Tal). A factory for the construction of Hitler's
new wonder weapon is to be built nearby. Wendelgard's
family is allowed access to the woods near where the factory
will be. From the stone quarry there they see that another
camp is being built, this one ringed by barbed wire and watch
towers. Wendelgard's mother is sure that it is not for military purposes, but her father cautions his wife and daughter
to mind their own business. When emaciated Jewish prisoners are brought to the farmyard for straw and beans, Mother
knows immediately that their newest neighbor is a concentration camp. She cooks potatoes for the starving prisoners.
When she announces that they are ready, a melee breaks out:

> ... The prisoners dived for the kettle. It tipped
> over. The hot potatoes rolled on the ground. They
> grabbed for them, fell on them, began to bite into
> them, pressed them into their faces, as boiling hot
> and dirty as they were. They stuffed potatoes into
> their mouths with both hands and kneeled down in
> the muddy, wet earth to scrabble for more. They
> fought over every last potato. There was an up-
> roar around the overturned kettle. The guards
> swore and thrust with their rifle butts into the
> teeming mass.
>
> "What kind of people are they?" asked my hor-
> rified mother. "They aren't even human any more!"
> "Those are Jews," answered the guard, "sub-
> humans. You can see that for yourself." [p. 69]

Only one young prisoner stands aside, burning into his memory the scene of degradation for which both guards and onlookers are responsible and for which they must someday be
made to pay.

Wendelgard's mother throws herself into the struggle
to bring food and medicine to the prisoners. It is a desperate, lonely battle against starvation, disease, and indifferent
authorities.

Martin Gray writes of concentration camps from personal experience (Au nom de tous les miens). In Treblinka
he learns that to survive one must work quickly with head
down. The SS use humiliation and terror to keep the inmates
servile. Working on a clothing detail, he rifles the pockets
of the clothing he sorts. He slips bits of food into his mouth
but has to swallow without chewing or attract attention and
death (pp. 118-126).

Gray bypasses his first chance to escape and is assigned to the death camp (pp. 126-139). He knows that he
has reached the bottom. From here no one escapes, no one
survives. They must remove bodies from the gas chambers,
explore their mouths for gold teeth, throw them into pits.
When they can do so without being caught, they strangle infants not killed by the gas so that their deaths will not be a
lingering horror. Gray writes:

> I would need another voice, other words to ex-
> plain the shame which washed over me in waves
> sometimes, a nausea to be still alive, and then I

would be overcome by a rage to live, to live to tell
what we had seen, what they had done, what they
had forced us to do.   And the more savage they
were, the more firmly anchored became my conviction that they would be defeated, that it was not
possible that this kingdom of death would become
the kingdom of men.   Their plague would cease one
day.   I had to be there, witness and judge, for
those strangled infants.   For those I loved.   [p.
130]

Additional titles:

Del Castillo, Michel.   Tanguy.
Karau, Gisela.   Janusz K.
Kerr, Judith.   When Hitler Stole Pink Rabbit, p. 81.
Lacq, Gil.   Les enfants de la guerre, pp. 130-132.
Uris, Leon.   QB VII.

The Aftereffects

Those inmates who did manage to survive the concentration camps were wretched skeletons at war's end.   They
had risen from the abyss but would never be free of the horror.   Nothing remained of their former lives.   Homes, friends,
families, and professions were gone.   They faced scorn and
resentment for the accusation of guilt they embodied.   Two
of the books in this section give examples of this devastating
attitude.   The third shows the fate of two broken victims.
The two books under "Additional titles" address the problems
of readjustment.

In Gudrun Pausewang's Auf einem langen Weg, two
boys become separated from their mother as they flee west
from their Schlesien home.   They come across a file of prisoners looking tired and thin, almost dead.   Achim and Werner, 6 and 10, feel pity for them but wonder what bad things
they did to deserve such punishment (pp. 58-69).

A kindly couple takes in the two boys, treating them
as their own sons and becoming Uncle Karl and Aunt Else to
them.   When Karl learns that a group of concentration camp
survivors has recently stayed at a nearby farm, he tries to
explain to Werner why they are so angry with everyone:

... "Because we didn't defend ourselves against

Hitler. Because we let him be our leader. But
most of us realized too late where he was leading
us, namely into war, and by then there was nothing
more we could do unless we wanted to end up in a
concentration camp ourselves. A lot are supposed
to have been killed there. Did you know that?
Even children. We only heard rumors. Aunt Else
always said she didn't believe it. But now, after
the war, everything is coming out. Apparently it
was even worse. No wonder they hate us." [p.
103]

With the war at an end and things returning to normal,
Werner wants to find their mother before Achim becomes too
attached to Uncle Karl and Aunt Else. They slip away in the
night and become a part of the ragtag stream of refugees and
soldiers. In a town along their road, they take refuge for
the night in a vicarage. It is full of men with shorn heads
and prison-striped clothing. Wishing to be especially polite,
Achim gives the greeting he was taught in school, "Heil Hitler!" As the boys run from the wrath of these concentration
camp victims, Werner tries to explain why that greeting is
no longer used (pp. 126-136).

Pausewang's book is galling in its insensitivity toward
the victims of Nazism. Each time they are mentioned it is
in such a negative context that it seems to excuse their treatment, raising sympathy for those who allowed them to be
abused and who are now faced with having to deal with them
again.

One of the sections which Anthea Bell omitted from
her English translation of Die Zeit der Jungen Soldaten by
Hans Peter Richter is similar to those cited above. In the
confusion and panic at the end of the war, two German soldiers come across concentration camp victims being evacuated before the Russians:

We met them completely unexpectedly. We were
supposed to clear the road. We placed ourselves
on a rise beside it. From there we could hardly
see the end of them. Four and five abreast they
dragged themselves along in endless lines. Filthy,
ragged, all in striped clothing. Right and left the
worried figures of single, armed guards.
No one noticed us. The men being driven by
were too exhausted to look up. "What's that?" I
asked my companion.

He shrugged his shoulders. Then he climbed
down from our view point and walked up to one of
the guards.

"The concentration camp is being cleared out, "
he explained when he came back, "so that they, "
he pointed with his thumb at the passing figures,
"don't fall into Russian hands. "

We looked at the passing faces, lifeless, shriveled,
starving. . . .   "They look terrible, " I said.

My companion nodded. We watched for a while
longer and then looked for a path away from the
road over which the prisoners toiled westward.

"It's not really surprising, " my companion began
abruptly.

"What?" I asked.

"That those guys out of the concentration camp
look so miserable. "

"How's that?"

"Well, " he replied, "it's simple reckoning.
We're in the service. For a day's ration we get
a tenth of a loaf of army bread and 50 grams of
horse sausage. That's barely enough to keep us
upright. But them, " he pointed backward, "they
were put into the camp for punishment. It's only
right they get less to eat. --No wonder they all look
like that. " [pp. 146-147]

A book which shows empathy for those who suffered
most cruelly Hitler's perverse wrath is Damals war ich
vierzehn, a collection of war remembrances. Two eloquent
stories tell the ordeals of a young boy and an artist.

The first, "Jari, " by Käthe Recheis (pp. 92-96), is a
moving episode about a boy who knows only concentration
camp life. Käthe's father sets up a hospital for concentration camp survivors in an abandoned barrack. To this is
brought 10-year-old Jari, who has been in a children's camp
in Poland since his early childhood. He has never known his
parents or even his own name and fears everyone. One day
Käthe brings him a hardboiled egg. He does not recognize
it, and when she tells him it is edible, he tries to bite
through the shell. He is terrified of Käthe until his fever
mounts again, and he holds her hand for comfort. To try
to cheer him, she brings him a toy mouse. He looks at the
mouse, slowly relaxes, reaches for it, and begins to laugh.
With relief and joy, everyone in the barracks turns toward
the child and laughs with him.

The second story, "Der Maler Imre, " by the same author (pp. 96-100), tells of a Jewish artist who is also in the barrack hospital. His wife and three children starved and froze to death as the family was driven from Hungary. Though always polite, Imre never speaks of them or himself and shows no interest in life. Käthe's mother suggests she take him paper and drawing pencils. For days he does not use them and then begins pouring out the anguish and horror of the concentration camp into his drawings. His sketches are of people with staring eyes crowded behind barbed wire, of people starving, screaming, of women being beaten. Purged of his trauma, Imre smiles gently one day as he draws a picture of Käthe. That night he dies peacefully.

Additional titles:

> Des Pres, Terrence. The Survivor: An Anatomy of
> Life in the Death Camps (shows what it took to
> survive in the camps).
> Murray, Michele. Crystal Nights (adjustment of a
> survivor to life in the United States).

Chapter 4

THE FATE OF THE JEWS

In The Artists of Terezin, Gerald Green places the persecution of the Jews squarely in the middle of the Nazi program:

> ... It is my conviction that what was paramount, mandatory and central to Hitler's program was murder. As I study the evidence, I am persuaded that the generative force of Nazism, the very core of their movement, was the killing of Jews. All other aspects of Nazism--employment, rearmament, world domination, Aryan supremacy--all these were secondary, and grew out of the compulsion to murder. [p. 26]

In most textbooks for young people, the annihilation of six million Jews is almost a footnote. The numbers are there but not the anguish. Objectivity is inappropriate when examining inhumanity. To understand the special fury Hitler reserved for the Jews, one must look beyond statistics to the experience of the victims, the attitudes of the persecutors. The books in this chapter reveal personal dramas. The authorized monstrosity they show is staggering. Yet among them, too, are accounts of goodness, of people who refused to share in the lust for slaughter.

Two books written for young people which explain anti-Semitism and the Nazi persecution of the Jews are Milton Meltzer's Never to Forget and Arnold P. Rubin's The Evil That Men Do.

Meltzer first examines the history of Christian persecution of the Jews, tracing it through the Crusades, the anti-Semitic writings of Martin Luther, and the official anti-Semitism

of some political parties in Germany in the late 1800's. He
answers Hitler's charges that Jews had infiltrated industry
and that the government was riddled with Jews by pointing
out that when Hitler became Chancellor there were no Jews
in power in any major company and only three of the Weimar
Republic cabinets contained any Jews.

The diabolical build-up of repression, which kept Jews
weakened and confused, is traced through the "Jude verrecke"
("Down with the Jews") week of terror in 1933, the Nurem-
berg Laws of 1935, the tightening of immigration laws by
foreign countries. Meltzer describes the plan of the Final
Solution. Perversely, the Nazis brought the victims to the
killers by forming ghettos and transporting Jews to labor and
death camps. By putting Jews in charge of their own destruction through the Judenrat (Jewish Councils), the Nazis were
able to speed up their annihilation. Meltzer lets the victims
speak for themselves whenever possible, through diaries,
memoirs, letters, songs, and poems.

In The Evil That Men Do, Arnold P. Rubin devotes a
number of chapters to the fate of the Jews. The first chapter, "Of Sorrow and Pity," is an overview of the singling out
of the Jews for destruction. In "The Nightmare Begins"
Meltzer shows the cunning with which the Nazis gradually
clamped down on the Jews. German Jews were so thoroughly
assimilated that they refused to believe rumors of what was
in store for them. Crystal Night was a turning point. The
horror which had been growing like a cancer could no longer
be ignored. Though news of concentration camps and Crystal
Night reached beyond Germany, the Western powers reacted
with such a lack of concern that the Nazis were encouraged
to carry out their plans.

Ghettos, mass deportations, and concentration camps
were key elements in "The Final Solution," which Rubin describes in his fifth chapter. As members of the master race,
the Germans planned to rule over all inferiors. Slavs, Russians, Poles, Czechs, and gypsies would be slaves. Jews
would die. By the end of the war an estimated 72 percent of
all Jews in German-occupied lands had been killed.

In his last chapter dealing specifically with Jews,
Chapter 8, "The Jews, the Church, and the Nazis," Rubin
discusses the history of Christian anti-Semitism. This chapter complements that which begins Meltzer's book. Rubin
points out that ghettos, laws against intermarriage, and the

wearing of special badges did not originate with Hitler but
dated back 2000 years. Rubin is particularly interested in
the question of the complicity of the Protestant and Catholic
churches, whose silence in the face of atrocities has been
debated by churchmen and historians for the past forty years.

The question of who was to blame for what has come
to be called the Holocaust is well explored and on a level
appropriate for high school students in Rubin's last chapter,
"A Question of Guilt." He examines it in terms of "the killers (the Nazis) ... the killed (the Jews) ... [and] the onlookers, such as the Allies and the neutrals." In considering
whether or not Jews were partly to blame for their wholesale
destruction, he writes:

> ... the situation facing the Jews--in terms of
> choices--was really a very basic one. An army
> of noncombatants, with no weapons, starved, ill,
> tied to families, with no outside support, isolated,
> is faced with the choice of fighting a well-organized,
> well-fed, well-armed, experienced foe. Not to re-
> sist might prolong survival, whereas resistance
> might well hasten death for both the combatant and
> his family. His entire family. [p. 188]

Another author to deal with the question of guilt and
complicity between oppressors and oppressed under the Nazis
is Gerald Green in The Artists of Terezin. He disagrees
with such scholars as Bruno Bettelheim, who wrote that the
Jews were responsible for their own fate because of their
lack of resistance. At the same time, he does not seem
satisfied to say that the Jews could not have been expected
to act in any other way. Though he speculates throughout
the book on whether or not they could have prevented their
annihilation, those passages which are most germane are
found on pages 79-83 and 142-153 and would serve well as
a springboard for classroom discussions, particularly in combination with "A Question of Guilt" from Rubin's book.

THE DECISION TO FLEE

To accept the unbelievable, that they had been chosen
to die, and then to leave everything behind for an uncertain
future, was overwhelming. Those Jews with the foresight,
the means, and the opportunity to flee were a tiny minority.
Young adult authors have told some of their stories.

Charles Hannam (A Boy in That Situation) is 14 when
he leaves Germany. Until the Nazis give him no choice,
Karl, as he is called then, has never felt Jewish. He is a
very ordinary child, fat, fair-haired, blue-eyed, and not particularly likeable. He scorns people with Jewish noses and
dark, curly hair. To Karl, the restrictions placed on Jews
are both grimly fascinating and debilitating.

One day in his geography class the teacher uses Karl
as an example of the perfect Aryan ideal because of the shape
of his head and his coloring. The teacher is mortified to
learn that this perfect head belongs to a Jew. The boys hate
the teacher so they congratulate Karl. The end to his isolation is distressingly temporary, and Karl is relieved when he
is no longer allowed to attend school.

In 1939 he is sent to England, where he learns that
to officials there he is as welcome as a Nazi. Because of
his age, however, he is not deported to Australia. On the
whole the officials charged with carrying out anti-German laws
treat him kindly. As he matures, he outgrows the stealing,
practical joking, and deceptions of his childhood. Leaving
Germany gives him the chance to gain confidence in himself
after the devastating experience of being despised in his homeland.

In writing of her own experience in World War II,
Judith Kerr chose the novel form. In the first of her trilogy,
When Hitler Stole Pink Rabbit, Anna is 9 and learns from her
father that she is Jewish. As the daughter of a famous German drama critic who never attends synagogue, Anna is not
quite sure what that means. It soon becomes clear. Ten days
before the election of 1933 a policeman who admires her father's works calls to warn that his passport may be revoked.
He heeds the warning and takes the train to Prague. The
election is just getting underway when Mother boards the train
with Max and Anna and starts the journey toward Switzerland.

The family is reunited in Switzerland, but they have
lost all of their possessions, and the neutral Swiss are afraid
to publish Papa's works for fear of offending their German
neighbors. In order to work in a land where his writing will
be published, he moves the family to Paris. After two years
of poverty there, he sells his script on the life of Napoleon's
mother to an English film company. With the money from the
sale, the family moves to England.

The Other Way Around tells of the family's years in
London in World War II and is further proof of the marvelous
adaptability of children.   The story is completed in A Small
Person Far Away.   When her mother tries to kill herself
years after the war, Anna hurries to Berlin to be with her.
There she comes to grips with her past and the war years.
When she returns to England she leaves the shadow of the
Nazis and the Holocaust behind.

Another German Jew who finds refuge in England is
Judith Ginsberg (Martha-Maria Bosch, Judith).   Judith and
the narrator are best friends until the anti-Semitism of Nazi-
Germany drives the first wedge between them.   The narrator
begins to cool toward her Jewish friend.   In 1938 Judith's
physician father sends her to England, but both he and his
wife stay and later die in concentration camps.   Twenty years
after the war Judith is on her way to Palestine with her husband and children.   She no longer needs the strength of her
hatred of Germany so stops there to reforge the link with her
old friend and to tell her all that befell her and her loved
ones in that terrible time.

The book has a double perspective, that of a victim
and that of one on the side of the oppressors.   Its impact is
lessened by the remove at which it is told, but it is appropriate for a reader whose reading or maturity level makes
other books inaccessible.   One offhand comment on page 149
should be challenged.   The narrator implies that the Israelis'
attitude toward the Arabs is like that of the Germans' toward
the Jews during the war.   Since Germany has done so well
making restitution to the Jews after a much more serious
rupture, the Jews can surely work out their problems with
the Arabs.   The statement is a red flag, an example of ex-
cusing the Nazis by making the others look bad.

The Platt family finds refuge in Brazil in 1936, but
Mrs. Platt is unhappy, Lisa ill, and Mr. Platt unemployed,
so they return to Berlin (Sonia Levitin, Journey to America).
In February 1938 Mr. Platt leaves for America.   Once settled there, he sends for the family.

Using the ruse of a holiday in Switzerland, the Platts
leave nearly everything behind and take the train to Zurich.
The Swiss refugee agency refuses aid because they left Germany voluntarily.   Unable to feed the three of them, Mrs.
Platt arranges for the girls to be placed in a children's camp,

not suspecting that the director keeps the children on starvation rations while she clothes herself with agency money.   The
camp is a boring prison.   The girls do not complain to their
mother, but she knows them well enough to hear what they
are not saying when they come for a visit.   Though it means
putting them in separate homes, she removes them from the
camp.   Nearly a year goes by before all documents are in
hand, and they board a ship for America.

Additional titles:

> Klüger, Ruth.   The Secret Ship.
> Little, Jean.   From Anna.
> Rose, Anne.   Refugee.
> Uhlman, Fred.   Reunion.

CRYSTAL NIGHT

On November 7, 1938, Herschel Grynszpan, a 17-year-
old Polish Jew, shot Ernst vom Rath, an attaché in the German embassy in Paris.   Throughout Germany Jews held their
breaths, hoping that the diplomat would survive.   On November 9 vom Rath died.   The controlled German press issued in-
flammatory statements such as, "Das Weltjudentum reisst die
Maske vom Gesicht" ("World Judaism rips the mask from its
face"), and Reinhard Heydrich issued orders for a pogrom to
take place that night.   The pogrom would be touted as a
spontaneous reaction of the German people in retaliation for
the perfidy of the Jews, whose conspiracy against the nation
was revealed in the murder of vom Rath.

Kristallnacht, so called because the streets were lit-
tered with broken glass, was a resounding success for its
planners.   Hundreds of synagogues and apartments were
burned, thousands of shops plundered.   Of the 20,000 Jews
arrested, 10,000 were put in the concentration camp at Buchenwald.   The arrests and destruction continued throughout
the night of November 9 and into the following day.   Many
Jews committed suicide or went mad.   Both Protestant and
Catholic churches remained curiously silent.   The Nazis ordered the Jewish community to pay for all of the damage
caused by the SS and SA plus an additional fine of one billion
Reichsmark.

The narrator of Hans Peter Richter's Friedrich becomes

involved in the exhilarating orgy of destruction in spite of his friendship with Friedrich Schneider, a Jew. As he comes out of his school, the 13-year-old sees that Dr. Schneider's office has been torn apart, his medicines scattered. Abraham Rosenthal's shop is knee-high in goods ripped from the shelves; all glass is broken, wallpaper shredded.

Then the narrator sees a group of five men and three women with crowbars heading for the home for Jewish apprentices. He joins the group and becomes caught up in the excitement. They force the door and begin tearing the home apart. A middle-aged man stealing tools presses a hammer into the narrator's hand. Swinging it nonchalantly, he inadvertently breaks the glass in a bookcase. At first he is startled:

> ... But almost at once my curiosity awoke. Gently I tapped a cracked pane of glass and it fell out of its frame. By now I was enjoying myself. I swung so hard against the third pane that its splinters fell in bursts to the floor.
> With my hammer I cut myself a path through the corridors, smashing aside whatever barred my way: legs of chairs, toppled wardrobes, chamber pots and glassware. I felt so strong! I could have sung I was so drunk with the desire to swing my hammer. [Translation by Edite Kroll, p. 92]

On he goes, searching for anything breakable to satisfy his urge to destroy. Then he can find nothing else.

> Disappointed, I was about to leave the room, but by the door I looked back one last time. Against the far wall stood a large blackboard. I pulled back my arm and hurled the hammer. It struck the center of the blackboard. The head remained stuck. The light handle projected from the black surface. All of a sudden I felt tired and disgusted. On the stairs, I found half a mirror. I looked in it. Then I ran home. [Translation by Edite Kroll, p. 93]

Shortly after he arrives home, he and his mother hear shouting people rushing up their stairs. They break open the Schneiders' door, beat Friedrich and his mother and rip apart the apartment. In the night Frau Schneider dies of her injuries. As a final blow, Herr Resch, the landlord, makes

Dr. Schneider pay for the rosebushes the looters damaged
(pp. 88-95).

Richter returns to Crystal Night in his book Wir waren
dabei. The narrator and Günther both admit that they took
part. Heinz, whose father is a wealthy Party functionary, is
disgusted with them and shocks them by telling them that the
action was not spontaneous, that his father had had to provide
the list of Jewish apartments and shops. Later Günther tells
his story. He had gone to Abraham Rosenthal's shop to buy
a new math notebook. The door was locked, but Günther insisted he needed to buy the notebook. Mr. Rosenthal tried
to give it to him and push him out quickly, but the mob arrived. They filled the shop, shook Mr. Rosenthal by his
goatee, and pushed him against a shelf so hard that everything fell off. A man pushed a jar of chocolates into Günther's hands and ordered him to throw it. When he hesitated
the man kicked him. Old Mr. Rosenthal nodded to him, and
he threw the jar. The mob cheered and began pulling everything from the shelves, dyeing the old man's goatee with blue
ink, shredding notebooks. Then they punched Mr. Rosenthal
and dragged him out of the shop as others threw junk into
the street. Günther looked for his notebook but could not
find it and went home (pp. 94-97).

The dilemma of those not supporting Hitler but caught
up in the rush of events is described by James Forman in
The Traitors. Together with his best friend, Noah Engel,
the son of a Jewish doctor, Paul Eichhorn plans a first-class
prank. In the middle of the showing of the Nazi film, Triumph of Will, the boys release a bag full of moths. Timed
to fly free just when Hitler and his general appear on the
screen, the moths are a roaring success.

That same day a Jewish refugee shoots Ernst vom
Rath in Paris. The Ravenskirch Nazis use the freeing of the
moths as an additional excuse for their destructive rampage.
Hitler has been insulted by the Jews, and Ravenskirch explodes.
The SA rush around "like bleating herds of bloodthirsty sheep,"
setting fire to the synagogue and destroying shops. Paul
watches in horror as a man with a petrol can suddenly turns
into a human torch. He is crushed that his practical joke
has provided an excuse for the barbarism of Crystal Night
(pp. 57-70).

One of the narrator's questions to his father in Horst
Burger's Vier Fragen an meinen Vater is what happened to

the Jews and why. As part of his answer Walter Jendrich explains how as a ten-year-old he felt proud and secure to be German. His teacher had inspired him with accounts of Germany's glorious past and of the perfidy of the French.

After Crystal Night the children come to school excited and filled with rumors, the teacher with red eyes. The children have heard that the SS learned of a Jewish revolt and were protecting the citizens from it. Others say that the police were looking for Communists and found them hiding in Jewish stores. The fighting broke out when the police tried to arrest the Bolsheviks. Other children are sure that the Jews burned their own synagogues.

The only thing that all the children agree on is that the Jews must be punished. To the children's eager talk of Jewish treachery, greed, and subhumanity, Fräulein Waller objects vigorously. She tells the children that had the Führer known of Crystal Night, he would never have allowed it.

During the long recess the children have something besides the events of last night to discuss. Something is happening in the gym, and no one is allowed near. When the bell rings Walter hides. As soon as no one else is around, he sneaks up to the gym window. The room is filled with Jews being forced to do exercises by SS and SA men. Each time they fall, they are whipped.

Not until the director catches him can Walter take his eyes from the blood-encrusted faces. The swats he receives are a relief and an expiation. The director swears him to secrecy because the Führer's opponents might treacherously use the information against their beloved leader. The men being punished in the gym are all thieves and criminals from whom the SS and SA are protecting the people. Walter does not really understand the director's talk but soon forgets the episode (pp. 22-32).

The response of many German citizens to Crystal Night is typified in Werner Toporski's Mädchen mit Stern. Jonas is awakened in the night by unusual sounds, men calling to each other, shouting, people running. Looking out, he sees men in brown uniforms beating a man. He slips fearfully back into his bed and the next day asks his mother if SA men were involved. His mother's reply echoes many others:

"It must have been ordered from above, although I
can't believe the Führer knew about it. I think he
has bad advisers. " [p. 26]

The evidence that Crystal Night was not spontaneous
lies in official Nazi documents. In <u>Howl Like the Wolves</u> (pp.
151-160), Max von der Grün cites three of these. The first
is a message to all police stations throughout Germany:

Berlin No. 234-404, November 9, 2355
To all police stations and police headquarters
To all chiefs or deputies

This telegram is to be passed on [to all person-
nel] immediately, by the swiftest possible means.
1.   In the immediate future action will be taken
against Jews throughout Germany, and particularly
against their synagogues. You are not to interfere
with these actions. However, you are to cooperate
with the security police to prevent looting and other
excesses.
2.   You are to take immediate measures to safe-
guard any important records that may be found in
the synagogues.
3.   You are to make preparations to arrest some
20,000 to 30,000 Jews throughout the Reich. The
primary criterion of selection is that they be Jews
of some wealth. More detailed orders will be issued later tonight.
4.   If, during the coming actions, any Jews are
found to be in possession of weapons, the most severe measures are to be taken against them. SS
reserve troops, as well as the regular SS, may be
called upon to participate in these joint actions.
In any case, the necessary measures are to be
taken to ensure that the actions are led by the State
Police.   [Translation by Jan van Huerck, p. 155]

The second document is a detailed account of the synagogues
attacked in one area, with a brief note as to how thoroughly
each was destroyed, and the third is Chief of the Security
Police Heydrich's own summary to Göring of the reports he
had received by November 11, 1938, from police stations
around Germany.

Additional titles:

THE HYDRA OF ANTI-SEMITISM

The authors of the books in this section tell a story
which is corroborated over and over. In every country the
Germans occupied, the Jews shared a similar fate: restrictions, persecution, death. Only Denmark acted with such
unity that most of its Jewish citizens were rescued. American Jews, too, shared the calumny of the prejudiced, though
not with the same virulence as those of Europe. Each act,
each word of hate, no matter where done or spoken, helped
to desensitize people to the plight of the Jews.

Austria

On her thirteenth birthday Inge Dornewald starts re-
cording her "real and true feelings" (Doris Orgel, The Devil
in Vienna). With the Nazis becoming ever bolder, anti-
Semitic incidents are on the rise. Inge's parents are not
religious, but they are still Jews to the Nazis. When Hitler
marches to the border and forces Austria to capitulate, both
Inge's father and grandfather are picked up and made to clean
the streets.

Mr. Dornewald's business partner commits suicide
when his brother is sent to a concentration camp. The Nazis
put a 23-year-old boy in charge of their import-export business and insist he be paid a salary three times that of Mr.
Dornewald. Naturally when the firm goes bankrupt, Mr. Dornewald will be accused of sabotage.

Mr. Dornewald's old wet nurse threatens to denounce
the family if they do not pay her 10,500 shillings. Just one
day before she carries out her threat, the family gets fake
baptismal certificates from a Catholic priest and flees to
Yugoslavia.

Denmark

The story of the Danes' response to the German threat
against their Jewish citizens is a proud chapter in Denmark's
history.   Denmark was a stable country united under a beloved king.   No other country was able to organize so well
against the occupiers.

In Nathaniel Benchley's Bright Candles Jens Hansen
is a month shy of 17 when the men in grey uniforms march
into Copenhagen.   Though they look capable of any evil, Jens
cannot believe that they will harm Danish Jews.   He muses:

> ... It was up to their superiors what they did about
> the Jews, but none of us had ever thought of the
> Jews as being anything but Danes, so it was hard
> for us to make the distinction in our minds.   It
> would have made as much sense for them to come
> for everyone who was left-handed, or who sang
> bass, or liked pomegranates.   I couldn't think in
> their terms, so I decided not to try.
>   "Well, anyway, the Jakobys are safe," I said.
> "They've been here for three generations." [p. 17]

Nothing saves the Jews, even in Denmark, from becoming targets of the Nazis' lust for murder.   The action
against the Danish Jews is to be secret and swift.   On September 17, 1943, Germans in civilian clothes steal the membership list of the Jewish Community Center in Copenhagen.
On September 18 Eichmann sends SS men to the city.   Fortunately, a consular officer passes a message to the Danes,
telling them of plans to round up all Jews.   When time for
the action arrives, the Danes snatch their Jewish citizens
from under the noses of the Germans:

> People telephoned their Jewish friends and acquaint-
> ances, then went through the telephone book and
> picked any names that looked Jewish; others roamed
> the streets, telling any passerby who appeared likely
> to be interested; and one man, an ambulance driver,
> took the day off and went around picking up Jews in
> his ambulance, taking them to places where they
> could hide.   In this case, the only people who didn't
> get the word were the Germans; they thought their
> operation was still a secret.   [p. 159]

Only 202 Jews are caught in the well-organized raid

and another 270 later. All others are in hiding, and the
Danish population is firmly united in its determination to
keep them out of German hands. Even those who have urged
cooperation with the Germans until now are incensed, with
the exception of the relatively small number of Danish Nazis.
The Danes are ideally located and begin shipping the Jews to
Sweden, using every possible craft for the task. Both Jens
and his father are involved. The Gestapo become savage in
their search for the missing Jews, killing everyone in an
operating room because they suspect that Jews are being hidden as patients. By the end of October 1943 all but 472 of
the Danish Jews have been transported to safety (pp. 157-189).

A similar account of the Danes' evacuation of the Jews
is in Eva-Lis Wuorio's To Fight in Silence (pp. 153-193).
Coming to Gormsgaard has always meant family reunions and
good times for the Jensens and Eriksons, but this visit is
different. On September 29, 1943, Aunt Minna drives up in
a delivery wagon with seven passengers. Then Mrs. Jensen
arrives, bringing seven more and sends Thor to invite Dr.
Holstein and his family. Mr. Jensen comes with a full car.
A Copenhagen taxi brings twelve more, and friends in two
more cars bring yet others. Until this time no one in the
family has shared his/her resistance activities with the vol-
atile Grandfather Gorm, for the old man refuses to guard his
words in front of anyone. With his house filling with strangers, he comes storming in for an explanation and is shaken
to learn what is happening in his beloved Denmark.

Two German transport vessels steam into Copenhagen
to take Jews to concentration camps. The Danes decide to
act first. The Germans have timed their action to find everyone home on Rosh Hashanah. On September 30 the family
divides up the tasks. Some stay at Gormsgaard to take messages and receive guests. Three of the children deliver messages in Copenhagen because their age makes them less suspicious. The adults arrange for transporting all guests to
Sweden.

In Copenhagen the children persuade the manager of
a popular men's tailoring shop to give his employees a holiday so they can picnic in Helsingor. A banker agrees to let
his workers go but says he and his family will be at the
synagogue that night. A woman at their next stop is happily
preparing the festival dinner.

At Helsingor people wait for boats to Sweden. A

doctor sedates the children so their cries will not betray their
families.   Crowded in freight cars that are then loaded onto
ferries, the Jews of Denmark sail to refuge in Sweden.   Hundreds of fishing boats take others.   Aunt Minna is further up
the coast helping to arrange boats when she is stopped by a
German patrol.   Not being Gestapo, the soldiers simply look
the other way.

On October 1 Werner Best, the German plenipotentiary
in Denmark, is so confident of success that he sends Hitler
a telegram declaring Denmark judenrein (free of Jews).   The
special troops and Gestapo begin their rounds.   They find almost no one at home.   Exasperated, they try to break into
neighboring houses and apartments but are stopped by the
Danish police.   Best is humiliated and furious.

In an epilogue to the book Wuorio states that by the
end of October, only 472 Jews had been captured.   Most of
these survived in concentration camps because of the constant
badgering of Danish and Swedish officials.   At the end of the
war, they were among the first released.   As they passed
through Denmark on their way to Sweden, these Jews were
greeted with a tumultuous welcome.   When they finally returned home, they found their homes cared for and as they
had left them.

Additional title:

Rubin, Arnold P.   The Evil That Men Do, pp. 130-131.

Eastern Europe

The Jews of Eastern Europe were not as assimilated
as those in the west.   They suffered the double burden of
isolation within their own lands and persecution by the German occupiers.   The high percentage of Jews killed in Eastern European countries is evidence not only of the efficiency
of the Nazi murderers but also of the cooperation they received from local anti-Semites.

One frequently printed and horrifying account of the
cold-blooded murder of Ukrainian Jews is the testimony of
Friedrich Gräbe, chief engineer of a branch of the Josef Jung
Construction Firm of Solingen and inspector of construction
sites.   Max von der Grün includes his account in Howl Like
the Wolves, pp. 238-240.

Near Dubno, Gräbe witnesses the massacre of Jews, who are forced to strip and place their garments on piles of shoes, underwear, and outer clothing. Family groups stand together talking quietly, saying their goodbyes without weeping or crying out. Wave after wave, they are ordered into the pit and shot. New victims have to trod on the bodies of the dying, then lie down on them to be shot in turn. The SS murderer sits at the edge of the pit, smoking a cigarette and dangling his feet over the edge as each group marches in front of his submachine gun.

Next day Gräbe returns to the site and finds workers of his firm staring at the survivors and corpses that lie outside the pit. An SS squad arrives. They make the survivors throw the corpses into the pit and then shoot them.

The cold brutality of the Nazis is further revealed in a document written by the SS Leader of Warsaw concerning the destruction of the ghetto. It is a carefully detailed report concerning a major action. The bureaucrat Stroop gives a thorough outline of the killing of Jews, "subhumans, bandits, and terrorists." His account is totally dispassionate and businesslike. He had a job to do and is reporting its successful outcome (pp. 206-207).

A surviving eyewitness to the destruction of the Warsaw ghetto is Martin Gray (Au nom de tous les miens). When the bombs begin falling on Warsaw, Gray's non-Jewish appearance helps him in the savage struggle for survival. Jews very quickly become the objects of hate. Poles denounce them if they try to stand in line for water or food.

The day after the Germans enter Warsaw, they distribute bread but order the Jews out of line. A small, dark man stands quietly with the others until he is denounced by a Pole. A soldier grabs his beard, shakes and kicks him. Everyone in line laughs as he runs away. Another Jew is forced to take off his shoes and hop like a frog. A German soldier tosses his shoes to a Pole, and everyone laughs. Gray examines the faces of the denouncers, trying to memorize them, but there are too many (pp. 18-19).

The end of November 1939, the Jews of Warsaw are required to wear armbands with a blue Star of David. Nowhere is the armband better or more simply described than by Gray: "... Un brassard qui veut dire: homme à voler, à battre, à tuer ..." ("... An armband which means: a man to rob, to beat, to kill ..." p. 21).

Before they are herded into the ghetto, the Jews have
to build the wall around it.   On the day they fill the ghetto,
the Germans make great sport of humiliating the Jews.   Gray
remembers seeing Germans laugh as a Jewish policeman hops
on one foot and a woman kisses the sidewalk.   There is no
end to the torments they can devise.   One makes an old man
do knee bends and then slowly walks over his prostrate form
when he falls.   Others beat a young Jew who enters the ghetto
wearing a hat and order a Jewish policeman to urinate on
him (pp. 46-47).

So determined is Gray to survive to bear witness that
he soon organizes a regular contraband route, his smuggling
helping to keep at least some of those in the ghetto alive.
He hardens himself to pass by those who are dying.   To
avenge their deaths he must live.   He manipulates street
punks both inside and outside the ghetto to act as his bodyguards and porters.   Time and again he is caught, tortured,
flees.   No one can stop him, but when he sees his parents
caught in a roundup, he turns himself in and is transported
to Treblinka.

On September 1, 1939, the Germans march into Poland.   Mendel the water carrier continues his deliveries as
usual (Yuri Suhl, On the Other Side of the Gate).   His customers in the small Polish town depend on him, and on this
day he dispenses comforting words along with the water.   For
himself there is no comfort, for he remembers 1914 when
the Cossacks flirted with the girls and gave biscuits to the
children and then raped Jewish women and looted Jewish
stores.   Mendel is drawing water with his same methodical
rhythm when two hooligans start tossing his cap back and
forth.   An old woman who confronts them becomes their next
target.   Then a railway man grabs Mendel's cap and quietly
tells him to leave.   It hurts Mendel to be leaving with empty
water cans, but he walks slowly away.   Before he can leave
the square, a German soldier stops him.   Urged by his
friends, the soldier starts sawing at Mendel's beard while
his comrades take pictures.   That is too much for a pious
Jew.   Mendel twists the bayonet out of the man's hand.   The
soldier with the camera shoots him, calmly puts away his
pistol, and takes one last picture, of the corpse (pp. 1-10).

The Germans appoint a Jewish Council to carry out
their orders.   Many consider its members traitors; others
would rather deal with them than with the Germans.   The
Jews are given 24 hours to prepare to move into the ghetto.

In the meantime, they are to report to work as usual. As
the Jews are herded into the ghetto, Polish onlookers stare.
Some jeer. Some cry. Others fight over abandoned belongings. Two thousand people are packed into two and a half
streets, six to ten in each room:

> ... Total strangers were thrown together in the
> most intimate settings. The floor became a com-
> munal bed. Occupants became known by the smell
> of their bodies, the sound of their snores. To
> open a window meant to freeze; to keep it closed
> meant to suffocate. Infants wailed. Men fought
> over an inch of space. Women quarreled over the
> use of the stove. To get into the hallway toilet
> was a major achievement. People would have gladly
> parted with a most precious possession for a little
> privacy. [p. 38]

The fifth week, barbed wire encircles the ghetto, and
the Jews are billed for the wire. Not even in the streets
can they escape the crowding.

Hershel and Lena Bregman are expecting a child. Although it is illegal to be pregnant in the ghetto, Lena bears
little David. For a year and a half they hide him, but when
the transports start it becomes too risky. Hershel devises
a daring plan to smuggle David out in a water barrel. With
the help of Poles on the outside, the barrel swap takes place
and David starts out for a new life.

The heroes of Suhl's Uncle Misha's Partisans are
Ukrainian Jews who have built a strong center of resistance
in a deep forest. At the first camp wedding, Commander
Zissman tells the story of another time when Jews sang "Lomir Zich Iberbeten" ("Let's Make Up"), the song with which
the young violinist starts the celebration.

Whenever the Germans occupy a town, they celebrate
with a pogrom. In Commander Zissman's town a pogrom is
not enough. They want to be amused as well. After slaughtering many of the town's Jews, they march the survivors
into the square. With the graves of their loved ones still
fresh, they must sing and dance. "Louder! Faster!" cry
their tormentors, and the Jews fall over each other in the
confusion. The Germans are delighted and film the grotesque
celebration so they can show the people back home how de-
praved the Jews are. Suddenly in the middle of singing

"Lomir Zich Iberbeten," a young woman substitutes the words, "mir velen zei iberleben" ("we shall overcome"), and the singing becomes an act of resistance (pp. 120-123).

A proud, civic-minded Jewish family in Czechoslovakia is gradually and inexorably destroyed in Ein Haus in Böhman by Hanna Demetz. Helenka's mother is one of three strong-willed daughters of the family patriarch. All of the daughters have defied their father, Helenka's mother in order to marry the scion of a rich local family. The old man refuses to see his daughter wed to a German law student but softens with the arrival of Helenka.

The Nazis take over, and Helenka's father loses his job because he refuses to divorce his wife. A teacher tries to seduce Helenka, and her parents dare not object. Tante Klara is shot by the Germans, her husband and daughter arrested. Grandfather loses his house, and his friends are afraid to be seen with him. Onkel Fritz and his family are deported; Onkel Rudolf is taken away. Onkel Fred dies in a concentration camp. The time comes when only Helenka's mother remains free. All of her deported relatives turn to her with pleas for help and food.

Helenka falls in love with a German soldier. Her mother is crushed. Not understanding what has happened to their relatives, Helenka becomes cool toward her. Denied access to a hospital, Helenka's mother dies, leaving Helenka to repent bitterly the pain she caused. At the end of the war her soldier is dead. Her father is killed trying to heal the breach between the victors and the losers. Her gentle aunt is killed because she is German. Those freed from occupation now turn their wrath on those who made them suffer, and the cycle of inhumanity remains unbroken.

Additional titles:

> Brand, Sandra. I Dared to Live.
> Bruckner, Winfried. Die toten Engel.
> Hautzig, Esther. The Endless Steppe.
> Uris, Leon. Mila 18.
> Werstein, Irving. The Uprising of the Warsaw Ghetto.
> Ziemian, Joseph. Sag bloss nicht Mosche zu mir,
>   ich heisse Stasiek.

France

     As with many assimilated families, the Niemans sel-
dom think about being Jewish until the Nazis remind them
(Marilyn Sachs, A Pocket Full of Seeds). The parents travel
the open-air markets around Aix-les-Bains selling sweaters
and blouses. Until Nicole is eight, she and her sister Jacqueline live with the Durand family. In May 1938 the family
is reunited in an apartment with four dark rooms and a tiny
kitchen.

     Françoise Rosten, rich and admired, chooses the out-
spoken Nicole to be her special friend, but it is Lucie whom
Nicole longs to have as a friend. From her veranda, Nicole
never tires of gazing across at Lucie's apartment, imagining
what she is doing. She cannot understand why Lucie loathes
her, for she has had no experience with anti-Semitism.

     Through their daughters, the rich, educated Rostens
and the working-class Niemans become friends. Mr. Nieman
joins the military, sure the war will end soon, and then is
sent home without seeing any action. The Rostens become
targets of anti-Semites. Their cook quits because it is de-
grading to work for Jews. One of Dr. Rosten's patients
switches to a Christian doctor and refuses to pay his bill,
by now several years old. The same man once dragged the
doctor out of bed in the middle of the night when his son fell
off a roof.

     The Germans occupy Aix-les-Bains in June 1943 and
act just like summer tourists. Mrs. Nieman wants to leave
for Switzerland, but Mr. Nieman balks. That November the
Rostens do leave. Nicole and Françoise are so sad to be
parting that Nicole is allowed to stay with the Rostens on
their last night in France. As Nicole starts after the Rostens she remembers she has forgotten to kiss her parents
good night, but the door is already shut.

     Next day Jacqueline is not in school. Nicole returns
home to find her apartment in a shambles. The landlady
tells her her family has been arrested, and she must hide.
She bicycles to the Durands. At first they welcome her, but
then they worry about their own safety and send her away.
She goes to friends of her parents. One couple will not answer the door. At the next home, the woman says she is
sick and her husband has a bad heart. Nicole bicycles the

whole day and then falls asleep in the doorway of her school.
Next day her teacher finds her there and takes her in without
hesitation.   Although some of the girls say Mlle. Legrand is
a collaborator and is only helping Nicole as insurance for
when the Nazis lose the war, what is important to Nicole is
that Mlle. Legrand dared to take her in.

Hélène Ray's Ionel, la musique et la guerre is the
story of a child prodigy, a cellist who at age seven wins
first place in a competition in his Romanian Conservatory.
Paris, City of Lights and civilization, is the city of his heart,
but his dream of studying at the Paris Conservatory comes
true too quickly when the Germans enter Poland.

At first, the fact of his being Jewish is secondary to
his being a talented musician, but gradually even in Paris
the noose around the Jews tightens.   The invective of the
German-controlled press invades the Conservatory.   One
morning Ionel overhears one of his classmates hurling insults
at the Jews while another defends them.   Signs begin to appear on stores: "Ici, maison française, interdite aux Juifs."
("This is a French store.   No Jews allowed.").   Hoodlums
are hired to stand at the doors of Jewish shops and harass
customers.   Then the Jews are ordered to post their own
signs: "Maison juive" ("Jewish store").   Ionel is amazed
by the French capacity for laughter and fun even as the
events around them are grim.

The time comes when the cousins with whom Ionel is
living decide to flee.   With a new name, Ionel remains in
Paris until the end of the war, his identity kept a secret by
those who love him.   Ionel's obsession with his Jewishness
and his guilt at not sharing the fate of others is echoed in
other books about Jews who survived the war, such as those
by Sachs, Ciravegna, and Brand.

Additional titles:

    Friedländer, Saul.   Quand vient le souvenir.
    Joffo, Joseph.   Un sac de billes.

Germany

Books written for young people from the perspective
of German Jews are rare.   More frequent are books in which

children are witnesses to acts of anti-Semitism. Inge
Deutschkron's autobiography, Ich trug den gelben Stern, is
one of the former. Deutschkron tells how she and her mother
survive nearly impossible odds, thanks to their own courage
and intelligence and to the help of brave friends.

When Hitler comes into power, the Deutschkrons are
active Socialists whose politics mean more to them than religion. The Nazis soon change that. Jews are required to
carry a "J"-stamped identity card with a photograph showing
their left ear, since that is supposedly a mark of Semitic
origin. By 1939 they are required to turn in radios; their
telephones are disconnected; an 8 p. m. -5 a. m. curfew is
imposed. They must turn over furs, binoculars, cameras,
and electrical appliances, including irons. Public laundries,
beauty salons, barber shops, museums, parks, concerts, and
theaters are off limits.

Though slated for destruction, Jews are important to
Nazi war preparations, for they provide hard labor in factories. Deutschkron points an accusing finger at IG-Farben,
where Jews were kept isolated and given the worst work and
ordered to wear a yellow star on their work smocks even before the stars were required by law.

Mr. Deutschkron reaches England in April 1939, but
by the time he can arrange passage for his wife and daughter,
England and Germany are at war. In September 1941 all
Jews are ordered to wear yellow stars. Inge, who does not
fit the Nazi stereotype of a Jew, keeps two different coats.
In her star-free coat she can buy food, have laundry done,
visit theaters, concerts, and movies.

Inge and her mother evade the transports that the
Nazis force the Jews themselves to organize. At one point,
with the help of forged identity cards, Inge works for a Nazi
bookseller while her mother tutors the children of SS fathers.
Inge is still vulnerable at the end of the war. She must hide
repeatedly from Russian soldiers looking for German girls to
rape. Living in the Russian sector of Berlin, she is dis-
criminated against by her Communist colleagues because she
is a Socialist. The British make it difficult for her and her
mother to rejoin her father in England. Once she is there,
they discriminate against her because she is from an enemy
land. In the years following the war, she sees former Nazis
rise to positions of power in the government. When she protests she is reviled by people who want to forget what happened. Only as a citizen of Israel does she find a home.

Other books in which the Jews of Germany play a part
take the point of view of onlookers, some sympathetic, others
unmoved. In this context Willi Fährmann's book Es geschah
im Nachbarhaus is significant. Although the events take place
at the end of the nineteenth century, they reveal a deep core
of anti-Semitism which existed in Germany long before Hitler
tapped it.

The low value placed on Jewish lives becomes clear
to 6-year-old Walter Jendrich on the day of Hindenburg's
death in 1934 (Horst Burger, Vier Fragen an meinen Vater).
The boys are playing Take-the-President-to-the-Graveyard
and arguing over who will be Hindenburg, who the horse,
when Walter drops out of the game and wanders over to the
stream. Soon the others join him on the bridge. Gerhard
Wandres, poorer than the others and something of an outcast,
approaches them hopefully. Günther claims to see a fish in
the stream, so Gerhard leans over the bridge and points enthusiastically to the imaginary animal. Suddenly Walter has
an irresistible urge to push Gerhard. He closes his eyes,
approaches, and when he opens them Gerhard is gone.

A crowd forms around the bridge, and Günther runs
for his father. Walter confesses, but Herr Breitner insists
that Walter tell the police that Gerhard fell by himself. As
Walter is struggling with his conscience, the SS-Führer who
lives on his street appears and sends him home. Behind him
Walter hears talk of "Buchbinderei Wandres ... Juden ..."
("Wandres' bindery ... Jews ..."). After all, Gerhard was
only a Jew. His death is no more interesting than that of a
stray dog. Certainly no Aryan boy should get in trouble for
such a trifle.

Karl-Heinz Weber is only three years older than Walter when he learns that Jews are poisonous (Hans-Georg
Noack, Die Webers). He reads that in the Nazi newspaper
posted outside the optician's office in April 1933. It surprises
him. He had never realized that his friend Ernst Heine was
dangerous, but he decides to shun him anyway. Across the
street, two SS guards block the door of the Heines' notions
store. A third grabs an old woman who is just leaving and
puts a sign in front of her saying she buys only in German
stores. He takes a picture of her for the Nazi newspaper,
and bystanders just laugh (pp. 20-22).

Ernst Heine becomes an outcast at school. With a
Jew among them, his class will never have a chance to be-

come 100 percent Jungvolk (pp. 39-41). The day after Crystal
Night, the Heines return to find their shop destroyed. Without a word, they set to work to salvage what they can. Curious people look on. Occasionally someone expresses sympathy, but only Karin Asmus, daughter of a Nazi, offers to
help. Her brother is furious when he sees her in the street
picking up buttons. What would people think if they saw her
kneeling beside a Jew? (pp. 68-70). In 1939 the Heines are
arrested, but the SS overlook Ernst, hidden in a pantry. By
the time they realize their error, the Webers have taken him
in (pp. 77-80).

The heroine of Renate Finckh's Mit uns zieht die neue
Zeit is completely unmoved at seeing Jews become the brunt
of irrational hatred. One day her mother sends her to buy
horse meat, for which no ration cards are needed. With a
folding stool and a book, Nela joins a line that she judges to
be one and a half to two hours long. Frau Schmidtke, the
half-Jewish mother of Nela's friend, quietly takes her place
in the queue. "Die Ziege" ("the goat") sees her and becomes
livid. Here is a Jew buying meat away from real Germans.
As "the goat" continues to vent her spleen, only two women
dare to speak up in opposition. Frau Schmidtke calmly says
they really should eat less meat and walks away. Nela feels
no sympathy, no emotion (pp. 16-21).

Now that the Nazis are in power, Nela is no longer
allowed her once-a-week café visit with two Jewish ladies.
The loss is meaningless to her. The only thing that stays
in her mind is that one day one of the ladies sat her on a
toilet stool in the café's bathroom, something her mother
never allowed. Only a Jew would do that (pp. 28-29).

A long-time member of her parents' tennis club is
expelled because he has a Jewish mother. Nela's parents
are incensed, not because the man was thrown out of the
club, but because he did not have the grace to leave on his
own (p. 53). With such examples, Nela very happily accepts
the idea that Jews are inferiors, appropriate objects of scorn
and hatred.

Dieter Borkowski depicts himself as a victim of Nazi
propaganda in his reconstructed journal, Wer weiss, ob wir
uns wiedersehen. He believes the anti-Jewish doctrine but
has occasional twinges of conscience. In May 1943 he travels
from Berlin to his uncle's home in Zernsdorf, Poland, now
part of the Reich. At a time when gas is available only for

war-related purposes, Dieter is thrilled to ride in his uncle's
truck.   On May 14 an important Party functionary rides with
them on an official mission, clearing out apartments that appear to Dieter to be occupied.   His uncle explains that they
will be given to people who have been bombed out by the Jewish war mongers.   Both his uncle and the Party official put
aside goods for themselves while they go about their work.
Dieter knows Jews are inferior but feels uneasy about the
day, even after his uncle explains that it is only right that
good Germans like himself should be able to take a few things
from enemies.   His aunt assures him that the deported Jews
are lazy and work shy and have been put to productive work.
Though their reassurances seem reasonable to Dieter, a small
shadow of doubt remains (pp. 37-41).

          Hans Peter Richter's account of the systematic perse-
cution of a Jewish family remains one of the best and continues to be reissued in many languages.   In <u>Friedrich</u> Richter
relates episodes of grim consequences with a disconcerting
lack of comment.   Friedrich Schneider is born in 1925, one
week later than the narrator, and grows up in the same apartment building.   In 1929 the narrator watches with envy as
Friedrich and his mother play happily in the new snow.   After
a while Frau Schneider comes back into the house, and Friedrich tramps through the piles of snow on his way to the door.
Herr Resch, the landlord, bellows at him, "Willst du wohl
meine Rosen in Frieden lassen, du Judenbengel, du!"   ("Will
you leave my roses in peace, you dirty Jewboy you!")   The
narrator's mother pulls her son away from the window without
comment.

          In 1933 the narrator takes Friedrich to a Jungvolk
meeting.   A hunchback visits the group that night and delivers
a special harangue against Jews.   In graphic detail he tells
of kosher butchering, murder of children, crimes, wars.
Seeing Friedrich's rapt attention, he directs his talk to him.
He ends his speech with, "Die Juden sind euer Unglück!" ("The
Jews are our affliction!"), and orders Friedrich to repeat
the phrase.   Friedrich sits in silent agony until the man
jerks him from his seat, makes him repeat the curse, and
steals his swastika ring.   Friedrich walks out.   The narrator
stays silently in his seat.

          That same year the narrator accidentally tosses a ball
through a shop window.   He admits the deed, but both the
shop woman and the policeman she calls insist it was Friedrich and march with a gathering crowd to the Schneiders'
apartment to demand payment.

The narrator's father joins the Party, but he cannot convince Herr Schneider that terrible things are in store for the Jews. The unheeded warning of 1936 becomes the grave reality of 1938, when Frau Schneider dies after being beaten on Crystal Night.

The landlord is gleeful when Herr Schneider and the rabbi he was hiding are arrested in 1941, as he has tried since 1933 to evict the family. He sacks the apartment and then turns on Friedrich. Friedrich goes into hiding but in 1942 risks leaving his refuge to ask the narrator's family for a picture of his father and mother. The sirens wail, and fear drives him to take cover in the bomb shelter. When several people show Friedrich sympathy, Herr Resch threatens to report them. Thrown back out into the night, Friedrich is in an agony of terror. When the raid is over, he is sitting in the shadow of the porch. Herr Resch kicks him, but the boy is dead. Richter ends his book with a chronology of the crushing of the Jews.

Additional titles:

> Forman, James. The Traitors, pp. 48-56.
> Hardey, Evelyn. ... damals war ich fünfzehn, pp. 65, 68-69.
> Oker, Eugen. ... und ich der Fahnenträger, pp. 102-105, 156-164.
> Seiffert, Dietrich. Einer war Kisselbach, pp. 61-67, 121-123.

Holland

Germany invades Holland in May 1940, and the Brenners are caught in the middle. The Dutch mistrust them for being Austrian, the Germans for being Jews (Marietta Moskin, I Am Rosemarie). Jackbooted soldiers goosestep into Amsterdam, and the sanctions against Jews begin. Special ID's are required. Jews are expelled from public schools. Then they must wear yellow stars and pay for them with clothing coupons. The Brenners are stripped of their Austrian citizenship, and Mr. Brenner loses his job. Silverware and jewelry have to be turned over for the war effort. By the summer of 1942 they must travel once a week to a distant food market where the food available to Jews is "wilted cabbages, stale bread, and shriveled potatoes."

Security police barge into the Brenner home and take
an inventory of all the possessions that will soon no longer
belong to "dirty Jewish pigs." They give the family three
days to move out, allowing them only two suitcases each.
As the Brenners walk away from their home, a truck pulls
up, and men begin carrying out furniture.

One hot summer day the Gestapo and a Dutch NSB
(National Socialist) officer pick up Rosemarie's parents. A
friend intercedes and arranges for them to return for Rosemarie. They cling to the South American passports they have
acquired. These passports and a gritty determination carry
the family through the dark years in concentration camps.

In James Forman's The Survivor the Ullman family
celebrates the seventieth birthday of its patriarch, Moses,
in August 1939. Around him are his sons: Abraham, with
his family of four children, and Daniel, who had been an
outspoken lawyer in Berlin until his wife was murdered on
Crystal Night. The following May the Germans invade.

Ruth, the oldest of Abraham's children, is an enter-
tainer and uses her talents to help the resistance. Holding
no illusions about the Germans, Daniel joins the underground.
Ruth and her grandfather urge the family to hide, but Abraham is trapped by bewilderment and inertia. Not until the
twins, Saul and David, are caught in a raid and released
only because of Ruth's contacts, is the family ready to hide.

By this time the list of restrictions against Jews has
grown to absurdity. Kosher slaughtering is forbidden. All
Jewish professors and civil servants are fired. Restaurants,
cinemas, universities, and the giving of blood are off limits.
They must abide by a curfew. The Dutch see their naive
hope of peaceful coexistence crumble when the Germans round
up Jews and send them to the transit camp at Westerbork and
the concentration camp at Mauthausen. To substitute for those
who hide when they are ordered to report for deportation, the
security police snatch substitutes off the street.

Late in the night an SS car drives up to the Ullman
house. The officer who steps out is Uncle Daniel in disguise,
and he takes them into hiding. After they have gone, Moses
calmly commits suicide.

The Gestapo close in on their hiding place, and the
Ullmans are forced to run. Ruth has already been arrested.

Mrs. Ullman has died as a result of a freak accident.   Ra-
chel has been taken to a safer refuge   Mr. Ullman and the
twins are caught.   In Westerbork they meet Ruth, then all
four are transferred to Auschwitz.   When the death camp is
liberated, only David is alive to tell the story and to start
a new life in Palestine.

United States

Though physically far removed from the events in
Europe, the Jews in the United States were still affected by
them, whether because of friends and relatives in Europe or
because of the anti-Semitism they experienced at home.   The
books in this section are all notable for the depth of the authors' sympathy for flawed humanity.

The few Jewish families in Ashlymine, Pennsylvania
are mostly merchants (Felice Holman, The Murderer).   They
own the hardware, jewelry, dry goods, variety, furniture,
drug, and candy stores.   The laborers are Polish miners,
always in debt to the merchants, a natural setting for con-
flicts.

Because the Jewish boys have to go to Hebrew school
after their regular school, they always get last choice of the
baseball diamonds.   The Polish boys are also stronger and
have control of the most desirable area of the school playground.   One day four of the Jewish boys decide to take over
the hill.   That the face-off ends without blows is due in part
to the fact that Lorsh, the leader of the Polish boys, is
caught offguard by Hershy Marks's frank admiration of him.

The Polish boys try to make Hershy admit he killed
Christ.   Though he longs to please Lorsh, Hershy just can't
bring himself to make such an absurd confession, but the demand troubles him.   Why do the Poles say they killed Christ?
Why does Hitler want to destroy the Jews?   If the rabbi is
a Pole, why isn't a Polish Jew the same as other Polacks?
How can he make the Poles admire him?   The new, young
rabbi in Ashlymine is willing to deal with Hershy's questions.
At last the boys have someone who will take them seriously
and attempt to give them straightforward answers.   He cannot stop the anti-Semitism or put an end to the cycle of poverty that puts the children of miners underground at an early
age, but he does try to help the boys understand themselves
and the others a little better.

Patty Bergen's father is also a member of the merchant class in a small American town (Bette Greene, <u>Summer of My German Soldier</u>). Unlike Hershy Marks's quietly accepting father, Patty's father rails against life in general and 12-year-old Patty in particular. As a Jew in Jenkinsville, Arkansas, Patty is already an exception and is made more of an outcast by her restless, questing mind.

The big event of the summer of 1944 is the arrival of twenty German prisoners of war. The whole town turns out to see them unloaded. After years of hearing about the brutality and treachery of Germans, Patty is disappointed to see how ordinary they look. Without the "POW" stenciled on their blue work shirts, they would look like ordinary folk.

Patty recognizes the xenophobia that lurks beneath the placid surface of the town. She is not sure what happened to the Lee family and does not want to believe what she suspects. "The Chink" and his wife had a grocery store and then suddenly left town. Patty overheard Mr. Jackson telling her father about "the farewell party" and heard her father's weak, unconvincing laugh. She knows that the Japanese have been suspected of disloyalty, but why the Lees, who were Chinese?

On a dull summer day ten of the POW's are brought to the Bergens' store to buy straw hats so they will stop fainting in the cotton fields. One of them speaks perfect English. Before he leaves the store, he has befriended Patty. When Anton escapes from the POW camp, he takes refuge with her. Hungry for love and understanding, Patty unfolds like a flower in the warmth of Anton's friendship.

Before he leaves, Anton gives Patty what he treasures most, his great-grandfather's ring, and a gift beyond price when he tells her, "... I want you to learn this, our last, lesson. Even if you forget everything else I want you to always remember that you are a person of value, and you have a friend who loved you enough to give you his most valued possession" (p. 155).

Anton is killed, and Patty's part in sheltering him becomes public. Her father grieves, but it is over his own shame rather than his child's pain. This is wartime, and Patty has evoked the specter of anti-Semitism in the town. As she is taken away by FBI agents, a spitting mob screams, "Jew Nazi--Jew Nazi--Jew Nazi!" Patty stays with her grandmother in another town while awaiting the legal process against her. She learns that her parents are being harassed in Jenkinsville. Patty's lawyer has to be pressured into taking the case. He feels embarrassed by her. She has called into question the loyalty of Jews everywhere. Even in the reform school to which she is sent, she is treated as an outcast and a traitor, a Jew Nazi lover.

The smallness of those confined by the blind, narrow view of the world is in sharp contrast to Ruth, the Bergens' black helper, Anton, and Patty. Each of these three stands tall and dignified in her/his own way. Their weapons are love and compassion at a time when both are in short supply.

Anti-Semitism is apparent in a book set in New York City in 1944, Myron Levoy's Alan and Naomi. Twelve-year-old Alan Silverman lives in a mixed neighborhood and has one good friend, a Catholic not afraid to like him because he is Jewish. Shaun Kelly is strong enough and sure enough of his own identity that he is not turned away from his friend just because the bully, Joe, taunts him for being a Jew lover.

Mr. Silverman worries constantly about the war, following its progress on maps and listening in fear to radio reports. Two victims of Hitler's occupation of France have moved in with a family upstairs, and the Silvermans ask their son to take on the task of trying to bring the daughter, Naomi, back to health, to teach her to play, to trust. She watched the Gestapo club her father to death and has withdrawn into a protective shell. With loving sensitivity Alan is able to draw her back out. Although the book ends in tragedy, Alan Silverman has triumphed in a battle to restore a human soul.

Additional titles:

> Cohen, Barbara. Benny.
> Colman, Hila. Ellie's Inheritance.
> Murray, Michele. The Crystal Nights.

HELPING HANDS; THE SHELTERING OF JEWS

The decision to hide Jews was sometimes made deliberately, other times accidentally. Anyone who dared to help not only ran the risk of losing his own life but also endangered his family and friends. It was far easier to avert

one's eyes and close one's ears. Those who put their own
lives on the line are the heroes and heroines, sometimes reluctant, of a number of books for young adults.

Czechoslovakia

In a Slovak town in 1942 a good-natured carpenter is
torn between decency and fear for his life (Ladislav Grosman,
The Shop on Main Street). His Party-member brother-in-
law is embarrassed that Tono does not support Hitler. As a
surprise, Kolkocky makes Tono the Aryanizer of the widow
Lautman's shop. Tono's wife, Eveline, dreams of wealth
and sends him off to the shop with lots of advice.

Rosalie Lautman is old and hard of hearing. She is
delighted with the well-mannered, well-dressed gentleman
customer but hasn't the foggiest notion what he wants. Tono
is trying vainly to explain that the shop now belongs to him
when Mrs. Lautman's old friend, Imre Kucharsky, arrives.
He tells Tono that Kolcocky has saddled him with a tiny shop
that cannot even support one old woman. For the sake of the
widow Lautman, the Jewish community will continue to support
the shop and even slip something to Tono.

Tono knows nothing about selling bric-a-brac, but he
does know about carpentry and soon is happily puttering about
the place, mending and renewing. Poor Tono can please no
one. Kolkocky accuses him of being a "white Jew" and gives
him one week to hang up a new sign, "Anton Brtko, Tailors'
Accessories." Eveline is greedy and steals Saturday's take
from the widow. The Jewish Mutual despises him for taking
money from an old woman. Only Mrs. Lautman is pleased
with her fine assistant. In her refuge he feels at home.

When he learns that Jews are being rounded up, Tono
tries to warn Mrs. Lautman. He feels fiercely protective,
but he wavers between wanting to save her and his own skin.
When he sees his brother-in-law coming, he pushes the
frightened and uncomprehending old woman into the back room.
After Kolkocky passes Tono discovers that he pushed Mrs.
Lautman too hard. She is dead. That is too much for the
honest carpenter, who has never harmed anyone. He hangs
himself from a hook.

France

In a village in France a group of 14- and 15-year-old

boys organizes minor acts of resistance in response to the
shooting of 50 hostages (Odile Yelnik, "V" comme Victoire),
They chalk "V's" on walls and print flyers with a print set
from a toy store.   When the Jews are ordered to wear yellow
stars, they make yellow stars for everyone in the class.   The
director sympathizes with their gesture but warns them that
gesture could bring reprisals but little else.

The parents of a Jewish classmate, Luc Abraham, are
arrested.   The boys stop chalking walls and distributing tracts
and concentrate on hiding Luc.   Claude lives alone, so his
room becomes the hiding place.   A German SS officer takes
the room next to Claude's and inadvertently saves Luc's life.
Knowing that the officer lives there, German soldiers don't
bother searching the building for Jews.

Luc has relatives in France's free zone.   Pierre,
whose grandmother lives on the other side of the line of demarcation, volunteers to smuggle him across.   The Germans
give Pierre a pass to visit his grandmother, and the two boys
take the train south.   At Chateauneuf-le-Roi the train is bombed,
and they lose the pass.   They approach the curé of the village
that straddles the line.   His flock is on both sides of the line,
but burials are always in the cemetery in the free zone.   Next
morning, Luc becomes one of the curé's mourners, walking
to freedom in a funeral cortège.

Additional titles:

> Ciravegna, Nicole.   La rue qui descend vers la mer
>   and its sequel, Aldo et Sarah.
> Stokis, Claude.   Réseau clandestin.

Germany

In the rubble of a German village, a small band of
children finds a secret cache of food (Leonie Ossowski, Stern
ohne Himmel).   A suspicious noise sends them all into hiding.
An emaciated youth steals into the room and starts eating
their food.   Incensed, they jump him.   In the stranger's
pocket Willi finds the yellow patch that identifies him as a
Jew.   Only Ruth shows sympathy for the boy.   Antek is too
afraid to show weakness in front of his friends.   Willi wants
to turn him in immediately, but Paule vetoes that because the
boy could give away their food supply.   For the time being,
they leave him locked in the dark cellar.

The group's dynamics are upset by Abiram. Willi,
with the key to the cellar, has control. Paule is busy trying
to figure out how to make a profitable deal with the Jew.
Antek is jealous of Ruth's empathy for Abiram and bothered
by her scorn for his cowardice. He cannot understand how
Ruth could defend a Jew and cannot bear the suspicion that
her pacifist grandfather plants in him that for twelve years
Germany may have been lied to by Hitler.

When Ruth is not there the boys decide to give Abiram
a hearing. He tells them of concentration camps and Nazi
brutality, of his father's being gassed, his mother shot as
she stood beside him. The boys are astonished that Jews
have been killed just because they are Jews. Willi screams
that they are all traitors for believing Abiram and locks
them in the cellar.

This is Willi's chance to prove himself to his father
and his Fatherland. He runs to Blockleiter Feller to tell him
about the Jew. Feller returns with him reluctantly. The
cellar is empty. Willi has made a fool of himself and lost
the food supply, which Feller demands as compensation for
his trouble once he stops beating Willi.

Willi vows revenge on his friends. Even as the Russians surround the city, he and the school's fanatic headmas-
ter believe in Hitler's victory and plot to destroy Abiram and
all those who are helping him. Only Russian occupation of
the village puts an end to their zealotry and restores an uneasy peace.

Jonas Partell is a happy 14-year-old who envisions
himself as a future Olympic gymnast and is proud of Hitler's
victories (Werner Toporski, Mädchen mit Stern). One of his
best friends vocally opposes the government, but Jonas decides not to abandon him. Uwe himself turns from Jonas out
of concern for his friend's safety.

Stung by Uwe's rejection, Jonas is walking home when
he sees a group of Hitler Youth tormenting a young Jewish
girl. A military vehicle lumbers by, and she sees her chance
to escape. Jonas pretends to be after her but watches for his
chance to steer the gang away. It is a part of town he knows
well, and it does not take him long to find her hiding in a
shed. The die is cast, and he takes Agnes home.

Jonas and his mother adjust to living with fear. Agnes

has been on the run for five years. Her stories of her family's arrest and of concentration camps shake Jonas's comfortable beliefs, and he becomes disillusioned with the Hitler Youth. His change of heart makes him think of Uwe. He goes to his friend and is picked up by the Gestapo along with Uwe's family. Though he is freed, he is stripped of his Hitler Youth leader's scarf and knows he has endangered Agnes. Through a prostitute he makes a down payment on a passport for her, but when he picks it up it is a worthless document that would fool no one.

The front nears the city, and bombing raids increase. One night in the air raid shelter someone recognizes Agnes and informs the SS. Three men tear apart the apartment looking for her. She is safe in the small room behind the pantry, but when she hears Jonas crying out in pain she cannot bear it so comes out. The SS shove them both out into the street and fall into the hands of the Americans. The Allies have saved them, but Jonas is overcome with grief that in his cowardice he betrayed Agnes.

The strain of hiding someone is also illustrated in James Forman's The Traitors. Though both want nothing more than to survive the war, neither Paul nor Astrid hesitates to hide Noah Engel, a Jew. Paul's ties to Noah have been formed through long friendship, but Astrid's are more complicated. She suspects Kurt, her boyfriend and Paul's brother, of having betrayed Noah's family.

In January 1943 the streets of Ravenskirch are quiet. No Jews remain, so there are no noisy, late-night raids. In the hope of finding firewood, Paul steels himself to visit the Engels' farm. A hoarse, formless sound frightens him away. Two days later he returns and finds a thin, starving, but grimly determined Noah. Paul promises to help, knowing he will despise himself if he does not. Astrid helps him to take the emaciated boy through the maze of sewers to his father's church.

Noah becomes healthy, restless, and bored. He eagerly awaits Paul's visits, and Paul comes to resent him in spite of his affection. The pressure and fear Paul feels become an almost unbearable burden. He is a reluctant hero, but when the SS move into Ravenskirch, he joins a plot to keep them from destroying it. Forman has little to say about Noah's feelings but a great deal about the decision to hide him and its consequences on people who do not see themselves as

brave or special but who cannot turn their backs on someone
in trouble.

Additional titles:

Haugaard, Erik.   Chase Me, Catch Nobody!
Lazar, Auguste.   Die Brücke von Weissensand

Holland

Just twenty minutes from the German/Dutch border
lives the de Leeuw family (Johanna Reiss, The Upstairs Room).
The fate of the Polish Jews makes radio news in the winter
of 1939-40, but Mrs. de Leeuw cannot be persuaded to leave
her comfortable home for the uncertainty of refugee status.
When on May 10 the Germans occupy Winterswijk, the time
for flight has passed.

The Germans impose sanctions on the Jews immediately.
The posting tree in the marketplace becomes the focus of
their diminishing possibilities.   Mr. de Leeuw is not allowed
to sell cattle.   Jews cannot rent hotel rooms or go to beaches
and parks and must carry identity cards marked with "J."
After autumn 1941, Jews are not allowed to attend public
schools.   Annie, who at 9 has never felt Jewish, is taunted
by former classmates as she returns from the synagogue
school.   The girl who was her best friend joins the chants
of the hecklers:

Jew, Jew, ugly mole,
Stick your face in a dirty hole.
Stick your face in a mustard pot,
By tomorrow Jew will rot! [p. 14]

Jews are fired and then because they are unemployed
are sent to labor camps.   Unable to escape to Switzerland,
Mr. de Leeuw searches for people to hide the family.   To be
safe they must go separate ways.   Annie and Sini go to the
Hanninks, where they feel safe but confined.   The Hanninks
are a way station for other Jews.   After a German soldier
follows Mr. Hannink one day, they insist on moving the de
Leeuw girls immediately.

The next night Annie and Sini are taken to the Oostervelds' farm.   The week or two they are to stay stretches
until the end of the war.   As Dientje serves the girls coffee,

Johann grumbles about the war.   Annie listens with wide eyes
to Johann's fascinating string of expletives.

During the long, boring days, Opoe (Johann's mother)
darns socks and keeps the girls company.   She is astonished
that Sini has a milking diploma and enjoyed working on a farm.
Crazy girl.   Why, Opoe could have a chest full of diplomas
--a planting-potatoes diploma, a manure-spreading diploma,
a feeding-cattle diploma.   Such a strange world.

Though the Oostervelds know they probably seem like
dumb farmers by comparison with the refined Hanninks, they
are proud and clever people.   In spite of the frustration of
confinement, the girls and the Oostervelds grow to love each
other deeply.

In the fall of 1944 the Germans requisition part of the
house.   Johann feels pretty cocky hiding Jews in the same
house.   "How's that for a dumb farmer?" he often repeats.
From October 17 on the girls have to stay in bed in the back
bedroom.   Then one day the Germans are gone.

When the Canadians march through Annie is reluctant
to greet them.   After so many years inside, she is afraid to
emerge.   On this day the Oostervelds' neighbors learn for the
first time that there were Jews on the farm.   Thanks to the
bravery of all those who hid them, all of the de Leeuws survive the war.

Eleven-year-old Dirk wants to help the resistance in
Holland just as his 15-year-old brother is doing, but Sebastian is always telling him he is too young (Gertie Evenhuis,
What About Me?).   When the chance comes to do something
important, Dirk suddenly longs for the innocence of a child.

All day long Dirk has been trying to get rid of a parcel of incriminating papers.   He is bicycling home with a
package of the newspapers still in his saddle bag when a
strange man comes peddling the wrong way up the street, a
frightened child clinging to his back.   Suddenly the street is
filled with German patrols in search of a Jew.   Dirk freezes
to the spot but instinctively resists the soldier who steals his
bicycle to pursue the fugitive.   The parcel of papers falls
onto the street, but the soldier does not take time to investigate.

A small, dark-haired girl standing behind Dirk tells

him he has lost his parcel. He looks at the child and sees
a yellow star sewn carelessly on her coat. Matter of factly,
she tells him that she was hiding when her family was dragged
away. Now she has fallen off her uncle's bicycle. Part of
Dirk wants to leave her and run, but he cannot just abandon
her. He remembers hearing his aunt say that she would take
in a Jewish child the next time the chance arose. Delivering
Hadassa to her, Dirk feels like a frightened child. Once
safe in his aunt's arms, he feels free, free from the terrible
need to help fight the Germans, free from the enormity of
his courageous act, and free to be a child once again (pp. 79-
83).

NO END IN SIGHT

        The insidious persecution of the Jews did not stop
with the death of Hitler, as is made clear in "Nadine's Geschichte" in the collection, Damals war ich vierzehn (pp. 108-
111). Nadine cannot recall the years she, as a Jewish child,
was sent from house to house. Her parents had joined the
French Resistance, and it was not safe for them to keep her.
Her father was killed, and when her mother came for her in
August 1944, she was just the tenth strange woman to Nadine.
She also does not recall her first years in Vienna with a new
stepfather or her elementary school.

        Nadine's memories begin on the day she comes home
and asks the meaning of the name the children call her, "Jud,
Jud!" One day three boys come into the class in brown
shirts to celebrate Hitler's birthday and say it is too bad
the Jews in the class were not gassed. It is five years after Hitler's suicide. Some of the parents take a boys-will-be-
boys attitude. Others claim that what happened during the
war was not really all that bad. In school Nadine is never
just Nadine but also "the Jew," who is tolerated as long as
she is helpful, cheerful, useful. When a classmate is ill,
she writes out the notes for him, but his parents insist she
send them rather than enter their home. When the class is
shown a pile of glasses outside a gas chamber, several laugh.
It never ends. The hate, the prejudice are always there.

        Years after the war Gabriele Berger, the child of
concentration camp survivors, starts school (Aliana Brodman,
... und du bist ab). She becomes an object of curiosity.
The other children want to know what a Jew is. She is different from them. She has no extended family. Her relatives
were all burned by the Nazis.

Her classmates are not even aware that their rhymes are anti-Semitic, that they hurt Gabi deeply with their casual cruelty. At a birthday party for Doris, Gabi's best friend, two little girls whisper together. Doris crossly tells them, "Wer flüstert, der lügt, und nur Juden lügen." ("Who whispers lies, and only Jews lie.") (p. 30). When the children play hide and seek, their countdown is, "Hinter einer Bude sitzt ein Jude, hat den Kopf voll Läuse, La La Läuse--" ("Behind an old house-y sits a Jew all lousy, La La lousy--") (p. 45).

Always, the unspeakable stories, the unanswered questions lie between Gabi and her parents. They can never understand her need to truly know them or to be like the other children nor can she comprehend their pain, the past that haunts them. A sensitive new uncle brings the family closer together, helping Gabi's parents to understand their child and Gabi to feel pride in a heritage that has been tinged with fear and shame for her. Gabi's adolescent search for identity is explored in the sequel, ... damit die Welt nicht stumm bleibt, a fine, sensitive book.

Chapter 5

TO THE VICTOR BELONG THE SPOILS

Early victories gave the Nazis a feeling of invincibility. Hitler's grandiose plans appeared realizable. The SS and the Gestapo moved in behind the troops to eliminate any opposition. In the eastern lands special Einsatz troops slaughtered whole villages, clearing the countries of Jews and other unwanted life. A book by Helmut Krausnick and Hans-Heinrich Wilhelm, Die Truppe des Weltanschauungskrieges: Die Einsatzgruppen der Sicherheitspolizei und des SD 1938-1942, points out that even the ordinary combat troops played a much greater role in the massacres, looting, and oppression than was previously thought.

After the disastrous Russian campaign, the Germans began retreating. Russian troops took revenge on German civilians in their path. The Germans now stripped of possessions and driven from their homes cared little that Russians or Poles or Czechs had suffered at German hands.

In this chapter are books from the perspectives of the occupied and their occupier. The books in "The German Attitude Toward Eastern Lands" show how the Germans were taught to think of people to the east. Under "Occupation" are experiences of Czechs, Danes, French, Greeks and Dutch when the Germans marched into their lands. The last section, "The Tables Are Turned," brings together books which portray the plight of German civilians who were made homeless by the fall of the Third Reich.

THE GERMAN ATTITUDE TOWARD
EASTERN LANDS

The lands to the east of Germany were to provide

132

space for the Reich to grow.   Their inhabitants were in the
way.   On August 22, 1939, Hitler declared:

> I have given orders to my Death Units to extermi-
> nate without mercy or pity men, women, and chil-
> dren belonging to the Polish-speaking race.   It is
> only in this manner that we can acquire the vital
> territory which we need.   After all, who remembers
> today the extermination of the Armenians?"

The authors in this section show how effective the Nazis were
in eliminating empathy for Russians and Poles and preparing
the ground for mass extermination.

The propagandists of the Third Reich declared that the
Russian people were subhuman.   Therefore, any crime visited
upon them was justified as a means of making more room for
the superior Germans.   Max von der Grün quotes an official
SS document in Howl Like the Wolves:

> Just as the night revolts against the day, just
> as light and shadow are eternal enemies--so the
> greatest enemy of man, the master of the earth,
> is man himself.
> The subhuman man [Untermensch]--that creation
> of nature appearing wholly identical in all biological
> respects, with hands, feet, and a species of brain,
> with eyes and a mouth--is in reality something
> quite different, a dreadful creation, a mere first
> draft of a human being with facial features resem-
> bling those of human beings--but mentally and spir-
> itually inferior to any animal.   The inner life of
> one of these people is a hideous chaos of wild and
> uninhibited passions: a nameless will to destroy,
> desire in its most primitive form, the most mani-
> fest vileness.
> A subhuman--and nothing more than that!
> . . .
> And this underworld of subhuman creatures found
> its leader: the eternal Jew!... [pp. 200-201]

From the minutes of a meeting with Hitler, Grün draws further evidence of this savage campaign:

> Thus we will once again emphasize that we were
> compelled to occupy, secure, and establish order in
> a given region; we will say that in the interests of

the native population we were forced to provide for
law and order, food, methods of transportation, and
so on, and that it is for these reasons that we
stepped in and took charge. It should not be apparent that we are thereby paving the way to take
charge permanently! Nevertheless, we can and
will take any measures necessary--shootings, deportations, etc. . . .

Basically it comes down to cutting up this gigan-
tic cake into manageable slices, so that first we
can control it, second we can administer it, and
third we can exploit it. . . .

We must cling to one iron principle: Anyone
who is not a German must never be permitted to
carry a weapon! . . . The area around Leningrad
is being claimed by the Finns; the Führer wants to
reduce Leningrad to rubble, and then turn it over
to the Finns.

> July 16, 1941
> Minutes of a conference with
> Adolf Hitler
> [Translation by Jan van Huerck,
> pp. 201-202]

The effect of the official policy was to reduce all enemies to a position of such degraded humanity that their ex-
tinction was of no more significance than swatting a fly. Hermann Göring elaborated on this policy on June 30, 1942:

"... it is a matter of indifference to me if you
say that your people are dropping dead from hunger.
Let them do so, as long as no German has to drop
dead from hunger ... if people starve, then it will
not be Germans who starve but others ... as far as
the people in the occupied territories are concerned,
I am interested only in those who work in munitions
factories or help to supply food; they must be given
just enough to eat so that they can do their work...."
[pp. 216-217]

Grün includes numerous other examples of the Nazis'
contempt for non-Germans. The following is an excerpt from
a speech which Heinrich Himmler made to SS group leaders
at a meeting in Poland:

An SS man must observe one absolute principle:
We must behave with honesty, decency, loyalty, and

true comradeship toward members of our own blood,
but not toward anyone else. What happens to the
Russians, what happens to the Czechs is all the
same to me. Those members of other nations who
possess good blood of our type, we will assimilate,
if necessary by stealing their children and raising
them among Germans. Whether other people live
in a state of prosperity or die of starvation interests me only to the degree that we may need them
as slaves for our culture; otherwise I have no interest in them at all. Whether or not ten thousand
Russian women collapse from exhaustion while con-
structing an antitank trench interests me only as to
whether or not the trench is completed for Germany.
We will never be brutal and heartless when it is not
necessary to be so: this is clear. We Germans,
who are the only people in the world who have a
decent attitude toward animals, will also adopt a
decent attitude toward these human beasts, for it
is a crime against our own blood to worry about
them and to instill ideals in them so that our sons
and grandsons will have even more trouble keeping
them under control. If someone comes to me and
says, "I can't build the antitank trench with children
or women. That would be inhuman, for it would
kill them," then I must reply, "You are a murderer
of your own blood, for if the antitank trench is not
constructed, then German soldiers will die, and
they are the sons of German mothers. They are
of our blood." This is the attitude which I would
like to instill and--I believe--have instilled in the
members of the SS, as one of the holiest laws of
the future. Our concern, our duty, lies with our
people and our blood. For them we must be concerned, for them we must think, work, and fight,
and for nothing else. We may be indifferent to
everything else. I wish the SS to adopt this attitude toward the problem of all foreign, non-Germanic
peoples, above all, the Russians. Everything else
is hogwash. [Translation by Jan van Huerck, pp.
229, 234]

To prepare the country for war with Poland, the German propagandists pour out reports of Polish atrocities in
the summer of 1939 (Renate Finckh, Mit uns zieht die neue
Zeit). Nela Keller is horrified to hear of German schools
in the Polish corridor being closed, teachers shot, German-

speaking children's tongues nailed to desks. She knows that
all Germans have a right to live in an expanded Reich. Hitler has already put a protective arm around Austria and the
Sudetenland, but the Poles, who have stolen German land,
fail to recognize the justice of this (pp. 101-102).

Nela's mother has the job of testing Polish and Ukrainian women for their worthiness to become Germanified. The
women have been forced from their homes to work in German
industries. Now they are subjected to humiliating examina-
tions which, if successful, can result in higher pay and a
small measure of freedom. Mrs. Keller receives these instructions from her women's organization concerning her duty:

> "... the monstrous sacrifices in human life that we
> have suffered through the enemy terrorist attacks on
> German cities oblige us to secure the necessary po-
> tential of our population. Because it is hard to put
> a check on the large influx of laboring women from
> the east, these women should, wherever possible,
> be integrated into the German folk. Of first im-
> portance in testing their worthiness to become Ger-
> man are health, hair color, and industriousness.
> Jewish types are excluded from this process."
> [p. 137]

Nela is thrilled in the summer of 1943 to be chosen
to work in (former) Poland with German settlers out of the
Ukraine, West Prussia, and the Black Sea area. These are
the Volksdeutsche, Germans who had settled in the east and
are returning to the Reich. Before she is sent, she is taught
how to work with these people who will need retraining in
German culture and civilization, who will not have had the
benefits of advanced technology and enlightened thought. She
is, of course, to remember while there that all Poles are
Untermenschen and that any diffidence or civility shown them
is treasonous. Nela learns her lesson so well that when she
is told to beat a Polish boy for being careless with the cows,
she barely hesitates (pp. 144-148).

Thousands of children are evacuated from German
cities to keep them safe from Allied bombing. The narrator
of Hans Peter Richter's The Time of the Young Soldiers goes
with his class and their teacher to a small village in Poland.
Looking out at the hills and woods, the teacher is inspired:

"Lovely!" he said, enthusiastically; he made an

expansive gesture. "And all of it German land,
won back for us again! Beautiful!" he repeated.
Then he began making plans. "We'll get to know
the villagers! Do our best to bring these people
a bit of German culture! They've had to do without it too long. We'll have social evenings with
them!" His voice was rising. "Put on amateur
theatricals for the locals! Train their boys and
girls to...."

"I shouldn't think you'd have much luck," said
the warden of the hostel, coming up. "Most of
them don't speak anything but Polish." [Transla-
tion by Anthea Bell, p. 22]

One of the most cynical accounts of the German attitude toward the Poles is Wolfgang Kirchner's Wir durften
nichts davon wissen. The family's sentiments are typical of
those who recognize their guilt yet angrily refuse to admit
it. The father of Diti and Wolfgang is a captain in the army
when the Germans chase the Poles out of Danzig in 1939.
Now in March 1945, with the SS transmitting messages from
the kitchen and parking tanks beside the house, Mother up-
braids him for having been a party to it. Father is still trying to believe that the Poles had designs against the Germans
and that Hitler will win the war.

On March 27 the Russians move into Danzig. On the
prowl for watches and women, individual soldiers break into
the cellar where the family and their friends are hiding.
Each time, all twelve children cry to the commandant for
help. He does not usually come, but it scares the soldiers
away.

Papa is arrested and Danzig is burned. The family
gathers what little each can carry and starts west. For the
first time, Wolfgang learns what happened to Klara, their
housekeeper's, brother-in-law. The Germans arrested him
because he was a Pole and threw grenades into the house.
Klara's mother died in the fire. Wolfgang worries that his
father may have been responsible in spite of Klara's attempt
to reassure him.

Bribing one of their Russian guards, the family turns
back and returns to Danzig. Their house is still intact, but
they move in with a friend across the street. Food runs out
quickly. When they hear of a dead horse in the woods, Diti,
Wolfgang, and their mother cut away chunks of it. They

return for more, but it is gone. By mid-April everyone
around has diarrhea. On one of his foraging trips, Diti finds
a supply of pills like his grandparents used to take for diarrhea and is soon able to feed the family with what he receives
in trade for them. He pretends to be requisitioning for the
Russian commandant and is able to steal more food for the
family.

Two Poles come looking for Papa. His wife is almost
relieved that he is already a Russian prisoner of war. She
is not sure of his innocence and knows he will fare better as
a Russian prisoner of war than he would if the Poles got him.
Klara has little sympathy for her fears, given what the Poles
suffered under the Germans Papa commanded.

When the family's food supply dwindles, Diti has no
qualms about stealing from the store of a young Polish couple,
reasoning that the Poles stole everything from the Germans
after the Russians took over. Diti is unmoved when Klara
reminds him who started the cycle of stealing.

The tables are clearly turned. The militia beat Achim
because they suspect him of being a Werewolf, one of the
children Hitler used in his last desperate attempt to win the
war. Street names change. Danzig becomes Gdansk. Diti
wonders if their own names will be changed and if they will
have to learn Polish. Poles begin making regular visits to
the apartment to buy or steal things they want. Existence
becomes precarious because only those with work permits are
allowed to stay in Danzig, and jobs for Germans are scarce.
Grandfather sends the family to relatives in the country.

Wolfgang feels deeply ashamed the first night. The
Koschalkes talk of the nearby concentration camp, and his
mother denies knowing anything about such things. They remind her that in January 25,000 prisoners were marched almost directly by her house. She remarks weakly that those
were cold days, and they rarely left the house.

In September the family receives permission to migrate
to Germany. Diti callously calms his brother's fears. Wolfgang worries that with so many refugees streaming into Germany, there will not be enough food for them all. Diti answers:

            "Don't think for a minute that all Germans were
        as dumb as we were!" says Diti. "A lot of them

got their valuables into the Reich in time--but not
us! Our grandfather didn't even open a bank account in West Germany. The Danzigers shipped
whole moving vans into the Reich. And something
else...." He lowers his voice so that Klara won't
hear. "Do you have any idea how much they stole
from the Poles and the Jews? Where is all that?
They didn't leave that in Danzig so that Ivan could
get it. That's been in the Reich for ages--in safety.
With that money they will rebuild Germany, bigger
and better than ever!" [p. 136]

Additional titles:

Hardey, Evelyn.   ... damals war ich fünfzehn.
Korschunow, Irina.   Er hiess Jan.

OCCUPATION

The character of German occupation varied only slightly
from country to country, depending on whether official policy
categorized the subjugated people as subhumans or merely
inferior. However, in every country, the Germans eliminated
opposition, rounded up Jews, stole resources, and imposed
harsh restrictions. The books in this section show how young
adult authors have depicted the occupation and people's re-
sponses to it.

Czechoslovakia

Czechoslovakia was used as a refuge for German children, whose presence added a heavy burden on scarce supplies. The children were largely young and naive and astonished to be treated with open animosity.

Ilse Koehn (Mischling, Second Degree) is eleven when
she is sent to a children's camp. The couple who own the
hotel where they are to stay have to be forced to allow the
girls in. When some of the girls are taken to a nearby hospital because the doctor decides they have scarlet fever, none
of the medical staff will speak to them. They are kept totally
isolated, given food that is sometimes crawling with bugs,
and treated as though they do not exist (pp. 44-57).

By February 1944 Ilse is in another camp. In groups

of 10 the girls ski to the barn where a film is being shown
to the villagers.   Czechs keep colliding with them and staring
at them with hatred.   After the film the girls have to search
for two hours to find their ski equipment, and then a group
of local boys torments them as they ski home (pp. 136-137).

Ilse does have one positive contact with a local.   She
is sent to help in the fields of a frail old woman.   She never
acknowledges the girls' greeting but serves them ice-cold
milk, bread, and blueberries.   When the work is completed
the girls say goodbye to the silent woman for whom they have
worked.   She rewards them with fresh bread and butter, a
smile, and praise in fluent German (pp. 144-149).

In Sybil Gräfin Schönfeldt's Sonderappell, a BDM camp
is not allowed to evacuate until they can hear the sounds of
battle from the approaching front.   During a stop in Prague,
Charlotte and Tilly impulsively decide to play the part of
tourists.   They make up a story to get permission to leave
the group and set out to explore the city.   No one will give
them directions.   The tram conductor mocks them and scat-
ters their German coins.   The one woman who admits to understanding German chides them for their naive belief in German justice.   Monuments and museums are closed to them.
The girls are abashed but cling to their superiority as Germans (pp. 118-120).

From the Czech point of view, Jan Procházka has
written Long Live the Republic.   Twelve-year-old Olin's
fellow villagers are an envious, mistrusting lot.   They have
hated the rich Bavarian family the Germans installed on an
estate in the village.   In the last days of the war, the Germans pile everything they can into official vehicles and flee.
Fair-minded, naive Olin watches with disgust as peasants loot
the estate, stealing a wagon, an electric motor, a threshing
machine, and anything else they can carry.   He knows none
of the thieves needs what he is taking.

Following Olin's father's lead, villagers paint "TYPHUS"
on their gates, hoping to frighten away any soldiers coming
through.   They send their boys to the woods to hide the
horses and then rush to the estate to finish plundering it.
In spite of their fear of both German and Russian soldiers,
the village boys take time to wait in ambush for the feisty
Olin as he rides out of town with his father's horse and
wagon.

The villagers greet the Russian victors with red flags
and jubilation then turn on Olin's only friend, a collaborator.
Amid cries of "Long live the Republic!" they stone, taunt,
and finally drive the man to his death.

Olin runs away from the scene, but more pain awaits
him on this first day of peace. His parents have locked their
gates and don't want to let anyone in while they are hiding
their stolen goods. So Olin is out on the street and vulnerable when the gang of boys catches him. They beat him and
then humiliate him utterly by urinating on his prostrate form.

Additional titles:

> Baer, Frank. Die Magermilchbande.
> Noack, Hans-Georg. Die Webers, pp. 95-98.

Denmark

Nathaniel Benchley describes the anger and bewilder-
ment the Danes felt when the Germans occupied their country.
In Bright Candles the normally cheerful, polite Danes search
themselves and the invaders for a place to direct their rage.
Only their love and respect for their king keeps them from
showing open contempt and resistance. However, the Danish
Cold Shoulder they give the Germans is so unnerving that the
Germans petulantly complain the Danes don't even see them.

As Danish resistance and acts of sabotage increase,
the Germans drop all pretense of benevolence. On August
28, 1943, they declare martial law. The underground responds by becoming more organized and coordinated. The
attempted roundup of the Jews hardens all but Danish collaborators against the Germans. Sabotage and counter-sabotage
and new orders from the frantic Germans lead to a general
strike the end of June 1944. Werner Best, the Nazi puppet
at the head of the government, cuts off all utilities, brings
in troops, and vows to break Copenhagen. The Danish response is a wall of solidarity. Rather than knuckle under
and end their strike, those who have food and access to water
and those without combine resources. Benchley tells of an
elderly couple's filling a washtub with water to share with
neighbors, of a butcher who roasts a carcass and passes out
the meat, and of a restaurateur's distributing food parcels.

When the Allies push into German territory, German

refugees stream into Denmark. Having believed stories of
their happy Danish cousins in the model protectorate, the
refugees are arrogant and astonished to find themselves unwanted.

Eva-Lis Wuorio (To Fight in Silence) also writes of
the Danes' cold shoulder toward the Germans:

> ... Everybody in Copenhagen had always been hygge,
> a special Danish quality of gayness which came
> from a secure feeling about themselves and their
> country. Now in the streets there was unfriendli-
> ness. Nobody was afraid. After all, the Germans
> had been told to behave, Karen's and Kristian's fa-
> ther had said. However, he had also said, "We
> have no cause to act friendly. They are like peo-
> ple who walk uninvited into your house, sit down
> at your table and expect you to prepare them a
> feast and say thank you for coming. It is more
> Danish not to be friendly." [p. 33]

On the day of the king's birthday in autumn 1942, the
Danes defy the curfew to gather at the Royal Palace. The
Germans make scattered attempts to arrest curfew violators
but are overwhelmed by the numbers. In the blue glow of
hundreds of blackout lanterns, the people sing to their king.
Then the king appears on the balcony, carrying his own blue
flame. He thanks the silent crowd, linking them as a family
with his quiet words (pp. 128-131).

Additional title:

Arnold, Elliott. A Kind of Secret Weapon.

France

In the mountains of the Isère the Germans make their
presence felt even while the area is still a free zone (Paul-
Jacques Bonzon, Mon Vercors en feu). Food supplies are
scarce. Gasoline is unavailable. Children begin to look like
harlequins in their patched clothes. The censored newspapers
blame the shortages on the Allies, but M. Chastagnier, the
baker of Combe-Froide, is sure the food is going to Hitler's
troops.

During the dark days the voice of General De Gaulle

brings hope. In November 1942 German tanks roll through
the valley below Combe-Froide. The mountains fill with
young people hiding from the threat of transport to labor
camps. Hundreds form resistance groups and go underground.
All of these people must be fed, creating an even greater
burden on food supplies.

One day the Germans occupy the village. Troops
lodge in the barns. Guards with machine guns watch each
end of the village. A 6 p.m. to 6 a.m. curfew is imposed.
If anyone defies orders, the village will be burned down.

As resistance to the occupiers increases, the Germans
take bloody reprisals all through the Vercors. Villagers are
massacred. Combe-Froide is destroyed. The vengeance only
serves to harden people's will to resist.

The war comes slowly to the small village in northwest
France where Ouf lives and even slower to Ouf's conscious-
ness (Minou Drouet, Ouf de la forêt). The boy is so tender-
hearted he is incapable of automatically associating the Germans he sees with something evil. One day he helps a young
soldier with blistered feet, so when his teacher asks the class
to explain what a German is, Ouf replies, "Un Allemand,
m'sieur, c'est un gar qu'a mal aux pieds ... comme nous...."
("A German, sir, is a guy who has sore feet ... like us....")
(p. 92).

The Germans requisition the château in which Ouf's old
friend, the marquess, lives but grant the guileless boy's request that she be allowed to stay. With his old sailor friend,
Loup de Mer, Ouf listens to the radio and hears of battles
and deaths. That night he cannot sleep so he goes to the
dump outside the church to collect flowers. The war has
made people more religious. The church is always filled
with flowers, which the housekeeper throws out every night.
Ouf collects them from the dump and lays them in holes
covered with branches so that the prayers they represent will
keep going toward heaven.

Village boys try to involve Ouf in stealing from the
Germans, but he refuses. He is willing to give his body for
his country, as the marquess and Loup de Mer have explained
can be demanded in wartime, but he wants to do it for something worthwhile. The boys go ahead and steal bicycles without him. One night Ouf is out burying flowers when a German patrol is looking for the bicycle thieves. One of them

falls into a flower tomb. Convinced they have found the cul-
prit, the Germans grab Ouf. He patiently explains about his
flowers and then lovingly re-covers them when the bemused
soldiers leave.

The village splits into two factions: those who have
performed petty acts of sabotage against the Germans and
think the others are cowards and traitors and those who think
the first have endangered the whole village for insignificant
gains. The latter gain strength when a whole group of hostages is shot.

Ouf's forest changes. Each night it is filled with activity. Resisters wait for drops from Allied planes, and the
Germans patrol to capture goods and people. Now Ouf, who
has never seemed of much use to the villagers, becomes important, for he knows every path and tree of the forest. The
recognition brings him no pleasure, for he is called on to
perform a deed which breaks his heart.

Additional titles:

> Fonvilliers, Georges. L'enfant, le soldat et la mer.
> Held, Jacqueline. La part du vent.
> Meynier, Yvonne. Un lycée pas comme les autres.
> Ray, Hélène. Ionel, la musique et la guerre.

Greece

Through the eyes of Petros, ten when the war with
Germany begins, the occupation is particularly vicious (Alki
Zei, Petros' War). German troops march into Athens six
months after the war breaks out. Someone takes down the
swastika flag from over the Acropolis. In retaliation, the
Germans impose a curfew and threaten to execute the flag
desecrater.

By summer 1941 water is low and garbage collection
spasmodic. There is too little food to satisfy a growing
boy's hunger. That November snow falls in Athens for the
first time in Petros' life. People collapse in the street from
hunger and cold. Petros' friend Sotiris leads him to see a
man dying of hunger. The crowd feeds the poor wretch, but
Petros is distraught. His own stomach hurts from hunger,
and the man's pain frightens him.

Petros wanders in an unfamiliar part of the city after
helping paint slogans on walls.   For the first time he sees
someone eating garbage.   The old woman guards the can as
though Petros were a threat.   Wizened children crouch over
a subway grating.   Moving to make room for Petros, one boy
shoves another, who flops over dead.

Sotiris asks Petros to help him hide his dead grandmother so he and his mother won't lose her ration coupons.
They feel no horror as they "walk" the tiny woman down the
twilit street.   At the cemetery they decide to leave her outside the gate but first remove her good shoes and cover her
with leaves.

Petros' grandfather starts taking long walks and seems
to put on a little weight.   Curious, Petros and Antigone follow
him one day.   When he thinks no one is watching, Grandfather
changes into rags and then draws on his experience in the
theater to make himself into a successful beggar.   He stands
in front of mansions and begs for food.

The slogan painting campaign pays off.   The Germans
distribute free soup.   No one is absent from school when the
cauldrons are brought in.   Petros brings his soup home to
share, and Grandfather signs up with the "Aged and Incurables"
for the free soup at the Unitarian Church.

At the end of February 1944, everyone but Petros'
mother makes up an excuse to go out early.   All of Athens
seems to be in the streets for a huge demonstration against
the occupiers.   They throw small, green bitter oranges at
the enemy.   Suddenly a carabiniere opens fire and kills one
of the demonstrators, Petros' friend Drossoula.

The Italians are defeated.   Gradually the Germans
disappear.   On October 12, 1944, Greece is once again free.

In another story Crete falls to the Germans shortly
after Greece.   The characters of Lou and Ernie Rydberg's
The Shadow Army lose their freedom abruptly when Germans
turn their house into headquarters, leaving them one bedroom
and the kitchen.   They cart off many of the family's belongings and kill the pet goat.   They force Maria Makakis to cook
for them.   Her sons escape and join the resistance.

As with Petros' War, The Shadow Army is a story of
resistance, though told less skillfully.   The more successful

the underground becomes, the more viciously the Germans
react.   To punish a village for hiding 20 Englishmen, they
burn it down and shoot all of its inhabitants.   The resisters
stand firm and are able to capture the commander of all the
German forces on Crete.

Holland

The Everingens respond to the German occupation by
making their farm a refuge for the hungry and hunted (Els
Pelgrom, The Winter When Time Was Frozen).   Each day Aunt
Janna cooks enough to feed any strangers who come asking
for food.   Unlike some peasants, she does not believe in
profiting from the war so never accepts more than a fair
price when people ask to buy supplies.   Other peasants are
less generous.   One sees two children hiding from a fighter
plane and chases them away with a pitchfork because they
might be beggars.   Villagers are cold and mistrustful.

Noortje Vanderhood and her father come to the farm
by chance when Britain loses the battle over Arnhem in September 1944.   Soon after, the Wolthuis family of parents, two
grown daughters, and an elderly neighbor, arrive asking for
shelter.   In the woods Aunt Janna hides a young Jewish family in an underground hole.   When a German deserter seeks
refuge, the Everingens feed and clothe him.   A young resister hides on the farm until it is invaded by 60 German soldiers, who demand temporary housing for themselves and
their Hungarian prisoners.   The soldiers are sent on to the
front and are replaced by pink-cheeked lads who transmit
messages to the front and dig foxholes on the farm.   The
Everingens spend all of their time and resources helping
others.   They are almost too good, unfailingly generous and
courageous.

Michel's family also feeds hungry strangers and friends
(Jan Terlouw, Michel).   His father is the mayor of Vlank.
Because he is not sympathetic with the Nazis, he becomes a
key contact for resisters wanting to know the condition of the
bridge over the Ijssel, which marks the boundary of the Allies' advance.   Michel, too, becomes committed to the resistance, not out of a love of heroism or adventure but because
of his loyalty to a friend.

Michel's father is shot as a hostage when a German
soldier is found dead.   Shortly afterward the Germans march
through town with young men they have taken from the streets

of Amsterdam. As they pass, townspeople give the boys
food and hide any who escape. A retired forester pulls five
out of the line and spirits them away. One man is recap-
tured. The SS make him dig his own grave and then shoot
him.

There are more heroes and less pettiness in Michel
than in The Winter When Time Was Frozen, yet somehow
the book is more believable. Both people and events ring
truer.

Additional title:

    Janssen, Pierre. A Moment of Silence.

Norway

By 1942 the German presence could be felt throughout
Norway. Margaret Balderson's description of their occupation
of Norway could be applied to any of the western European
countries under the Nazi thumb (When Jays Fly to Bárbmo):

> So much had happened since the outbreak of the
> war. The Germans now occupied the whole of our
> country and it was no longer possible to go anywhere
> without catching a glimpse of their heavily armed
> boats patrolling our once tranquil waters, or hear-
> ing the sound of their militant footsteps as they
> crunched confidently along the streets of our towns.
> For some time now, we had even felt their presence
> in our own little village. The school had been
> closed, a swastika fluttered ominously above our
> small community hall, and all farm folk had been
> forced to hand over a large proportion of their
> foodstuffs for the consumption of the German army.
> Among the Norwegian people the seeds of hate
> were growing--almost undetected--into something
> strong and united. We gossiped little to one an-
> other about our plight, but our faces, our eyes,
> our very actions transmitted to one and all the in-
> tensity of our feelings. We knew for certain, and
> without the use of mere words, that we were all
> one people and of one mind--and that mind was to
> dispel the Germans ultimately and drive them from
> our country.
> No longer did we pay any heed to our own radio

broadcasts or newspapers, which could be bought
(though nobody purchased them) at the village stores.
These were now under the strict censorship of the
Germans themselves, who would have had us believe
that our government was false, our king a traitor,
and that they, the Nazis, had come as friends to
help us build our country into something new and
powerful. But we were not deceived. Every even-
ing from our hidden radio sets we heard the real
news--from the BBC in London and from the radio
in Stockholm--and at times this news was all too
blunt, leaving us with nothing more to think about
than the cold hard reality of our own dilemma.
[p. 145]

The Norwegians remain firmly opposed to the Germans.
Rumors of resistance give them hope though patriots are arrested, Jews are deported, and Germans are everywhere.

Ingeborg's father is killed ferrying Norwegian soldiers
to England. Ingeborg stays on the farm. When the Germans
find a Jew there, they burn down all but the house and slaughter the animals.

As they retreat from the Russians, the Germans destroy everything in their path and uproot thousands to slow
the advancing troops. In the wake of their destruction, Inge
joins her Lapp relatives, retreating to a life she idealizes
but has never known. With the end of the war and the birth
of new hope in Norway, she responds to the call of her old
life and returns to rebuild the farm.

Poland and Russia

The German invasion of Poland and Russia was one
of the most vicious in history. In Never to Forget Milton
Meltzer describes the fury with which the Nazis massacred
millions in their path:

From the first day of Hitler's invasion, the massacre began. The Einsatzgruppen--the "mobile killing units" of the SS, under the command of Reinhard Heydrich--moved into Poland with the regular
armored columns. Their instructions were to kill
as many civilians as possible, especially Jews.
... Most were professional men--teachers, artists,
lawyers, a physician, even a clergyman--and most

> were in their thirties. No one was asked to volun-
> teer, but once chosen, they did their job of mass
> murder with zeal and skill. [p. 64]

These were technocrats. Their business was murder. The
descriptions of their atrocities are so horrifying that if they
were fiction, no one would believe them.

A survivor of one such action in Russia is quoted in
the book. She tells of the killing squad arriving in Zagrodski
in August 1942. All Jews are ordered into trucks. Those
not finding room on the truck have to run behind. If they
fall they are shot. At their destination, the people are ordered to undress and stand at the edge of a pit while four
SS men shoot them. Those who try to run are shot. The
bodies of the dead pile up on those wounded but still alive.
Not bothering to finish off the wounded, the SS leave. The
naked survivors try to climb out of the pit.

The Germans return and order the survivors to pile
the corpses in a heap. Children who are still alive are
thrown on the heap and shot. Four Jews escape burial. In
describing her experience to the court, Rivka Yosselevscka
told of blood spurting from the grave, of her anguished wish
to join those already dead (pp. 65-70).

Martin Gray remembers that when the Germans marched
into Warsaw they gave a great show of military strength (Au
nom de tous les miens). From the back of a truck, soldiers
passed out bread--to Aryans. All the while an officer took
pictures to show evidence of the benevolence of the Germans
and the gratefulness of the Poles (pp. 17-18).

The horrible suffering of the people in besieged Leningrad provides the background for Jaap ter Haar's Boris.
Much of Leningrad lies in ruins. Each day thousands starve
or freeze, often dying in the street. Boris's mother is weak
from malnutrition. His father has drowned trying to drive
supplies across the ice. His friend Nadja's father and brother
have just died, and her mother is failing.

So desperate is their hunger that Boris and Nadja decide to gather potatoes from the snow-covered fields between
the Russian and German fronts. Nadja collapses long before
they reach the fields. German soldiers step out of their
blind. They take pity on the children and risk their lives
to return them to the Russian line. Soldiers there think the

Germans are trying to spy until Boris's desperate defense of his new friends convinces them that some enemies have not forgotten their humanity.

Boris's clean hatred for the enemy is tempered by his experience, but he remains ambivalent. While Nadja is being treated by an army doctor, Boris meets a soldier who has been wounded by the same Germans who saved the children's lives. Two days later Nadja and her mother die. Boris has only Nadja's diary to keep her memory alive.

Boris is determined to stay by his mother and avoid being evacuated with the other children. Before the evacuation can be arranged, the Russians break through the German lines, recapture the rails, and begin to turn the tide. A train brings food into Leningrad. Thousands of German prisoners are marched through the city. From both sides of the street people look on in silent hatred. Boris can hardly bear to look at the exhausted, frightened prisoners or the bitter witnesses. In the eyes of one young German he sees such pain and hopelessness that he cannot stand by. He runs to him and pushes a precious bar of chocolate into his pocket. The crowd is angry until an old woman speaks up:

> "You did the right thing," she repeated, and turning to the others, she added, "What good is our victory if we live in hate?"
> The people nodded thoughtfully, for people who have suffered much can forgive much. [p. 159]

Additional titles:

Brand, Sandra. I Dared to Live.
Grund, Josef Carl. Nachruff auf Harald N.
Hautzig, Esther. The Endless Steppe.
Ryss, Yevgeny. Search Behind the Lines.

THE TABLES ARE TURNED

After the decisive defeat of the German troops in Stalingrad, the Russian army began pushing back the German front. Hitler had done what he had vowed never to do, waged war on two fronts, and would now pay the consequences. As the Germans had swept across Russia, they had murdered, raped, looted, burned entire villages, lay waste the land. It

was back across the wasteland they had created that they had
to retreat.

In the path of their retreat were thousands of German
civilians. Many had migrated from Germany centuries earlier. Others had been part of the Nazi settlement policy. The
latter had been rewarded for service or loyalty with farms
and land stolen from people in the occupied countries. Still
others were children who had been sent to camps in Poland
and Czechoslovakia to keep them safe while the cities of Germany were being leveled.

Many Germans who had lived in Russia or Czechoslovakia or Poland for decades had nevertheless turned on their
countrymen when the Nazis assured them that these were subhumans. Others had continued to live in peace with their
neighbors, trying to cling to a life they had always known.
The Nazis considered all non-Germans as Untermenschen and
treated them abominably. The conquering Russians made
German civilians pay.

This section consists of stories of those Germans
caught in the path of the advancing Soviet troops. It would
be hypocritical to discount their suffering and losses even
though they can be disconcertingly blind to the perfidy which
led to their plight.

Nelly Däs's family was among the thousands of Germans whose forefathers settled in Russia and maintained pockets of German language and culture. In Wölfe und Sonnenblumen she complains of their treatment by the Stalinists and
the prejudice they suffered when the Russians began exiling
those of German ancestry.

In 1937 her father is sentenced to thirty years' hard
labor. When war is declared between Germany and Poland,
Emma Schmidt (Nelly's mother) begins hoping that the family
will be freed by the Germans. She idealizes Germany and is
thrilled when troops march into Russia. German soldiers
become regular guests of the Schmidts and assign two POW's
to work for them.

In the spring of 1943 the Germans order everyone of
German ancestry to flee. Although sad to leave homes and
friends, they place their hope on the Germany of their dreams.
The long trek is broken into many stages. In January 1944
they are packed onto trains and shipped into Poland. Though

Poland is part of the Reich, they are disappointed to be stopping short of their goal but at least have food, shelter, and security.

In Der Zug in die Freiheit Däs continues her family's story. The German government has taken away all of the refugees' horses and housed the wanderers in a displaced person camp in Wronke. Emma is distressed to learn that the land and homes being given to refugees are being stolen from the Poles. She is called before the authorities when she voices her concern. Her distress is somewhat suspect, for she sees no difference between the plight of the Poles under the Germans and that of the German settlers under the Russians:

> ... And this business with the Poles is a scandal for the entire nation. I placed so many hopes on this government--and now I see that it has dispossessed the Poles as mercilessly as the Russians did us Germans.... [p. 11]

Nelly is sent to an agricultural school to learn a trade. There she gets into trouble for slipping food to Lena, a Russian-speaking Pole who works in the school. Anni, one of the school's leaders, scolds her for taking bread from German comrades to give the enemy. From all the talk, Nelly understands one thing:

> ... The Germans were human beings who shouldn't suffer any hunger; the Poles, however, were enemies, and it was a crime to feed enemies, even if they were only children. Enemies were enemies, period!.... [p. 43]

Nelly conforms externally but secretly continues to slip bread into Lena's pocket.

The girls come to think of the castle as their home. The war is far away, their lives peaceful, until news comes of brothers, fathers, and friends killed in battle and of partisans killing Germans. (Däs paints the partisans as dangerous enemies of peace and freedom, an interesting contrast with Yuri Suhl's Uncle Misha's Partisans.)

Refugees from the bombings in Germany and the Russians in the east tumble over each other in Poland. The order comes in January 1945 for the castle to be evacuated.

Nelly is an experienced refugee. She knows what to take and
how to prepare the wagons and advises the girls and the peasant families with whom they are to travel. On a cold winter
night the trek begins. A horse slips on the ice. Only Nelly
knows how to bring it to its feet again. Many people freeze
in the bitter cold. Survivors scream out their grief or try
to commit suicide. As they crowd onto trains in Birnbaum,
Nelly and her friends throw out boxes and bags that those
already on board would rather save than other people.

Nelly and two friends escape from the others in Berlin, determined to join their families. They brashly claim
that Hitler Youth can ride trains free, push their way on,
organize enough food to survive, and at last reach home.
Only Nelly's father doesn't return from the war.

Nelly and others like her find that they are not really
accepted anywhere. In Russia they remained outsiders. In
Germany they are considered exotic but inferior. Nelly
grumbles:

> ... They also came down hard on Russia, about
> which they knew nothing. I had had a lot of bad
> experiences, but it upset me when anyone spoke
> against Russia. What did they know about that
> country? The Communists aren't Russia. For
> the people here, everyone who came out of Russia
> or still lived there was a third-class human being.
> Grandfather had always said: "Our forefathers
> were pioneers in Russia. We are their descendants
> and can be proud of them. They accomplished a
> great deal in Russia. They cultivated huge tracts
> of land. They were welcome in Russia."
> And now we seemed to be intruders in Germany.
> That bothered me immeasurably. The head of my
> workshop once asked me privately, "Tell me, Nelly,
> how do people in Russia walk?" I motioned him
> closer to me and said softly, "You won't believe
> this, but they walk on their hands." [p. 142]

Däs's books are considered dangerous by some critics
because they ignore the suffering of the Russians. However,
they are very well written and certainly explore an experience
and set of mind which were common to thousands. In the
hands of a good teacher they could provoke discussion.

Stefan and his father are among the German settlers

who flee the Ukraine when the tide turns against the Germans
(Maria Halun Bloch, Displaced Person).   Accustomed to Soviet repression, Stefan feels uncomfortable in Germany.   The
new freedom of the displaced person camp makes him suspicious.   Here people are speaking so freely that Stefan is
constantly looking for informers.

Stefan and his father leave the camp as the Russians
near and find that other Germans regard them as unwanted
foreigners.   Stefan's father is killed in an air raid.   Left on
his own, Stefan wanders on, wanting to reach the American
sector.   He uses his last legacy from his mother, a bar of
English soap, to bribe his way across the border.

Bloch's story pictures the German refugees as persecuted minorities driven from their homes for no reason.   No
connection is made with the Third Reich or German aggres-
sion and atrocities.   Suddenly these people became innocent
victims of the Soviets.

Gunhild Francke (Last Train West) has happy memories
of her childhood in Silesia.   Then in autumn 1944 hundreds
of horse-drawn wagons come through the town.   The pins on
her mother's map keep moving farther west.   That winter is
especially cold, but the children are happy.   Every day they
can choose something from the store of canned fruits instead
of just on weekends or special occasions.

On a Sunday morning in February 1945 they take the
last train out of Silesia.   After four nights and three days on
a cattle car, they reach northern Bavaria.   They are exhausted
and hungry but alive and safe.   The Americans impose such
tight regulations that it becomes nearly impossible to get
enough food.   All of their energies are spent on survival.

Being neither Bavarian nor Catholic, Father is pessi-
mistic about ever being able to teach in Helmbrecht.   Hopping
one freight car after another, the family works its way north.
Father finds a teaching job in Lübeck but no housing for the
family, so while he teaches there the others travel to Sweden
to live with relatives.

Willi Fährmann's Das Jahr der Wölfe tells the same
harrowing tale as the other books but with more sympathy
for the various sides involved.   Within the first few chapters
a young man reveals his disillusionment with the war.   He
has witnessed Ukrainian men, women, and children massacred
by soldiers of his own unit.

As the front approaches people begin packing up and
fleeing. Grandfather dies rather than leave his home. The
Bienmanns' flight begins in the heart of a cold winter. Progress through the mud and snow is unbearably slow. Father
keeps slipping back home to gather more provisions. Each
time he leaves, his pregnant wife is terrified, but he always
manages to return, even after being caught in a battle during
one foray. The Bienmanns join thousands of others heading
toward western Germany. Around them flows the front.
Crossing the frozen bay toward Danzig, the wagon train is
forced to spend two nights on the ice. By the time they
reach land, many young, old, and weak have frozen. Wagons
have broken through. Few have been willing to jeopardize
their own survival by helping others.

The family at the center of the drama is drawn closer
together by their ordeal. The father has been too ill to be
a soldier, so the family has remained complete. The author
sympathizes with the Bienmanns without losing sight of the
war which brought on the family's displacement.

They meet their first Russians before the baby is born.
Mrs. Bienmann's condition softens the hearts of the conquerors and helps the family through some difficult encounters.
The first soldier demands watches. Another insists that Father drive him to his unit and give up his horse, but he replaces it with another (which Poles steal the same day).

The battle troops move on, and the occupation troops
follow. They put Mr. Bienmann to work treating sick and
wounded horses and are pleased with his skill. When the
order comes for German civilians to evacuate, the corporal
in charge of the horses gives the Bienmanns a horse.

The family starts out again in pouring rain. Mother
and the new baby are lying in an open wagon. A miller gives
them refuge in his mill, and they stay there until the Russians once again rout the Germans. They are crowded onto
trains which roll on to Berlin. Someone on the train complains about their shabby treatment and terrible losses. An
old man snaps:

> "We all allowed injustice to take the upper hand
> and didn't try to stop it. All of us! Only people
> who spoke out loudly while others suffered violence
> have a right to complain now." [p. 163]

In Berlin the Bienmanns are reunited with relatives, but the

apartment is too small for so many.   A year after their flight
began they find a new refuge on a farm in western Germany.
Looking out at the fields, they are reminded of the home they
lost.

The book least sympathetic to the refugees is T. Degens's Transport 7-41-R.   In April 1946 a trainload of evacuees leaves the Russian sector to return to homes in Cologne.
Among them is a 13-year-old girl whose parents are getting
rid of her by sending her away to school.   The refugees are
a heartless, selfish lot, and the narrator mistrusts them all.
She is ferocious in her determination to free herself from
all adults.   Unlike many of the others on the train, she believes the documentary they were all forced to see.   She was
ashamed to learn of concentration camps, of people herded
and beaten into cattle cars, of piles of naked dead, mountains
of their belongings.   She feels little pity for the complaints
of the evacuees, who are returning to Cologne of their own
free will.

In spite of her determination to stay aloof, she is
drawn to an old man and his sick wife.   One night Mrs.
Laurentin dies peacefully in her wheelchair, and the girl
promises to help her husband bring her body to Cologne.
She lies, steals, and cheats to keep the dead woman from
prying eyes and to keep herself and the old man alive.   On
the last stretch to Cologne, only the smell of sauerkraut
masks the stench of the body's decomposition.   At a cemetery
behind the Cologne cathedral, Mr. Laurentin and the girl bar-
ter for his wife's funeral and then leave the cemetery together,
two people who have grown to love and need each other.

Additional titles:

      Baer, Frank.   Die Magermilchbande.
      Deutschkron, Inge.   Ich trug den gelben Stern, pp.
        178-186.
      Ecke, Wolfgang.   Flucht.
      Klingler, Maria.   Nimm den Diktator und geh.
      Ossowski, Leonie.   Stern ohne Himmel, pp. 5-15, 88-
       95.
      Pausewang, Gudrun.   Auf einem langen Weg.

Chapter 6

FIGHTING BACK: RESISTANCE TO THE NAZIS

Individual and organized resistance formed in every country which fell under Nazi domination. Acts ranged from subtle scorn, at which the Danes were gifted, to hiding enemies of the Reich, to carrying out acts of sabotage. Networks united thousands of resisters into small cells whose members knew only the person to whom they answered and that part of the task to which they were assigned.

A quotation from Hiltgunt Zassenhaus characterizes the minority who resisted while another minority willingly collaborated and the majority remained silent and cooperative. She was quoted in Die Zeit, June 19, 1981:

> ..."It was simply common decency.... The first thing I had to learn was, you are alone when you swim against the stream. And the second, every person has opportunities to show courage and to offer resistance. His chances are bound only by his fear and his lack of initiative...." [p. 53]

Belgium

Belgium's lack of wild or unpopulated areas made it difficult to form the sort of maquis which drew so many resisters in France. Nevertheless, by 1943 resistance had become common. Even young Gil Lacq helped to deliver tracts, as he tells in his Les enfants de la guerre.

One day a man for whom Gil's father prints anti-Nazi tracts stops Gil in the street and asks him to deliver a pistol. For the first time the boy gets caught in a raid as he rides the tram with his dangerous secret. Fortunately, no one bothers searching a 9-year-old. Everyone is ordered

off the tram.   As he steps off, Gil sees a young man stick
a gun inside a newspaper.   When the Germans search him,
they do not bother to check the newspaper he holds in his
raised hands.   The search ends without incident, and everyone climbs back on the tram.   The young man winks at Gil
and then stares in astonishment when Gil shows him his own
pistol (pp. 109-123).

     Lacq also tells the story of a Russian immigrant
couple in Belgium who send their son to live with his grandmother so they can join the resistance, unaware that Grandmother is hiding Jews, Russians, and aviators.   The boy's
mother disappears, and the father goes underground, joining
a group so involved in the adventure of resistance that they
refuse to turn over their weapons when the war ends.   Not
until the mid-fifties does the boy learn that his mother was
a heroine: When a German was killed in broad daylight, 50
hostages were taken.   Sure that her husband was responsible
and unable to persuade him to confess, she turned herself
in to save the hostages.   The Germans insisted she was too
small and weak to have murdered anyone, so she walked over
to a guard, took his bayonet, and killed him.   Decapitated
by the Germans, she became a heroine after the war, with
Communists, Belgians, and White Russians all claiming credit
for her act (pp. 134-145).

Denmark

     In a note prefacing his novel Bright Candles, Nathaniel
Benchley says of the Danes:

> It is a curious fact that Danes who were involved
> in the resistance are reluctant to talk about their
> experience, to the point where they become virtually
> mute.   They have a terror of appearing to boast;
> they are embarrassed when they hear of one who
> may have talked, and they prefer to treat the whole
> experience as though it had been a trip to the office.

     Jens Hansen is a month shy of his seventeenth birth-
day when King Christian orders an end to all resistance.
Four days later the Hansens receive a letter telling of the
Danes' valiant fight when the Germans crossed into Jutland.
It is their first news of Danish resistance.   They make ten
copies of the letter and send them anonymously.   Jens is
nearly caught posting them but escapes questioning by the
German soldier watching him by pretending not to understand.

In his worst German, he says, " 'Sie wollen das Herrenpissen-
platz, nicht?'" ("You want the men's bathroom, no?") and
leaves the soldier laughing.

Danes form the DKS, the Danish Cold Shoulder Society,
and pretend not to see the Germans. In the square a German
band plays oompah music as part of the plan to win the hearts
of the Danes:

> ... The only trouble was that the Danes wouldn't
> listen. They walked through the square as though
> the musicians were so many pigeons, and the only
> person I saw who even acknowledged their presence
> was one man who, without breaking stride, fished
> in his pocket and brought out a coin, and tossed it
> at them.... [p. 26]

Jens and his friend Ole are caught writing SSU ("drive
the swine out") on the wall of the German Army headquarters.
Ole tries to lie his way out of trouble by claiming that the
letters are really a compliment and that he admires the SS,
but only the fact that the Germans are new at occupying Denmark saves the boys from punishment.

Minor acts of resistance soon pale for Ole. He longs
for heroic action and persuades Jens to help him steal dyna-
mite from a construction site. Jens accidentally sees a type
slug hidden under a doily in a dental clinic, and Ole talks
him into making a second appointment to try to make contact
with an apparent resistance network. The boys are soon distributing flyers and compiling information on Danish collaborators.

As the occupation drags on resistance escalates to
violence, to which the Germans respond with yet more violence. Hitler sends the king a flowery telegram to congratulate him on his 72nd birthday. The king's reply is terse:
" 'Thanks. Christian X.' " The insulted Hitler brings down
his full wrath on the Danes. That only hardens their resistance. When at last the German troops are forced to withdraw, millions of candles glow once again in the windows
throughout Denmark.

Through the device of an extended family, Eva-Lis
Wuorio includes various facets of the resistance movement
in Denmark and Norway (To Fight in Silence). Resistance
begins with a quietly dramatic act of the king. On the day

that Denmark is occupied, King Christian rides as usual through
Copenhagen on his horse. He ignores the German soldiers
until he sees the swastika flag flying from an official building.
He protests the violation of the treaty and says that if it is
not removed by 12 o'clock he will send a soldier to bring it
down. The flag is still in place as he passes the building
again. He says that he is sending a soldier. The officer
warns that the soldier will be shot, and the king replies,
"I am the soldier."

Two months later Kristian Jensen becomes a part of
the Danish wall of silence when he refuses to respond to two
German soldiers who politely ask for directions. His father,
Svante, helps to organize underground communications networks for the inevitable time when the Germans' rule becomes
harsher. Relatives in Norway use their sea-going contacts
to get soldiers and gold to Canada.

Young Thor acts so rashly that in 1941 he has to be
spirited to Sweden for the protection of other resisters as
well as his own safety. The action shifts back to Denmark
when Thor runs away from his Swedish military school and
takes refuge with his aunt in Jutland. Aunt Minna, an important resistance fighter herself, sees the boy's potential
and persuades her nephew, Svante, to give him responsibil-
ities.

By fall of 1942 the whole family is involved in the
complicated resistance networks. A year later they play an
important role in the rescuing of Danish Jews. When informers turn the family in to the Gestapo, those members who are
in danger flee to London to continue the fight from there.

Peter Andersen becomes involved in the resistance by
accident when he is 11 and discovers his parents working in-
tently over a mimeograph machine in the basement (Elliott
Arnold, A Kind of Secret Weapon). In Liberated Denmark
Lars Andersen can print news that cannot appear in the newspaper for which he works. Peter quickly learns not to ask
questions, understanding the danger of knowing too much.

While Lars is away Lise falls ill. She insists on getting out the paper anyway and ends up in the hospital. She
is so worried that the papers be delivered on schedule that
she allows her son to take over the task. Peter hides all
the evidence he finds at home, packs the newspapers in his
school case, and takes the train to Copenhagen. He delivers

the papers like a professional.   Unfortunately, his contact is
being watched and is caught by the Gestapo, who send someone after Peter.   Seeing that he is running from Germans,
passersby manage to slow his pursuers.   He runs into Tivoli
Park.   The Germans block the entrance.   A Danish workman
beckons to him, hides him in his wagon, and calmly drives
him out of the park.

The head of the Gestapo in Snekkersten is the detested
Major Gruber.   It is one of Lars's keen desires to force him
to be transferred in ignominy.   After long thought he devises
a scheme.   He writes and duplicates an editorial for the underground newspaper, praising Major Gruber for his leniency
and humanity.   On his way home from celebrating this stroke
of genius with his family, Lars is arrested.   With the Gestapo watching his house, Peter and his mother have to hide
all evidence of the newspaper and seek refuge with the Pastor.
Major Gruber personally brings the Pastor news of Lars's
death, but his plan to flush out his quarry fails.   As a vale-
diction on his father's life, Peter insists on distributing his
father's editorial before he and his mother leave Denmark.

Major Gruber closes in on them, but just before he
can arrest them he is ordered to Copenhagen to answer to
his superiors for his apparent soft touch.   From the same
docks through which thousands of Jews, resistance fighters,
and wounded have been shipped to Sweden, Lise and Peter
start their journey to freedom.

Additional title:

Arnold, Elliott.   A Night of Watching.

Eastern Europe

It is interesting to note that while the Jews have been
accused of allowing themselves to be slaughtered, all of the
books in this section are about Jewish resistance.   As Milton
Meltzer points out in Never to Forget:

> ... The vanquished nations, all of them, had trained
> and equipped armies.   The Jews had nothing.   The
> Nazis killed myriads of people in the parts of Rus-
> sia they occupied, a territory whose population
> greatly outnumbered the German troops.   How much
> resistance did Hitler encounter there?

...

> The purpose here is not to criticize or demean
> others, only to indicate how hard it is for anyone
> to resist a ruthless totalitarian power which com-
> mands modern weapons and employs elaborate means
> to crush opposition. [p. 139]

Many did resist. Meltzer gives the example of a 12-
year-old girl who smuggled Jews out of the Minsk ghetto, of
shoemakers who put nails into German boots to cripple their
wearers, of rebellions in Jewish ghettos and revolts in death
camps, and of passive resistance. Unlike other resistance
movements, the Jews were not supplied with arms by the Allies. They were not treated as equals by other underground
movements in occupied countries. Their seasoned leaders had
been eliminated by the Nazis. Even if they were successful
in their struggle, they had no place to go. They were facing
an enemy which wanted nothing less than their total annihilation.

Of particular interest in presenting to young people the
story of Jewish resistance is the third section of Meltzer's
book. Under the title, "Spirit of Resistance," he makes clear
what was facing those who decided to oppose the Nazis. On
the same subject are pages 132-139 of Arnold Rubin's The
Evil That Men Do in which he tells of the heroic resistance
in the Warsaw ghetto and other ways in which Jews defied
their persecutors.

Two novels by Yuri Suhl show resistance by Eastern
European Jews. In On the Other Side of the Gate, the inhabitants of a Polish ghetto organize an underground. In
order to hide their activities they meet in the "Typhus Room"
of the hospital. The German guards are so afraid of contam-
ination that they never enter it. One of the ghetto resisters
slips out to make contact with the partisans. They rob him
of the group's only revolver and scorn his offer of Jewish
help. The Home Guard partisans are not only rabidly anti-
Semitic but also hostile toward the left-wing People's Front
and refuse to form a coalition against the Germans.

After the barbed wire goes up around the ghetto, the
Germans outlaw pregnancies. Lena Bregman is already expecting a baby. She and Hershel decide to defy the Germans
by bringing their child into the world. For the first year and
a half, little David is kept hidden. Then the transports begin.
If David is to live, he must be smuggled out of the ghetto.

Hershel contacts a member of the Polish underground, who
is embarrassed to learn that the partisans stole the Jews'
only weapon. Their daring plan to save the boy brings together members of all three resistance groups. The hopes
of his people go with David as he is carried out in a water
barrel.

Uncle Misha's Partisans was inspired by an actual
episode. The group forms when 19 escape from the Koretz
ghetto. They have only one weapon and no money or food.
They gain three more weapons by attacking Ukrainian policemen who are rounding up six boys for German labor camps.
The grateful boys bring them food and tips on who in the village can be trusted. Determined to avenge the deaths of their
families at the hands of the Hitlerites, the 19 partisans hide
in the forest and defy the enemy.

> Once, not so long ago, they remembered, they
> too had enjoyed the warmth of home and the love
> of family. Now their homes were gone. Total
> strangers sat at the tables they had sat at, slept
> in the beds they had slept in, wore the clothes they
> had worn. And their families--fathers, mothers,
> wives, children--were all heaped in some unmarked
> mass grave, together with cherished dreams and
> cherished hopes, a bulging mound of earth the only
> monument to their unlived lives.
> And they, the "lucky" ones, who by some mir-
> acle had managed to escape the executioner's bullet,
> had vowed to avenge them and destroy the destroyer
> of human life. Their home was the forest; the open
> sky their roof; their fellow partisans the only family
> they had; their most precious possession, their
> weapons. Each night, under cover of darkness,
> they would emerge from the forest in twos, in
> threes, in tens, and fan out in various directions,
> a silent, invisible army of Jewish fighters in search
> of the enemy. [pp. 61-62]

Two of them are returning from sabotaging a German
train when they find a boy in an oversized soldier's coat
clutching a violin. His parents and sister have been killed
by the Nazis. For the past year he has been wandering, finding work here and there. Now he is searching for Uncle
Misha's partisans.

Motele reminds the partisans of their lost children.

They are intrigued by this violin player who for a year has
passed as a Gentile, who can cross himself like a Christian
and speak Ukrainian without an accent.   Motele's musical talent proves invaluable.   The guards around Ovrutch relax their
vigilance on a Christian holiday so that people can enter the
town to celebrate.   Partisans dressed as beggars join the
crowds.   Motele plays his violin beside the real beggars outside the Greek Orthodox church and steals the show.   A German officer gives him a job playing in the officers' club from
12-2 and 7-11.

Motele is humiliated when he has to wear a specially
tailored Nazi uniform.   The German officer tells him what
an honor it is.   He is the only non-Aryan in all of the occupied countries who is allowed to wear one.

Motele plays his part so well that no one suspects him
of deceit, and he is able to plan how to sabotage the club.
Returning to Ovrutch one day with his violin case filled with
explosives, he is stopped at a road block.   In his German
uniform Motele boldly walks up to the Ukrainian guard and
demands to be allowed through.   Seeing his special identity
card, the guards let him pass.   He fears he will be late,
so he flags down a taxi full of well-dressed people and orders
the driver to take him to the club.

On the night the club is to be blown up, Motele has
the honor of playing for a German general.   He waits until
all the non-German help have gone home and then lights the
wick on the explosives.   As he and his comrades flee, they
take courage from the memorial candle Motele has lit for
their dead.

Sandra Brand is another who did not fit the Nazi stereotype of Jewish appearance.   She tells in her autobiography, I
Dared to Live, of feeling guilty to be surviving while her family and friends die.

She uses her fluency in Polish and German to help her
find work as an interpreter in a Polish warehouse in Warsaw.
As a clerk in the Vinetta offices, she is responsible for checking merchandise manufactured in the ghetto, obtaining work
cards for the BBH (ghetto factory) workers, and dealing with
the manager of BBH.   No one suspects she is a Jew, so she
soon becomes a conduit for people and information to and
from the ghetto.

Because of an illegal search of her boarding house she meets Rolf, a German policeman who eventually becomes her lover.   Time and again the two of them are able to save Jews who have been listed for deportation.

For his "illicit relationship with a Pole," Rolf is sent to the Russian front.   He returns thin and haunted.   Needing Brand to act as a contact, he reveals his membership in the Polish underground.   Their activities become more dangerous as various members of the resistance are arrested.   To test his loyalty, the Gestapo order Rolf to execute his interpreter. He manages to evade the order but knows he is under suspicion.   Not long afterward, he and his interpreter are ambushed.   Germans are to blame, but the Gestapo put the blame on the partisans and shoot twenty hostages.

Brand moves to Konstancin, where she is ordered to act as interpreter for the Ortskommandatur.   In this position she is able to free Poles who have been rounded up for labor camps.   Her status is always precarious.   The Polish underground considers her an enemy for working for the Germans. The Germans would kill her if they knew she was a Jew.

At war's end Brand searches in vain for her child. Then with nothing left to hold her to her native land, she immigrates to America.

Martin Gray dates his true birth from September 1939 when bombs began to fall on Warsaw (Au nom de tous les miens).   His father told his 14-year-old son to survive by any means, and Gray took his advice.

When the Jews are forced into a walled ghetto, Gray organizes a smuggling ring to bring food to its starving populace.   He hardens himself to pass by people dying in the streets.   He must survive to avenge their deaths.

During one of his sessions with the Gestapo, Gray is tortured beyond his capacity to withstand, and he agrees to talk.   He is released from the torture session and spits in his interrogator's face, hoping to be killed before he loses his will to resist.   Instead his enraged torturer strikes a bargain, treatment for his wounds in return for denunciations. A sympathetic doctor diagnoses typhus, giving Gray time to heal and a chance to escape.

Gray's will to fight is sapped when he sees his family

being taken away. He joins them in a cattle car headed for
Treblinka. Even there he is determined to survive. He escapes from the death camp and then from the work camp.
He tries to tell the Jews of Zambrow what awaits them, but
his warnings fall on deaf ears. Once again he is sent to a
concentration camp. He escapes and begins smuggling bread
to the camp but is caught again. This time he joins a detail
working outside the camp. Because most of those in the detail have families being held hostage, they refuse to let him
escape. He slips away from them and hides in an outhouse,
with soldiers urinating and defecating on him. When all is
quiet he takes refuge in the forest.

In the forest he finds a group of Jewish resisters,
who tell him of the fighting in the Warsaw ghetto. Trying
to return to Warsaw he is caught and escapes again. For a
short while he joins the Arma Krajowa, the anti-Semitic Polish partisans, who teach him how to handle weapons and wage
war.

He finds the Warsaw ghetto ringed by jackals waiting
to threaten, rob, terrorize, and finally denounce any Jews
who escape. Gray joins the fierce battle against the Germans,
only leaving when the Germans have nearly won and are systematically destroying ghetto buildings.

Again Gray joins a resistance movement, this time
the Arma Ludowa, which has Jewish members as well as
Russians, French, Czechs, and Poles.

Gray is an indomitable survivor, resurfacing each time
he is pushed under. After the war he becomes a successful
antiques importer in New York. Then he marries and lives
happily with his wife and four children in the south of France.
Life is good until his whole family perishes in a sudden fire
that sweeps through Provence.

Additional titles:

 Samuels, Gertrude. Mottele.
 Szábo, Magda. Abigail.

France

In the hills of Vercors in the summer of 1944, 3500
maquisards resisted German assaults for two months. Their

struggle is the subject of <u>Mon Vercors en feu</u> by Paul-Jacques
Bonzon.   When the Germans invade the free zone in 1942, an
active resistance movement forms.   Fourteen-year-old Luc
Chastagnier ignores his limp and joins his father and other
<u>maquisards</u> as they gather arms dropped by the English.   In
the ovens of his bakery, M. Chastagnier prepares bread for
the underground.

In the spring of 1944 the Chastagniers nurse a wounded
aviator in the attic above the bakery's ovens.   They have
passed him on to the <u>maquis</u> by the time the SS decide to
search their house, but the SS find his notebook in the attic.
They immediately take M. Chastagnier behind the house and
shoot him.

As soon as someone can take over the bakery, Luc
joins the <u>maquisards</u> and stows away on a sabotage mission.
The mission succeeds, but Luc falls into the Gestapo's hands.
He escapes with the help of a sympathetic guard and eludes
his pursuers.

In the bloody reprisals which follow the sabotage,
Luc's village is destroyed.   Luc is reunited with his beloved
Violette, a refugee who had found shelter with his family.
Years after the war, Violette's and Luc's daughter marries
the son of the German guard who helped him escape from the
Gestapo, thus symbolizing the reconciliation between the two
countries.

The book is primarily an adventure story, but along
with the action comes a thoughtful look at some of the decisions facing those in an occupied land.

Just as adventuresome but with more interesting characters is Claude Stokis's <u>Réseau clandestin.</u>   Two friends,
Roland and Godet, become involved in the resistance.   They
are filled with heroic dreams, but their escapades retain a
childishness even while they are acting with complete serious-
ness.

The flyers dropped over Paris by the English in October 1943 inspire them to start their own resistance group.
Their chance comes all too abruptly.   Two days later they
are sitting in detention when they hear fighter planes.   While
the other detainees hide under their desks, Roland and Godet
rush outside and watch a parachute drop.   Ignoring detention,
they rush over the wall and find the pilot.   With boyish inge-

nuity, they bring the wounded soldier to a hiding place. The doctor to whom they take Bob is a Jew and is horrified to learn that they know where he and his family are hiding.

The doctor's fears are justified. Two weeks later he and the family sheltering him are arrested. Only Bob and Dr. Lévy's children are able to hide. To bring them to safety, Roland must contact the resistance. Gaspard is sent to pick up Bob. His rescue attempt fails, and he becomes another of Roland's charges. Once again Roland travels into Paris to contact the resistance, this time in an office staffed by a large number of Germans. Bob and Gaspard are picked up by the network but not the three Lévy children, so Roland has to let his mother in on the secret.

Gaspard is arrested but escapes with Roland's help. He needs time to recover from his torture sessions with the Gestapo, so his resistance network presses Roland into service as a go-between. The boy becomes the arm to Gaspard's brain and is astonished to learn that Gaspard's contact is the physics teacher the boys have always found nice but ineffectual. M. Leret tells Roland, "'Le courage n'est pas l'apanage des grands jeunes gens costauds. La France a besoin de tous les bras pour se défendre.'" ("Courage is not the sole property of vigorous young men. France needs us all now.")

The heroism of these characters is that of ordinary people. Things do not always go right. On one trip to retrieve weapons dropped by the Allies, they have a string of accidents. The truck has a flat, their jack breaks, and for a while it looks as if they are stuck. Roland passes a message on to the Allies to bomb an arms shipment near his own home and learns afterward that the arms had already been moved out. In spite of setbacks they keep on trying, confident that their cause is just.

One small boy and an old woman show those around them that it is possible to remain civilized in wartime in Minou Drouet's Ouf de la forêt. Against their will they become involved in the resistance (pp. 195-255). Ten-year-old Ouf is so tenderhearted that he sneaks out at night to wash the slug poison off the lettuce in his father's garden. While others despise the German soldiers occupying La Guerche, Ouf empathizes with them.

In order to communicate with the marquess, whose house has been requisitioned by the Germans, Ouf works out a delivery system using Croche, his pet magpie, and Zoum, his squirrel. The two friends use the animals to pass notes back and forth to each other and at one point even use them to deliver a special message for the resistance.

The forest changes as the war nears its end. Each night it swarms with the counter activities of resisters and German patrols. The Germans acquire three vicious dogs, which the guileless Ouf quickly befriends. That helps him to save a parachutist but means that he must lie to the German commandant, who has become his good friend. That hurts Ouf. He is not accustomed to lying.

Ouf's knowledge of the forest proves valuable to the resistance. They teach him to plant explosives and give him the task of blowing up a munitions truck. When the war is over the villagers give Ouf a medal. The recognition brings him no joy, for in sabotaging the munitions truck Ouf killed his friend, the commandant.

Thirteen-year-old Pierre does not have Ouf's loving acceptance of all living things but does face a similar crisis of conscience when he becomes friends with a German soldier after his own father is killed escaping from a POW camp (Georges Fonvilliers, L'enfant, le soldat et la mer).

A German soldier is killed near Saulac in May 1944. The local government imposes a 5 p.m. curfew. Dodolphe, the village innocent, is caught out on the street after curfew and beaten. This enrages Pierre and his friends, who plot minor acts of sabotage against the Germans. When the boys' small revenges threaten to bring sanctions on the whole village, their teacher persuades them to stop.

A group of resistance fighters is discovered trying to blow up a stretch of tracks. One of them takes refuge with Pierre and his mother. Pierre realizes his teacher is a part of the same group and offers him help as well. At the same time, he is overcome with guilt because he has come to feel a reluctant love for a German soldier.

The saboteurs are arrested, and Pierre decides he will destroy the tracks. Twice his plan is stymied. He meets his German soldier again. This time the last of his reserve melts in the warmth of the older man's friendliness.

That night Pierre's plan succeeds, but it pales in comparison with Dodolphe's. The village innocent blows up the German garrison, killing Pierre's friend. Pierre is tormented with grief and throws himself on the body of his German soldier, oblivious to the sound of Allied bombers.

Another Pierre is the hero of Odile Yelnik's "V" comme victoire. The young people in the book are deeply disappointed in the adults, who appear to accept the occupation. They form their own resistance group but stop their acts of petty sabotage to take on a much more dangerous task, hiding a Jewish classmate.

Pierre comes up with a scheme to bring Luc to the free zone where he has relatives. As part of his cover, he brings along a chicken. The chicken serves its purpose, drawing attention to its own antics and away from the boys. Near the line of demarcation the chicken becomes even more important. A prisoner of the Germans is able to slip a message in its box. The boys never learn that they have saved a whole unit of resistance fighters just by delivering the message.

When the train stops, the boys climb down to find water for the chicken so are not on the train when it is bombed. Their papers are destroyed, and they become saddled with a French resistance fighter who was accidentally dropped on the wrong side of the line, but at least they have an excuse not to have to show Luc's forged identity papers. The local curé adds Luc and the freedom fighter to his funeral cortège and leads them into the free zone.

After so much excitement Pierre feels lost back in his own village. When the Allies invade North Africa, he and his friends come up with a new scheme. The father of one of the boys owns a laundry. By copying the insignia and unit numbers from the German uniforms brought in for cleaning, they supply the resistance with valuable information on troop movements.

When the father of one of the boys is arrested and shot, Pierre and his friends feel a sense of guilty relief. They are horrified and saddened, but their faith in adults is restored. Pierre says,

> "Yes, it's terrible for him, for all of us. And yet ... In a way I feel relieved. I'm proud. I'm

> almost happy. It's as if all of a sudden I had been
> given back glory, honor, and pride."
> "Yes," said Maurice, "finer than we could have
> believed. I know. There are still heroes among
> us. I thought of that, too."
> Without saying it, without daring to admit it,
> for a long time they had felt little but mistrust and
> scorn for adults. Now everything was back in place
> again. There were still people to admire. That's
> what they had missed the most. They had Michel
> [their contact with the resistance], of course, but
> he was a faraway image.
> Their captive enthusiasm once again took flight.
> This death reassured them. This death fortified
> them. They felt reconciled with the world of men,
> a world they often found hard to comprehend....
> [pp. 212-213]

Thanks to the information the boys gather, the Allies
are able to bomb a construction site. The factory that is
destroyed would have built the new V weapons. The boys are
at loose ends when the war is over, needing to resume the
normal patterns of their lives yet accustomed to living with
excitement and danger.

Additional titles:

> Antona, René. Et pourtant l'aube se leva.
> Cénac, Claude. Le printemps viendra deux fois.
> Ciravegna, Nicole. Aldo et Sarah.
> Durand, Pierre. Vivre debout, la Résistance.
> Guillot, René. L'homme de la 377.
> Lafitte, Jean. Nous retournerons cueillir les jonquil-
> les.
> Marignac, Jeannine. Têtu, agent de liaison.
> Solet, Bertrand. Les jours sombres.

Germany

In spite of such examples as the White Rose and the
attempt to assassinate Hitler, the resistance movement in
Germany remained small and splintered. Hitler's easy victories and apparent economic success bought many supporters.
Others preferred to ride out the storm as inconspicuously as
possible, hoping to stay out of trouble until it was over. Arnold Rubin in The Evil That Men Do gives a very thoughtful

discussion of what happened in Germany and why in the chapter, "A Question of Guilt." Concerning resistance, he quotes the historian Professor Louis L. Snyder:

> "There was opposition, there was resistance, there was conspiracy," said Professor Snyder. But, he added, "the opposition did not work, the resistance did not work--both have been overemphasized."
> [p. 168]
>   . . .
> An American Army newsreel shows the citizens of Weimar coming out of Buchenwald. One holds his head, giving the impression they did not know what was happening. Yet, you or I would ask, "Did you smell it? You lived alongside it, and you didn't even smell what was going on?"
> But the answer is this, that these people were suppressed by a dictator. We don't know what it means to live under a dictatorship, in either Germany, or Russia, or Italy under Mussolini, or any other totalitarian state. If one spoke up, it meant his life. And there were just not that many heroes around. If one dared to oppose this regime, he just threw his life right on the line. If one opposed this man, he lost his life [pp. 171-172]

Rubin cites examples of German resistance: the White Rose group in Munich, Father Lichtenburg, Pastor Dietrich Bonhoeffer. Whatever course of protest they chose, all paid with their lives.

Rubin further discusses the support the Nazis received from such pillars of society as the military, industry, medicine, religion, and law. In the face of such massive support, individual and group resistance was difficult indeed.

On February 22, 1943, Hans and Sophie Scholl were executed in Munich. They wanted no glorious martyrdom, no adulation. Their calm acceptance of their deaths, Sophie's firm statement that she would change nothing if she had the chance to act again, the unwavering conviction that they and the other members of the Weisse Rose exhibited have elevated them to the stature of heroes in Germany. Streets and squares are named after them. The anniversary of their execution is solemnly observed. Yet the question of why these young people, so full of life and laughter, would risk all at a time when few dared to whimper remains an intriguing puzzle.

In an attempt to answer that question, Hermann Vinke collected letters, journal entries, and interviews with peers, family, and friends in Das kurze Leben der Sophie Scholl. The Scholls were a liberal, progressive family which encouraged the children to think independently. Sophie showed a strong talent for art and music and writing. Yet when it came time to enter the university she declared, " 'Kunst kann man doch nicht lernen. Ich studiere Biologie.'" ("You can't learn art. I'll study biology.")

The Scholl children all joined Hitler Youth, achieved leadership positions, and became disillusioned. The Nazi ideology clashed with their strong religious beliefs.

Maximilian University in Munich was among the most tradition-bound and reactionary. It was here in the spring of 1942 that Hans and his friends decided that the time for action had come. After distributing two flyers, they were ordered to the Russian front. The suffering and destruction that the young medical students saw there were further impetus to resistance. When they returned to the university they began composing more flyers. Just how widespread their activities were is unknown because of the need for secrecy. What is known is that they were able to distribute their impassioned appeals so widely that they reached beyond the borders of Germany and alarmed the Gestapo.

In his address on the 470th anniversary of the university, Munich's top Nazi official, Paul Giesler, said that the girls should be home having babies for the Führer rather than wasting their time at the university. Several left the room angrily and were taken by the SS. A noisy protest followed the speech and made the Weisse Rose members feel they were not alone.

The group's last flyer was a fiery, hopeful call to action printed after the defeat in Stalingrad. Hans and Sophie decided to hand it out themselves at the university. They placed a copy on each of the seats in an empty lecture hall but still had flyers left. They climbed to the top of the glass-covered courtyard and dumped the remaining flyers, letting them float down the stairwell. A university custodian saw them, sealed the exits, and called the Gestapo.

That was February 18, 1943. Other members of the group were arrested shortly thereafter. Those carrying major responsibility for the Weisse Rose were executed--Hans,

Sophie, and Christl Probst within a few days. As was customary under the Nazis, their parents were billed for the cost of their executions. Except for Werner, who was in uniform at the time, the remaining members of the Scholl family were arrested and kept imprisoned for several months. Hans and Sophie were aware of the odds against their success but hoped their example would encourage others to take a stand.

Hiltgunt Zassenhaus used her position as a government censor to help Jews in concentration camps and then prisoners of war (Walls). Although her book sometimes bogs down in piety and didacticism, at its core it is an exciting example of courage and ingenuity. Zassenhaus's narration illustrates how effective careful, determined resistance against the Third Reich could be.

In January 1942 she is assigned to censor the mail of Norwegian civilian prisoners who have been picked up by the Gestapo. She begins making a file of their names and addresses and whatever personal information she can learn. The officials trust her so they put her in charge of monitoring visitors to the prisoners. They are allowed one visit every four months. The Norwegian Seaman's Pastor is their most frequent visitor. He greets Zassenhaus coldly until he realizes she intends to be useful to the prisoners.

Zassenhaus's special identification card gives her access to all penal institutions of the German Department of Justice. Therefore, when the prisoners are moved she not only continues her visits but is able to insist on better treatment for them. Zassenhaus and Reverend Svendsen build up a library for the prisoners, smuggle in medicines, bread, and chewing tobacco, and open a supply line through contacts with the German laborers who work alongside the prisoners in the munitions factory. The warden is sympathetic and gives apples to Zassenhaus for her friends but warns her to be cautious.

In January 1944, 300 Danish prisoners are added to Zassenhaus's workload, giving her 1200 prisoners to look after. They are transferred to widely separated prisons, but she continues her visits even though she has begun medical studies. Only Dresden refuses to let her see the prisoners. She complains to the Department of Justice and a year later is allowed to visit even these prisoners. She is astonished to find the city of Dresden untouched by war. During that first visit, Dresden is destroyed, but the prison is safely outside the city limits.

When Hitler orders political prisoners killed, a guard slips word to Zassenhaus. She contacts Swedish officials and the Red Cross and is able to help save all of the Scandinavian prisoners. So intensely has she lived and so completely have the prisoners absorbed her that she feels empty and purpose-less at the end of the war. With new resolve to continue to make her life count, she plunges into her medical studies.

Several novels also tell of resistance in Germany. Wilhelm Weber avoids his old Socialist contacts for the first two years after the Nazis take over, hoping to survive the storm without getting involved (Hans-Georg Noack, Die Web-ers). Then in the spring of 1935 a friend who is being watched by the Gestapo asks him to hide a mimeograph machine. Wil-helm does so as a favor but still remains aloof. In 1937 the friend is arrested, and Wilhelm can no longer stand aside. He begins printing and distributing tracts, trying to hide his activity from a son who is in the opposite camp. The war that divides the family kills his wife, but Wilhelm doggedly persists, needing to believe that the madness can be stopped.

In Horses of Anger James Forman traces the career of a cavalry officer who remains loyal even when he is forced to give up his Jewish wife. His blind faith is shattered by his experiences on the Russian front, and he becomes bitter and disillusioned.

While recovering at home from a leg wound, he com-mutes to the university in Munich where his disillusionment deepens. He is put back into service as the head of a flak battery, but his drunkenness and defiance get him transferred to France. When he returns to Bavaria minus a hand, he throws himself into organizing resistance against the SS.

In Forman's The Traitors a frail pastor and his adopted son become increasingly dismayed by the brutality of the Nazi regime. In the spring of 1944 they meet with the baron and a colonel, knowing that what they are consid-ering is treason. Although they cannot act until the Allies appear, they make a commitment to keep Ravenskirch from being destroyed by the SS or the young fanatics like the pas-tor's son, Kurt.

The plot against Hitler fails, and the SS arrive in

Ravenskirch. Their mission is to keep the Americans from passing beyond the town, even if it should cost the lives of everyone living there. The final struggle between the SS and the conspirators is more a war of wits than weapons. With the SS set to destroy the bridge and the town, the conspirators blow up the sandbags holding back the river, flooding the cellars in which the SS have planted explosives just as the Americans reach the town.

Additional titles:

> Bruckner, Karl. Mann ohne Waffen.
> Forman, James. Ceremony of Innocence.
> Grün, Max von der. Wie war das eigentlich?
> Scholl, Inge. Die weisse Rose.
> Vinke, Hermann. Carl von Ossietzky.

Greece

Wildcat Under Glass by Alki Zei deals with resistance in Greece from the start of the fascist dictatorship. Myrto and Melia's cousin is one of the first to join the underground. Niko calls on Melia to help him and does not even allow her to confide in Myrto. That is a heavy burden for Melia, who has always confided in her sister.

When Niko has to go into hiding to avoid arrest, the children become involved in the resistance. Because they are least likely to be suspected, they bring him supplies. They think of it as a game but understand that they must never allow the authorities to see them. The police try to trail them one day, but the children lead them so far astray that they have to admit defeat.

The wildcat that sits under glass in the parlor becomes a message center. One of its notes tells Melia to deliver a message for the resistance. She finds Niko waiting for her, and again he swears her to silence. Not being able to confide in Myrto is hard for Melia, but Myrto has joined a fascist youth league. Its members use Myrto until she realizes she is being duped. Niko helps her to sever her ties with them but then must flee. When authorities close in on him, Niko leaves the island to fight openly against the fascists in Spain.

Zei continues her account of the Greeks' struggle

against fascism with a new set of characters in Petros' War.
To 10-year-old Petros the start of war seems like a national
celebration. Then six months later the Germans invade. German and Italian soldiers strut through the streets of Athens
while Greek soldiers beg for enough money to get them back
home. Petros and his friend Sotiris are recruited by the
older Iannis to flatten the tires on German trucks. When
they run out of nails, they turn to subtly insulting the Italians.

The shortage of food becomes severe. People are dying in the streets. Iannis turns to painting slogans on walls
and uses Petros as his lookout. His zeal and discretion proven,
Petros is made a member of the freedom-fighting group of
beautiful Drossoula. The first mass demonstration against
the occupiers brings only a slight easing of the food situation.
At a second mass demonstration the tensions are yet higher,
and a carabiniere fires into the crowd with a machine gun.

Petros' father has been quietly working for the resistance all along, but his mother has withdrawn from all but
the daily struggle to keep the family fed and clothed. When
the Italians surrender and are taken prisoner by their former
allies, a deserter hides in Petros' basement. The woebegone
Italian draws Petros' mother out of her shell. He becomes
her shadow, following her like a puppy, and she becomes her
old, strong self again.

The Germans become even more vicious in 1944. Soon
Petros is the only one left of his original resistance group.
His friend Sotiris becomes cocky. He taunts a Greek girl's
German lover, Hunther, by yelling, "Reltih tupak!" ("Hitler
kaput" backwards). He brazenly torments the "little Czar-
inas," the fat daughters of a collaborator. As the Allies
make advances, the Germans fight over every inch of soil.
Sotiris thumbs his nose at the fleeing Hunther, who pulls
out his gun and coldly shoots him.

In spite of the tragedy, Sotiris' funeral becomes a
joyous affirmation of freedom and of triumph over the enemy.
The resilience and determination of the resistance fighters
have given pride and strength to a people bowed by a brutal
occupation.

Additional title:

    Rydberg, Lou and Ernie. The Shadow Army.

Holland

In the winter of 1944-45 Michel, whose independent
and taciturn nature make him ideal for the job, is pressed
into the resistance in Holland (Jan Terlouw, <u>Michel</u>). When
his friend Dirk is picked up by the Germans, Michel learns
that he has been hiding an English flyer, who then becomes
Michel's charge.

Michel's mother asks him to take two Jews to safety.
With the help of Baroness Wansfeld, whose estate lies right
on the river separating liberated from occupied Holland,
Michel brings the men into the free zone. The Baroness
dies defying the Germans, and Michel is sure his clumsiness
betrayed her.

In a complicated web of guilt and innocence, Dirk is
indirectly responsible for the death of Michel's father. The
man Michel has suspected of being an informer has actually
been hiding Jews, and the uncle Michel trusted has betrayed
them all.

When the war ends those who have most recently joined
the resistance, when it appeared safe to do so, are the most
vicious in punishing those whom they suspect of having been
sympathetic to the Germans.

The danger of carelessness and children's need to feel
a part of something important are illustrated in Gertie Evenhuis's <u>What About Me?</u> Dirk turns 11 in the fall of 1943 and
feels old enough to do his part in resisting the Germans.
His older brother, Sebastian, will not include him, so he decides to act on his own. Stealing part of Sebastian's supply
of secret newspapers, he delivers one to his teacher, two
to the milkman, another to a girl evacuated from Rotterdam,
one to his grocer, and the last one he pastes on a wall.

Next day he learns that his teacher has been arrested
with forbidden papers. Sure that it is only a matter of time
until he is arrested and horrified that he may have betrayed
his teacher, Dirk rushes home from school to destroy the
rest of Sebastian's newspapers. He tries to burn them, but
his mother thinks he is burning rubbish and stops him. With
many copies yet to get rid of, he runs to his friend Eddie
for help. Eddie's mother sends them to the country for milk,
and Dirk tries to eat the papers along the way. That proves
to be impractical, so he tries feeding them to a pig. Then

the brother of a Nazi-sympathizing classmate nearly catches him trying to burn more copies, and an SS man almost discovers what he is carrying.

He still is not home free when he has to hide a Jewish girl who falls into his hands. Dirk becomes achingly aware just how young he is. When he delivers the child and learns that he was not actually responsible for his teacher's arrest, he is relieved to drop his resistance activities and be a child once again.

A simple, stirring account of Dutch resistance is Pierre Janssen's A Moment of Silence. It portrays both the suffering of the Dutch under the Germans and the heroism of those who gave their lives for liberty. Each short chapter considers a different Dutch war memorial. Black-and-white photographs and spare text draw on the experiences of those who lived and died that others might be free. Among the stories are the Dutch workers' strike of 1941, the dauntless Dutch Merchant Service, Auntie Riek (the woman who started the organization which united the Dutch underground), and Queen Wilhelmina. The translator describes this slim little volume accurately:

> ... There is no false note, no exaggeration and, above all, no bitterness or hatred. [Janssen] is moved by the fear that those who have never known the horrors of war and what they do to the soul of a people, might assume that peace and freedom can be taken for granted.

Chapter 7

THE CANNON FODDER

With stirring marches the young men marched off to war. By the millions they died. The story of the battles they fought has been repeated in hundreds of history books, documentaries, and textbooks, many written specifically for school children. Less often do young people read the stories behind the uniforms. How did soldiers treat civilians with whom they came in contact? How did they view themselves? How did they handle their prisoners? There are clearly other questions to ask, but these three have been addressed by the young adult authors in this chapter.

The first two questions are the subject of "Soldiers on Both Sides." The second section, "Prisoners of War," includes the relatively limited number of accounts showing the treatment of prisoners by both the Allies and the Germans.

SOLDIERS ON BOTH SIDES

Both German and Allied soldiers receive mixed reviews from young adult authors. Their accounts range from sympathetic to condemnatory. The first four parts of this section deal with Allied soldiers, the final with German.

American

Gil Lacq of Belgium (Les enfants de la guerre) contrasts the hypocrisy of the Germans, who could lay waste a city and at the same time systematically dismantle a church tower so carefully that it could be reconstructed after the war, with the Americans. The latter were more indiscriminate and frank, destroying at random. They would blanket an area with bombs. Sometimes a whole section of a city would be

reduced to a rubble while a nearby military target was left
standing.   Lacq attributes that to the economic advantage of
creating a constant demand for more weapons.   After the
Germans left, the Americans took over his school.   They
destroyed a wall so they could drive their trucks through.
To the delight of the boys, they painted pin-ups on all of
the walls.   The walls were painted over after the Americans
pulled out, but materials were scarce and of poor quality.
Long afterward teachers competed with the walls for the attention of their pupils (pp. 169-175).

        Gunhild Francke's memories of the American soldiers
who occupied the village to which she and her family fled are
decidedly unfavorable (Last Train West).   They impose a curfew which makes it difficult to buy food.   People are allowed
on the streets only two hours a day.   The children forage in
the American garbage piles and watch with hungry eyes as a
soldier pours petrol over a loaf of bread.   Only the black
soldiers show sympathy for the villagers.   The others act as
though the Germans do not exist.   The British fare somewhat
better in Francke's eyes.   They are mostly friendly except
for those whose job it is to censor packages.   They are only
supposed to be preventing a black market from forming but
regularly pilfer the packages.

        When the Americans march into the Tirol, they oust
Bibi and her Uncle Felix from their home (Maria Klingler,
Nimm den Diktator und geh).   Bibi had imagined the arrival
of the victors would be full of drumbeats and glory.   Instead
the Americans arrive four to a Jeep, most of them chewing
something.   To humiliate Nazi Party members, they make
them sweep the streets.   They abuse Uncle Felix because a
refugee falsely accuses him of murdering a soldier.   Fortunately, they are also naive, and the children soon learn how
to work them for food.

        The soldiers use trees for target practice and shoot
Bibi's cat when it gets in the way.   Moses, a young black,
is the only one to show real sympathy toward the children.
He brings Bibi a kitten to replace the one killed.   He empathizes with the men who are now prisoners of the Americans,
for he, too, is a second-class citizen and has been since
birth.   Instead of burning the food that the Americans throw
out, as he has been ordered to do, Moses waits until Uncle
Felix's housekeeper can salvage what is still edible, for he
knows she is preparing it for the POW's.

Bibi's friend Michl hides a pistol in her attic. Bibi
is terrified. If the Americans living in the house find it,
they will take Uncle Felix away. That night the soldiers throw
a party in the house and invite women from the village. Bibi
decides to risk retrieving the pistol while the party can cover
her noise. She sneaks into the attic, slips the pistol under
her dirndl, and takes along a doll as an alibi. The trapdoor
shuts with a bang. The Americans rush up the steps, guns
ready. They are so touched by the child's wanting to retrieve
her doll that they invite her for cake and soda. She eats the
proffered treats like a soldier preparing to die and then sits
patiently while they show her photographs of their wives and
children. At last she can slip away and throw the pistol into
the stream and with it her fears for her uncle.

When the Americans move out, one of them takes Uncle
Felix's car. The troops which follow them are undisciplined
and loud. They blow up Felix's trout stream for sport, but
the war is over, and the family knows that good times will
come again. In spite of the suffering of the refugees who
flock to Uncle Felix and the battles which have devastated
much of Europe, Bibi has remained largely untouched and
unmoved by the war.

Additional title:

Ellis, Ella Thorpe.   Sleep-walker's Moon.

British

British soldiers make cameo appearances as parachut-
ists in French resistance stories, but only in Bel Ria are they
full-blooded characters, here not so much in contact with civilians as with a special little dog.

The dog who is destined to leave his imprint on so
many lives clings first to the only link with his past, Corporal
Sinclair of the Royal Army Service Corps (Sheila Burnford,
Bel Ria). The dog's gypsy masters save Sinclair's life by
making the dog dance to distract the German patrol. Sinclair
has just left them when a Stuka swoops out of the sky, guns
blazing. The old man and woman are killed. The little dog
and his monkey companion follow Sinclair. He is wounded
and passes on his charge to Neil MacLean, sick berth attend-
ant on a British ship. MacLean detests animals but takes
the dog as a sacred trust. While the monkey fends for itself

and thrives, the little dog suffers in the cold sterility of Mac-
Lean's care. He names the dog Ria, and by the time Sinclair
writes to ask for the dog again, MacLean has lost his heart
to the plucky beast. Still, he honors his promise and puts
Ria on land, where he can be sent on.

Ria despairs at being separated from MacLean. The
house in which the little dog waits is bombed. Ria survives
the most terrifying ordeal of his life. Afterward he finds an
old woman who is buried in her garage. The two give each
other comfort and strength until she can be rescued. With
something to care for, Alice Tremorne blossoms. She begins
knitting for soldiers in order to keep her fingers limber
enough to groom the dog she calls Bel. Nearly two years
later MacLean learns where Ria is and shows up to claim
him for Sinclair, for he still must honor his pledge. Bel
Ria divides his loyalty, leaving Mrs. Tremorne to spend
several days with MacLean on the military base and then returning to The Cedars. MacLean and Mrs. Tremorne become
fast friends through Bel Ria. Sinclair arrives for a visit,
bringing Bel Ria the collar bell which recalls his past to him
with such aching intensity that he must dance. One last time
he whirls in the strange little dance Mrs. Tremorne had never
understood and then sinks down for the last time.

French

Many Frenchmen left France to fight for their freedom
alongside the Allies. Only one appears in these books, un-
assuming but a hero. The inmates of the camp in Biberach
await the Allies with prayers and hope in Marietta Moskin's
I Am Rosemarie (pp. 170-176). Those Germans who have not
yet fled hang out a white flag, and the English camp leader
and German commandant go out to look for the Allied army
commander. Hours later the Englishman returns with a frail
French sergeant in grimy khakis, who self-consciously thanks
the cheering crowd and then returns to battle. Rosemarie,
who has survived Westerbork and Bergen-Belsen, muses:

> I stared after him, still under the spell of the
> moment. This little man with his self-conscious
> thank-yous had touched something deep in me. He
> is a symbol, I thought. He is Victory, the Libera-
> tor, Freedom, Peace--all rolled in one.
>   Peace! I suddenly laughed. To me peace will
> never be a dove with an olive branch, or an angel
> with golden wings. My symbol of peace wears a

khaki shirt and a dusty helmet and army boots!
[pp. 175-176]

Russian

Half of the following books give a negative view of Russian soldiers, half positive. To Koehn, Kirchner, and Forman, they are brutes in search of revenge. To Brand, Procházka, and Nöstlinger, they are human beings with both good
and bad qualities. The Russians did wreak vengeance on German civilians in return for what they had suffered. Such
abuse is never excusable, but the second three authors put
it into perspective.

When the Russians take over Berlin, people rush out
to greet them, happy that the war is over at last. Ilse
Koehn's grandmother knows better. She hides Ilse and her
mother and a neighbor in the cellar crawl space (Mischling,
Second Degree). For three days and four nights they cower
in the dark on the cold, damp sand while above them they
hear the sounds of the Stalin Organ, Russian voices, the
screams of women, laughter, and commands. Then Ilse's
grandparents take advantage of a short lull to hide them in
the attic of a pig sty. There they hide for a month while
what seems like the whole Russian army surges around them,
fighting, looting, raping, and celebrating (pp. 228-240).

The Soviet soldiers who break into Wolfgang's home
in Danzig have the same murderous intent (Wolfgang Kirchner,
Wir durften nichts davon wissen). They are in search of
watches and women. The cries of twelve children keep them
from raping the women, but they plunder the entire house.
Each time the looters leave the family hopes for peace, but
always more soldiers come. Each hopes to find something
the others have missed. They smash rows of canned fruit,
steal sausages and wine, search for vodka, and drop lighted
matches (pp. 14-22).

German men are marched off to prison. Most of their
families join the tide of refugees. Wolfgang's family stays
in Danzig. A friend offers them sugar, chocolate, and cocoa,
gifts from her Russian lover. She had been raped repeatedly
in front of her child until a Russian soldier moved in with
her. He is kind and generous, and she needs his protection
(pp. 71-75).

Throughout their ordeal and eventual flight, most of

Wolfgang's family members remain stubbornly blind to the reasons for the Russian occupation and Polish revenge. Wolfgang gives himself some credit for dawning awareness that the Germans may have been wrong but paints a very unsympathetic view of his mother and Diti, his brother, who refuse to admit that the Germans were responsible for atrocities in Danzig.

James Forman portrays the Russian soldiers as savage and primitive. In The Survivor a Russian soldier wants to rape Hannah and only relents when David convinces him that as a Jew she has suffered enough at the hands of the Nazis. The soldier and his comrades have killed an SS officer and stuck him in a vat of honey because he insulted them. They have never seen flush toilets so have been using one as a laundry. When they catch the SS officer using it for its intended purpose, they are furious and kill him. Now they want to celebrate and drunkenly insist that David and Hannah join them.

Sandra Brand in I Dared to Live contrasts the fates of the Germans and the Poles who fell into Russian hands. She is thrilled when the Russians drive the Germans out of Poland. The Russian soldiers are very civilized to her. She takes a job with the Agriculture Department and is sent to take stock of German businesses taken over by Poles. When she travels to Stettin, she is given both a weapon and a companion. There she learns to her astonishment that the same Russian soldiers who had treated her so well have raped, looted, and murdered in Stettin, which was populated by Germans (pp. 197-199).

A Russian soldier saves Olin's life in Jan Procházka's Long Live the Republic. German deserters have stolen Olin's horse, and he dare not go home empty-handed. Suddenly he hears what sounds like an order to stop. Looking around, he spies an unfamiliar uniform. Having enough bruises already, he isn't about to stop, but the Russian is faster than he is. He hurls Olin to the ground just as Germans start firing overhead.

When he realizes that the soldier is one of the liberators they have been waiting for (but from whom he was supposed to hide the horse), Olin wonders if maybe he should sing the national anthem or say something memorable. The lieutenant offers him bread and bacon and a wondrous glass bubble that looks just like snot when he sticks it up his nose.

Twice Olin tries to steal a Russian horse, and twice he has to run. He tells the lieutenant about a motorcycle that is hidden in the woods. Almost forgetting the war, the two go on a hair-raising ride. The lieutenant starts performing tricks with gay abandon. His arms are spread like an acrobat's when he is felled by a German. The dead soldier frightens Olin. He starts running; shots fall around him. He wants desperately to be home with his mother. Suddenly the shooting stops. The villagers pour into the streets to cheer the conquerors. Under the jubilation runs violence. The crowd turns on Olin's only real friend, a collaborator, and runs him to his death. All the confusion of injustices Olin has witnessed leads him to remark, "One person, no matter who he may be, is nothing on such a large earth."

Nazis begin streaming out of Vienna as the Russians approach (Christine Nöstlinger, Fly Away Home). Christel Goth's home is bombed, but the family is safe in a borrowed villa on the edge of town. Its Nazi owner has loaned it to them and fled. Father deserts from a military hospital and hides in the villa. They wait nervously for the Russians. Then one day the victors arrive in a long line of horses, carts, and soldiers. The neighbors hang out white sheets, but Mrs. Goth has a more pressing problem. She must burn her husband's uniform before the Russians find it. She is still trying to stuff the grey-green bundle into the stove when the first two Russians come into the kitchen.

The rest of the day group after group of Russians come through the house, opening cupboards and drawers, searching for watches, stealing whatever looks interesting, and then sometimes discarding it as soon as they are out of the door.

A major moves into the house with some of his men, much to the relief of the Goths and Frau Braun, who is also living there with her children. With the major there, the looting stops. Mr. Goth persuades the Russians that his legs were mutilated by disease, not battle.

The Russians' cook arrives to set up his kitchen in the summerhouse, and 8-year-old Christel falls in love. He is a tiny man with a round belly, thin arms, bowed legs, a bald head, and ears that stick out. He is dirty and smelly and repulsive to all but Christel. To her he is special:

But to me he was the first ugly, smelly, crazy

person I had ever loved.   [I really loved him, and
I hope he knew it because other than I, no one did
love him, not even the Russians.   The good-natured
ones hardly looked at him.   The less good-natured
laughed at him or made fun of him.   Once a drunken
sergeant gave him a kick that sent him flying clear
across the summerhouse kitchen.   He landed by the
door.   His glasses flew off into the ivy.   They were
hard to find.   I looked for them for half an hour.
When I found them I cleaned them on my smock and
brought them to the cook.   He put them on and said,
"Not matter, not matter, missus," and smiled.]
...

I would often sit beside the Russian cook; I liked
being with him, even if the others did think it was
silly of me.   I loved the cook because there was
absolutely nothing about him that had anything to do
with war.   He was a soldier, but he had no gun or
pistol.   He did have a uniform, but it looked more
like a rag-and-bone man's outfit.   He was a Russian, but he could speak German.   He was an enemy, but he had a soft, deep voice for singing lul-
labies.   [He was a victor and got kicks that sent
him flying clear across the summerhouse kitchen.]
His name was Cohn, and he came from Leningrad,
where he had been a tailor.   Cohn told me a lot of
things, and when he finished he would always say,
"Not matter, not matter, missus!"   [Translation
by Anthea Bell.   Passages in brackets are omitted
in the translation, pp. 64-65]

The soldiers celebrate May Day by getting roaring
drunk.   Christel and Gerald Braun steal the sergeant's pistol.
Next day he lines up the family and threatens them with a
submachine gun for stealing his pistol.   In order to calm the
still-drunken soldier, Herr Goth speaks to him in fluent Russian.   The Major's orderly witnesses the scene.   He knows
now that Herr Goth was a soldier in Russia, perhaps even
among those who destroyed his village, but he is so relieved
that no one has been hurt that he doesn't betray him.

Christel stows away on Cohn's wagon when he drives
into Vienna.   She wants to visit her grandparents.   While he
is wandering around looking for her later in the day, he is
arrested as a deserter.   She never sees him again.   Her
father has to risk coming into Vienna to find her.   On the
way back he is stopped because he does not have valid per-

mission to enter Vienna.   Christel runs home and frantically
tries to persuade the drunken soldiers to come to his rescue.
They are so pleased to see her back again that she has to
muster up all the fury her 8-year-old body is capable of to
convince them that her father is in trouble.   A wild ride and
fast talking free Mr. Goth, but it is the last time he can
count on the Russians for help.   The combat troops are moving out and the occupation forces moving in.

        Christel doesn't understand her father's comment that
it is lucky that the Russian soldiers have so little vacation
and receive so few letters that they have no clear idea what
the Germans have done in their land.   (Note: This observa-
tion is omitted in Bell's translation.)   To her the Russians
are friends and family.   When they leave the villa seems
empty and sad.

Germans

        In the first five books in this section German soldiers
are sympathetic protagonists in contact with enemy civilians.
Though as a whole they are feared and despised, as individuals
they could be anyone's father, brother, or friend.   It is not
insignificant that all five are set in western Europe.   The
remaining books, beginning with Horst Burger's Vier Fragen
an meinen Vater and including those listed as additional titles,
show the German soldier from his own point of view.

        A German soldier is one of the main characters in
Georges Fonvilliers's L'enfant, le soldat et la mer.   The
soldier tries to befriend a young French boy who could be
his own son.   He commiserates with Pierre, understanding
why the boy hates the Germans who killed his father.   He
tells him that the Germans will soon be gone and that it will
be better for everyone.   In spite of himself Pierre is touched
by this grave, humane man.   They meet again on the beach,
and the soldier understands Pierre's hostility, which masks
his desire to be friends.   On the day that Pierre is plotting
sabotage the two meet on the street.   The soldier talks to
Pierre of approaching peace and his hope for a better world.
Pierre's plan falls through, and the two meet again.   This
time Pierre's reserve and hostility melt, and the two talk as
friends.   That night Pierre sabotages a stretch of tracks, but
the village innocent goes after larger game.   From a distance,
Pierre hears the rumble of explosions and sees the German
garrison collapse in flames.   He forgets his own danger of
being caught and rushes to the garrison, where he falls sob-
bing on the body of his German soldier.

In another French village, Ouf is terrified when he
sees German soldiers coming his way (Minou Drouet, Ouf
de la forêt). He hides in the ditch until they pass and then
sees a young soldier sitting with his boots off. His bloody,
blistered feet touch Ouf's heart. The boy cannot ignore the
soldier's pain. He binds the soldier's feet with healing herbs.

The officer who sees Ouf help the young soldier warms
to the naive boy and grants him special favors. He will not
make Ouf's friend the marquess leave her home and will
order his men not to shoot the animals of the forest. When
his men accidentally kill Ouf's friend Daphne the commandant
allows Ouf to bury her in the woods.

Tension between the villagers and the Germans increases. The Germans shoot hostages and train three vicious
dogs. It hurts Ouf to have to lie to the commandant, but he
wants to be part of the resistance. Just days before the commandant is to leave, Ouf helps blow up a munitions truck.
To the villagers he is a hero, but his heroism is hollow,
for among those killed is the commandant he has grown to
love.

A young German officer befriends a small, ragtag
group of children in rural Italy in Erik Haugaard's The Little
Fishes. One day he and his men shoot down an English plane,
and the officer orders his men to shoot the pilot who has
bailed out. The guilt and shame of his order weigh heavily
on the officer. He can no longer face the children, witnesses
to his crime (pp. 154-169).

In Jan Terlouw's Michel a little Dutch boy crawls onto
his roof when no one is watching. The view is grand, so he
decides to go around to where he can look down on the street.
He is having a glorious time and is curious about the sudden
commotion below. When he realizes he is the center of attention, he becomes frightened. No one is quite sure how to
get him down. The gutters look too corroded to hold an adult.
Suddenly a German soldier appears. He puts his bicycle
aside, rushes through the house, and climbs out on the roof.
His boot crashes through the gutter, but he throws himself
down and inches toward the child. He grabs Jochem's leg
and slowly, cautiously leads him off the roof. Before anyone
can thank him he rides quickly away (pp. 135-139).

A German submarine crashes on the rocks off North
Devon in David Rees's The Missing German. All but one of

the soldiers is taken prisoner. Two young English boys find
the missing German and agree to hide him. The boy is afraid
of being locked up, afraid of losing his freedom. He is simple and uncomplicated, physical rather than cerebral. His
wanting to be free has nothing to do with politics or ideology.

Though he knows that Stefan is very much like him,
Simon suffers a crisis of conscience hiding him. He, too,
is uncomplicated and has considered all Germans to be enemies. Keith, whose mother has been interned by the Germans for two years, has no such reservations. To him Stefan
is simply a human being in trouble.

Stefan cannot bear the strain of hiding so turns himself in. Simon is tortured both by his part in hiding Stefan
and by his failure to protect him but finds within his family
the assurance of love he so badly needs.

The third question that the narrator of Horst Burger's
Vier Fragen an meinen Vater asks is: With so many soldiers
dying, why did thousands of Hitler Youth volunteer for active
duty? Walter Jendrich answers his son that information was
very controlled. There were many who did their best to oppose Hitler and to avoid military service, but they had no
support, no encouragement, no one to whom they could turn.
He says, "Es gehört Mut dazu, nicht mit den Wölfen zu heu-
len." ("It takes courage not to howl with the wolves.")

They were taught that to die for the Fatherland was
the highest glory. To avoid service was cowardice and be-
trayal. Soldiers home on leave seldom told how it really
was, and those who did were not believed. Even in 1945
fanatics believed in victory. Fear of reprisals should they
lose convinced others that Germany must not lose.

During this hopeless time, Walter and his friends,
14 to 16 years old, decide to save Germany. A thirst for
adventure and unbelievable optimism propel them. In the
fall of 1944 they volunteer for field service, digging trenches
for retreating troops. Rations are so insufficient that they
have to steal. The only rule is that they not get caught.
They are convinced that the Hitler Youth and SS will win the
war in spite of the cowardice of the general population.

In the spring of 1945 they build tank traps. Food becomes yet scarcer. The boys long for battle but are told
there are not enough weapons. They steal some and are

caught.   The sudden order to evacuate the camp saves them
from being court martialed.   As the camp marches further
from the front, Walter and his three best friends slip away
to join fighting units.

Suddenly their lives change.   They had had heroic
visions.   The reality is different:

> ... Until now they had lived an orderly, almost
> regulated life.   Duties were assigned.   They ate
> at a particular time, and nights they had a roof
> over their heads and lay in a real bed.
> Now they were soldiers on active duty.   No one
> knew what the next hour would bring, when they
> would get something to eat or what they would find
> to crawl under for the night.   They could no longer
> pull back to read a book or to wash when they needed
> to.   Even conversations ceased.   Their senses were
> wide awake, tuned to ancient instincts--to survive,
> to recognize and meet dangers in time.   So must
> the caveman have lived in some gray yesteryear,
> the Neanderthals, hunters and gatherers.   They
> were constantly on the alert.   When they weren't
> marching, they learned to use each brief pause
> for a refreshing nap, no longer waiting until night.
> War didn't stop for dark.   [p. 107]

Max kills his first human being by mistake, a baker
who is trying to warn the boys to clear out before all hell
breaks loose.   Ashamed and terrified, he runs, his friends
close behind.   They rejoin their company and march away
from the front.   Unpatriotic jokes which a few days earlier
would have made Walter seethe no longer bother him.   When
battle with the French is near, only Max and Walter are still
following their leader.   All of the others have taken cover.
In the middle of the fighting, Walter is filled with raw terror
and can go no farther.   He doesn't want to be a hero.   He
just wants to live.   What idiots they were to volunteer for
this murderous adventure.   In the darkness he crawls back
down out of the line of fire.   He nearly slides by a medic
who has stopped to treat Max.   He puts out his hand to touch
his friend.   Where Max's head should be Walter touches only
a warm, pulpy mass.

Walter's friend Werner is shot in the stomach; Beppo
is blown apart.   When the fighting stops and the survivors
inspect the bloody field, Walter's commander tells him that
war is war and now the Germans must pay:

> "I'm a professional soldier," said Becker, mak-
> ing a sweeping gesture. "And that includes all of
> this. Just so we understand each other, I'm no
> Nazi. With us it's a family tradition that the sons
> become officers. If I had another profession ...
> but I'm a soldier. I never learned anything else.
> Now I have to pay the consequences. We had our-
> selves a good day at the expense of others as long
> as it went well. I'd be a pig if I complained now
> that things have changed. You have to pay for
> everything in life." [p. 136]

Walter tells his son that they did not fight for Hitler,
or so they told each other, but for the Fatherland. They
were only doing their duty and following orders. Watching
their cities being destroyed, hearing of the barbarity of the
Russian soldiers, they could tell themselves they were fighting for their homes and families.

The idealism of the narrator of Hans Peter Richter's
novels on the Third Reich also shrivels in the heat of battle.
Although his friends Günther and Heinz are more realistic,
they share the narrator's dream of heroism when the three
volunteer for active duty in I Was There. Heinz precedes
his younger friends into the military so is in a position to
take them both into his unit when they join. The cold and
hunger and discomfort quickly take their toll. Günther dozes
on guard duty and gives away their position with an accidental
burst of machine gun fire. The book ends in a barrage of
explosions, terror, and death, with Günther screaming for
Heinz.

Richter begins the third book in the series, The Time
of the Young Soldiers, with a statement of chilling simplicity:

> When the war broke out, I was fourteen years old;
> when it ended I was twenty. I was a soldier for
> three years. I thought that the things I saw and
> the things I did were justified because no one spoke
> out openly against them. [Translation by Anthea
> Bell, Preface]

As with many soldiers the narrator's dreams of glory are
shaped by the Hitler Youth. When he turns sixteen he begins nagging his parents to allow him to enlist. A sergeant
major quickly cuts the recruits down to size. Then a corporal teaches them how to handle a civilian who dares insult
the uniform:

> "... This oaf has insulted the honour of the Army,
> and surely you know that a stain on your honour
> can only be wiped out with blood? What you do is
> kill the filthy swine! Make sure he's good and dead,
> though, or he may end up in court giving evidence
> against you." [Translation by Anthea Bell, p. 33.]

At every chance the officers humiliate the men, already miserable from the cold and damp and repulsive food. A corporal puts the narrator through a debasing half hour of exercises then calls him a sissy when his hands tremble from exhaustion. The bayonet instructor teaches them how to free their weapon from their targets by kicking them in the balls. In the name of training, recruits are wounded and mutilated with callous disregard.

Then they are sent to the front. The narrator is shot through the chest and arm. Most of the gun crew ignore his anguished screams. In the field hospital he watches as his amputated arm drops into a dirty ammunition crate. One of the wounded tries to rape the Russian cleaning girl, and all of the others gather around. Even as she struggles she is careful not to hit their wounds and tells them goodbye when she frees herself.

The narrator goes home from the hospital. No one looks at his arm, no one mentions his loss, and he wonders what to do with his life. (Bell omits this in her translation.) At least he is out of the military, or so he thinks, but as soon as he reports back to his base he is reassigned.

He trains in a military academy, receives his commission as a lieutenant, and is sent to France. The 19-year-old lieutenant asserts his authority by ordering his men to do grueling rifle drills. He soon learns to overlook minor infractions and to empathize with his motley crew of convalescents, draft dodgers, ex-prisoners, and men with no battle experience. They are constantly on the move, see and deal in death, have fleeting liaisons with women, hide their heads when aircraft fly overhead, and think only about surviving.

The narrator is transferred to the eastern front. He sees the booty stolen from Russian shops, the Russian women used as maids and whores, sees the body of a hated sergeant killed by his own men. The Russian troops close in. The surrounded German soldiers beg to withdraw and finally ignore orders and flee in disarray, jockeying with refugees for places

on the few boats that can take them to safety. The narrator
hardly dares walk through the hostile crowd that greets them
in Copenhagen. Then suddenly an old woman rushes up to
him. He ducks, but she throws her arms around him and
shouts that peace has been declared.

Written from the perspective of a boy whose father
was declared missing in Stalingrad, Tu n'es pas mort à
Stalingrad by Christian Delstanches tells of the horrifying
winter in which the German troops were left by Hitler to
starve and freeze rather than capitulate. The same year
that the Berlin Wall ends the escape hopes of thousands of
East Germans, a young Berlin archaeologist reads Dernières
lettres de Stalingrad and finds in it a letter he is sure was
written by his father. After months of inquiries Walter finds
his father with a new wife and family in Vienna. Both he and
Walter's mother have formed new lives, each thinking the
other dead. His own need to know satisfied, Walter is con-
tent to leave his father's new family intact and to give his
mother peace of mind by assuring her that her husband did
die in the war.

In the search for his father and the long conversations
with him, Walter learns what it was like in those last days
of Stalingrad. In January 1943, 30,000 soldiers watch the
sky, listening for rescue planes. They are sick, undernour-
ished, wounded, and freezing. Their hopes follow a Junker
as it lands and unloads a useless cargo. Instead of food,
medicine, and mail the plane brings barbed wire, dozens of
kilograms of paper, motor fuel, and bombs. Hundreds of
wounded try to board but must wait until their evacuation
numbers are called. Two who try to escape by hanging onto
the landing gear fall to their deaths. No one bothers with
them. Death is too common (pp. 28-35).

One division covers its vehicles with straw to camou-
flage and protect them and then discovers that field mice have
damaged them beyond repair (p. 36). A plane drops three
parachutes. Three men sitting in a bombed-out tank watch
them fall and run to retrieve them. In one of the boxes they
find bread and sausages. Angry officers make them turn over
the boxes for central distribution. The men are desperate.
They know that little or none of the food will reach them.
They crawl back into the tank, complaining bitterly that those
who distribute the food are fat cats. Several hours later all
men are ordered out of their makeshift shelters. The tank
is searched, and in it are found two sausages, one of them

partly eaten.   The officers ask no questions, give no trial.
They simply shoot the thief (pp. 43-46).

The seriously wounded are left to rot.   Food and medicine are reserved for those still able to fight.   In the cellar
of a hotel the wounded await death.   Their limbs are gangre-
nous.   They lie in their own feces.   Tetanus and typhoid are
rampant.   Parasites feed in their wounds.   Marauders steal
their food and clothing.   Some of them are given fatal mor-
phine injections as their comrades retreat (pp. 107-109).

The survivors curse Hitler for having abandoned them,
for sacrificing them without pity.   After a winter of eating
frozen food, all are suffering from diarrhea.   Their ears,
noses, and eyelashes are frozen.   At the end of their weapons
and food, they are finally allowed to capitulate, not by Hitler
but by their own commanders.   The tattered remnants of the
once mighty army are marched off to Siberia, but Walter's
father and a comrade escape.   They find shelter and food and
hide until winter breaks and then flee across the Crimea and
on through Turkey, back to their devastated homeland (pp. 157-
174).

For those who served in the war and who participated
in the authorized atrocities of the Germans in occupied lands,
there could be no peace.   In the collection Damals war ich
vierzehn, Lene Mayer-Skumanz tells of her own father's
troubled return ("Der fremde Mann," pp. 101-104).   She and
her sister are small when he goes off to war and is wounded
and becomes a prisoner of war.   Mother keeps alive his memory with stories of his days on the stage and pictures of him
in many roles.   In June 1946 she is taking the girls to school
when her husband recognizes her on the street.   To Lene the
man who approaches them looks strange, gray.   Gradually the
girls adjust to him.   He plays with them, sings with them,
tells them stories of the hospital and the prisoner-of-war
camp, but he will say nothing about the war.   Night after
night he dreams of it, his screams bringing the girls to his
side.   The family tries to comfort him, to protect him with
their love, but he is tormented.   Lene remembers the nightmares:

> "What did you dream," I asked, "that made you
> cry out so?"
> "About the war," he said and for a moment was
> the strange, gray man we had met on the street.
> "It's all over; everything is all right again," said
> Mother and took us back to bed.   "Go to sleep."

But for a man who was in the war, it could
never again be all over, or all right, or the way
it was. We knew that now, my sister and I. Each
time we heard our father cry out from his dreams,
we learned it anew. [pp. 104-105]

Additional titles:

Borkowski, Dieter. Wer weiss, ob wir uns wieder-
      sehen.
Forman, James. Horses of Anger.
Grund, Josef Carl. Flakhelfer Briel.
Limpert, Richard. Über Erich.
Seiffert, Dietrich. Einer war Kisselbach.

PRISONERS OF WAR

Relatively few books for young readers tell the fate
of soldiers who were taken prisoner by either side. Max von
der Grün and Bette Greene give a generally favorable impression of the Americans as captors. René Antona and Fania
Fénelon give quite a different picture of the Germans.

Max von der Grün is 18 years old and stationed in
France when the war ends for him (Howl Like the Wolves,
pp. 254-271). It is August 1944, and he is glad to be alive.
The black soldier who flushes him out of a radio van gives
him the first chocolate he has eaten in months. After a few
months in a camp in Scotland, he and about a thousand other
prisoners are shipped to the United States. The next three
years he spends in Monroe, Louisiana. He describes the conditions in the camp:

We had very good accommodations at the camp.
We slept in beds on clean white sheets, and we were
given plenty to eat. The American guards treated
us well and were even friendly toward us. The
Nazi propaganda machine had told us daily that soon
America, too, would begin to suffer from the effects
of the war. None of this was true, for every day
we were given meat, fruit, vegetables, salad, and
white bread--things we had only dreamed about in
Germany. We prisoners of war were fed better
than the German soldiers at the front.
America could even afford to waste food, while

in Germany and in the German-occupied countries
people were starving--and starving to death.   There
were several playing fields in the camp where, during our free time, we used to play soccer and hand-
ball.   We needed sawdust to mark the fields.   One
day when I asked the American commandant for a
few bags of sawdust so that we could mark out the
fields for our games, he was at a loss to know
what to do at first.   Where could he get sawdust
when there were no sawmills in the area? However,
he himself was a sports enthusiast, so he gave us
two bags of pure wheat flour, and on another occasion he gave us a bag of powdered sugar.

Mad as this may sound, it is true.   In Germany
the prisoners were stretching their arms through
the barbed wire and begging the people outside for
a piece of bread or a potato, but the people outside
had nothing to eat themselves.

Yet in the southern United States we were strew-
ing wheat flour and powdered sugar over a soccer
field.   [Translation by Jan van Huerck, p. 260]

So imbued are they with twelve years of Nazi propaganda that many of the inmates believe that President Roose-
velt's death on April 12, 1945, will prove the turning point
in the war, that German victory is now assured.   When they
are shown films of German atrocities, many are deeply
ashamed, but others laugh at the fairy stories invented by
the Americans.

The prisoners work in the fields on the farms around
the camp.   They are paid for their work and can buy such
things as chocolate, cigarettes, and stationery at the camp
canteen.   Max begins to read the works of authors banned in
Germany and to hope for a better tomorrow.

All of Jenkinsville, Arkansas, is waiting when 20 German soldiers arrive by train (Bette Greene, Summer of My
German Soldier).   In their denim pants and blue work shirts,
the POW's look disappointingly ordinary, hardly the rabid
beasts people expected.   They are put to work in the cotton
fields around the town.

Greene says little about the camp itself, for the important story is the loving friendship that develops between
an escaped POW and Patty, an abused child who shelters
him.   Anton's escape, however, is not motivated by mistreat-

ment but by a need to be free.   So deeply does Anton care
for the Jewish child who offers him her love that he nearly
gives himself away when he sees her father beat her.   Ruth,
the Bergen family's black helper, sees Anton but says nothing
until she can ask Patty later about him.   She tells Patty:

> ... "That man come a-rushing out from the safety
> of his hiding 'cause he couldn't stand your pain and
> anguish no better'n me.   That man listens to the
> love in his heart.   Like the Bible tells us, when a
> man will lay down his life for a friend, well, then
> there ain't no greater love in this here world than
> that. "   [p. 130]

Guy Lambert becomes a prisoner of the Germans when
Pétain orders the French soldiers to surrender to the Germans
or be shot as traitors (René Antona, Les évasions du brigadier Lambert).   The humiliated French are marched to a
prison camp.   The heat and their heavy loads slow them down,
but stragglers are beaten.   In their first camp the prisoners
get a taste of the barbarity the SS have in store for them.
Leaving there, they are housed for a month in airplane hang-
ars before being taken to Berlin and the camp called Stalag
II D.   Along their route they are stoned by jeering children.

There are 32,000 prisoners crowded into Stalag II D.
They are given a daily ration of one-fifth of a loaf of bread,
a tablespoon of jam, and watery soup.   Lambert's first escape is with a comrade, who hampers his progress and requires constant encouragement.   Ten days later they are
found by a troop of Hitler Youth and turned over to the authorities.

Guy is sentenced to 21 days of solitude, limited rations, and interrogations.   Every three days he is given a
small amount of food.   He tries to make it last the three
days, but by the next morning he has devoured every crumb
of bread and drop of soup.   Fellow prisoners help keep him
alive by smuggling bits of food to him and celebrate the day
of his release by cutting their own rations to prepare a special soup.   He finds a solidarity among these prisoners he
has never known before or since.

The days in the punishment camp almost never vary:
reveille at six a.m., roll call (often prolonged), breakfast,
sport (the SS version of it), then work, which the POW's
sabotage as inconspicuously as possible.   When the SS suspect

sabotage, they order men on "tours de baraques." The prisoners have to run 15 to 30 laps around the barracks in their
awkward wooden shoes. The space between the barbed wire
and the barracks is narrow, and at each corner stands a
guard with a bayonet. The SS take cruel pleasure in these
harrowing races.

All of the POW's in the punishment camp dream of
escaping. One day two are missing at roll call and are
never caught. Two others escape from a truck taking them
to and from their farm work. Another walks out the main
gate with a leather briefcase under his arm. Yet another
pulls the same trick holding a file of papers.

After four months Lambert is allowed to join the main
camp. The work is so hard, the rations so meager, that he
knows he will have to escape soon or he will be too weak.
Once again he is persuaded to include a comrade in his plans,
one who leaves the camp with his pack filled with books and
tobacco instead of survival rations. In spite of Faubert's
carelessness and naiveté, the two make good their escape
and join the resistance in France.

While Guy Lambert was himself a victim of SS brutality, he insists that the Russian prisoners were treated far
worse. They were tortured, starved, and murdered by their
captors. Those who survived were sent to concentration
camps and treated like beasts. Thus the story which Fania
Fénelon relates in Playing for Time (pp. 50-52) is all the
more touching.

One night she leaves her bed and looks out at the
snow falling on Auschwitz. On the horizon appears a troop
of twenty Russian soldiers, marching barefoot and in rags.
They march shoulder to shoulder with proud steps. Coming
abreast of an SS officer they raise their caps, and the SS
snaps a return salute. Fania stares in wonder at these unbroken men. Bronia, a young Russian Aryan, joins her at
the window and tells the legend of these men:

> "I heard about those men when I arrived in the
> camp in April '43. In '41 the German army in-
> vaded my country and took soldiers prisoner. They
> were brought here, to Auschwitz. At the time it
> was just endless marsh with an occasional birch
> tree on the horizon. The SS decided that the Rus-
> sian soldiers would build their own camp. But the

Russians said: 'No, we are soldiers and we will
not build our own cage.'' The Germans replied that
if they wanted to eat and sleep, they would have to
work. The Russians refused. 'Arbeiten, arbeiten,'
insisted the Germans. More blank refusals from the
Soviet soldiers. They wrapped themselves in their
greatcoats and lay down then and there, in the mud
of those swamps. The SS continued with their side
of the exchange but the Russians stopped answering.
They died of cold and hunger, one after the other.
We don't know what the Germans did with the corpses.
Perhaps they sank into the mud, this living Auschwitz mud--perhaps they are here, right under our
feet.... Twenty of them survived, still refusing
to work. The SS knew when they were beaten: they
offered them clothes and shoes, but the soldiers
wouldn't take them because they belonged to the deportees. The only job they agreed to do was to
distribute the bread, very early in the morning.''

Bronia was silent. It was impossible to disen-
tangle truth from legend in this tale.

"Look at those men, they are our bread passing
by.''

Our bread, our hope, our certainty.... [Trans-
lation by Judith Landry, pp. 51-52]

BIBLIOGRAPHY

For the convenience of teachers and librarians, this annotated bibliography contains the following information:

1. Original edition and translations. Paperback publishers are indicated in parentheses; an explanation of the abbreviations used follows the bibliography. Pages cited in the text refer to the editions listed first unless otherwise indicated. If the original edition is in a language other than English, German, or French, original language, title, and date of publication are given. If the title has changed between an earlier and later edition, both titles are given. All books published in France or Belgium are in French; those from Germany, Austria, or Switzerland are in German; those published in the United States, Australia, or Great Britain are in English.

2. Country in which the book is set.

3. Fiction (F) or non-fiction (NF).

4. Rating in terms of pertinence to a study of World War II and broadly defined reading level.

Pertinence:
1 Should be read by everyone
2 Of considerable interest
3 Moderately interesting
4 Useful if nothing else is available
5 Of little interest

Reading level:
E Easy to read: from age 10
A Of average difficulty: aimed at a young adult audience
M Mature: written at an adult level but appropriate for high school students

Example: (Germany, NF: 1A) following the annotation indi-
cates that the book is set in Germany, is non-fiction, should
be read by everyone, and is of average difficulty.

Alexejew, Sergej. Es war ein grosser Krieg. Tr. from
  Russian by Max Hummeltenberg. E. Berlin: Kinderbuchverlag, 1980. Orig. in Russian: Title not given,
  1975.
      A poorly written propaganda piece touting the heroism
  of the Soviet citizens against the fascist barbarians. The
  people display complete solidarity; everyone wants to do
  his part. The Soviet troops free Poland, Rumania, Bul-
  garia, and Hungary and fight valiantly in Berlin. They
  are helpful and generous to hungry children. Adventure
  without excitement, propaganda without redeeming literary
  or historical merit. The tragic, heroic story deserves
  a better telling. (Eastern Europe and Germany, NF:
  5E)

Allan, Mabel Esther. Time to Go Back. London: Abelard-
  Schuman, 1972.
  _____. In jenem Frühjahr in Liverpool. Tr. from
  English by Gertrud Rukschico. Recklinghausen: Bitter,
  1976. (Arena)
      Fascinated by the poetry of her Aunt Larke, who was
  killed in the bombing of Liverpool, Sarah jumps at the
  chance to accompany her mother to Larke's home in
  nearby Wallasey. She is about the age Larke was when
  she was killed. Reading her poetry and walking in her
  footsteps, Sarah begins to be displaced in time. She
  lives through two bombing raids on Wallasey, becomes
  fond of a young man, Hilary, and is with Larke on her
  last day. Back in her own time she meets and falls in
  love with another Hilary, son of the first. Shaken by
  her experience, she writes it down and gives it to her
  mother to read. Her mother is deeply moved because
  both she and Hilary, Sr., remember a Sarah who appeared several times during the war and disappeared
  without a trace. Original twist to a war story with vivid
  scenes of air raids in Merseyside. (Great Britain, F:
  3A)

Antona, René. Et pourtant l'aube se leva. Paris: Éditions
  Magnard, 1968. (Magnard)

Scenes from occupied France: the desperation of refugees and the bravery and ingenuity of those who dared resist the Germans. Antona credits his countrymen with
heroism and gritty determination. (France, F: 2A)

_____. Les évasions du brigadier Lambert. Paris: Édi-
itions Magnard, 1974. (Magnard)
The account of Lambert's escapes from German prisoner-of-war camps is written as though the biographee
himself were speaking. Vivid portrayal of the brutality
of the camps. An exciting story which ends with Lambert's reaching the unoccupied section of France. (France,
NF: 2A)

Arnold, Elliott. A Kind of Secret Weapon. New York:
Scribner's, 1969.
An entire Danish family becomes involved in the re-
sistance, publishing uncensored news for wide distribution.
Lars Jensen is killed, but his wife and 11-year-old son
carry out his plan to force the transfer of the local Ges-
tapo chief. Shows the solidarity of the Danes under the
Germans. An exciting, simply told story. (Denmark,
F: 1A)

_____. A Night of Watching. New York: Fawcett, 1973.
_____. La nuit de veille. Tr. from English by François
Ponthier. Paris: Presses de la Cité, 1968.
_____. Zwei Meilen über den Sund. Tr. from English
by Ilse V. Lauterbach. Gütersloh: Bertelsmann, 1968.
Fictionalized account of the Danish resistance move-
ment and the rescue of the Jews. (Denmark, F: 1A)

Baer, Frank. Die Magermilchbande. Mai 1945: fünf Kinder
auf der Flucht nach Hause. Hamburg: Albrecht Knaus,
1979.
A small group of children are thrown to their own de-
vices. Without adults to guide them, they make their
way across war-torn Czechoslovakia to return to their
homes in Berlin. Written for adults but with such story-
telling skill that high school students could read it easily.
Accurate picture of the grim struggle of civilians to survive in the middle of war. (Czechoslovakia and Germany,
1M)

Balderson, Margaret. When Jays Fly to Bárbmo. New York:
World Pub. Co. , 1969.
_____. Eichelhäher über Bárbmo. Tr. from English by
Hans-Georg Noack. Ravensburg: Maier, 1974. (Maier)

One of the few books to deal with the occupation of
Norway. Even the lives of the nomadic Lapps are changed
as age-old patterns are destroyed by the occupiers. The
indomitable spirit of the Norwegians shines through the
splendid characters. (Norway, F: 2A)

Bastian, Horst. Wegelagerer: eine Freundschaft in den Wir-
ren der Nachkriegszeit. Würzburg: Arena-Taschenbuch,
1979. (Arena)
In the years following the war an orphan becomes part
of the struggle to survive and rebuild. He experiences
hunger and cold, witnesses thefts, plundering, cheating,
and lying. Determined to remain free, he wanders from
town to town, always hiding from authorities but at the
same time holding fast to the small child he found in the
rubble near where his mother was killed. The story has
little to lighten the bleakness. Its characters are almost
universally base. Originally published in the DDR. (Germany, F: 4A)

Bawden, Nina. Carrie's War. Philadelphia: Lippincott,
1973. (Penguin)
_____. Hörst du, es ist ganz nah. Tr. from English by
Inka Steiger-von Muralt. Köln: Benziger, 1976.
Carrie and her brother are evacuated from London to
a small Welsh mining village. There the war is far
away and plays only a small role in their lives. A rare
blend of humor, suspense, and fine writing. (Great Britain, F: 3A)

Bayer, Ingeborg. Ehe alles Legende wird. Baden-Baden:
Signal, 1979.
Through primary materials and accompanying text, the
author traces the rise of National Socialism, the course
of the Third Reich, and the danger of neo-Nazism at
home and abroad. The editor, publisher, and others recall their own war experiences and try to explain how
young people became such willing followers of the Nazi
movement. Even today, when she sees a film of a Nazi
demonstration, Bayer remembers the excitement she felt.
By comparing the propaganda and atrocities of the Third
Reich with the rise of right-wing extremism today, Bayer
has written a powerful cautionary piece. (Germany, NF:
1A)

Benchley, Nathaniel. Bright Candles: a Novel of the Danish
Resistance. New York: Harper & Row, 1974.

Resistance of the Danes to the German occupation.
As the Germans become more vicious, the resolve of the
Danes hardens, and all of the Hansens become.involved in
sabotage. When the Germans start to round up the Jews,
the Hansens help to arrange the massive operation which
evacuates the Jews while German ships wait in the harbor
to deport them. (Denmark, F: 1A)

Berger, Peter. Im roten Hinterhaus. Stuttgart: Schwabenverlag, 1966. (Arena)
The various forces at play during the 1920's and 1930's
are mirrored in a working-class family from an industrial
city along the Rhine. Unemployment, poverty, clashes
between Nazis and Communists, fascination with Hitler,
anti-Semitism, and the outbreak of war all find echoes
in the large family. The narrator describes his family
in such picturesque, often humorous terms, they seem
to come alive. (Germany, F: 1A)

Bloch, Marie Halun. Displaced Person. New York: Lothrop,
Lee & Shepard, 1978.
German refugees from the Ukraine suffer persecution
under both the Soviet and German regimes. The story
is choppy, disjointed, and self-pitying. Interesting as
an example of an attitude still prevalent today: Innocent
German settlers in the eastern territories were set upon
by their neighbors and/or the Soviet military. They lost
everything and were forced to flee. The fault lies not
with Hitler or his followers but with the countries which
threw them out. (Germany, F: 4E)

Blume, Judy. Starring Sally J. Friedman As Herself.
Scarsdale, N.Y.: Bradbury Press, 1977. (Dell)
Sally, whose aunt and cousin were gassed in a concentration camp, becomes obsessed with their deaths and
convinced that an old man who offers children candy is
really Hitler in disguise. The story is set in Miami
Beach shortly after the war and is concerned primarily
with Sally's learning to cope with fears and uncertainties.
(U.S., F: 4E)

Bodenek, Ján. Ein Sommer in Rovne. Tr. from Slovak by
Barbara Zulkarnian. E. Berlin: Kinderbuchverlag, 1980.
Orig. Slovak: Leto na Rovniach, 1975.
A rich, greedy farmer uses an orphan boy as a slave
until brave partisans parachute into the area and force
the farmer and his fascist compatriots to surrender.

The equation is simple: fascist = capitalist = tyrant. A
didactic, lifeless propaganda piece. (Czechoslovakia, F:
5E)

Bonzon, Paul-Jacques. Mon Vercors en feu. Paris: Hachette, 1975.
    Superficial but adventuresome story of the resistance
movement in Vercors, a major center of the maquis.
The village of Combe-Froide suffers under the heavy
hand of the Germans. Luc's family becomes deeply involved in the resistance when they hide a Canadian aviator. The author has surprisingly little to say about the
massacre in Vercors, for which French collaborators
must share the blame. (France, F: 3A)

Borkowski, Dieter. Wer weiss, ob wir uns wiedersehen:
Erinnerungen an eine Berliner Jugend. Frankfurt am
Main: Fischer, 1980. (Fischer)
    Reconstructed diary of the author, a loyal Hitler
Youth member whose beliefs withstood severe tests but
remained intact until the end of the war. In rewriting
the journal that the East Berlin authorities confiscated
from him in 1960, Borkowski has let his adult experiences
and knowledge color his memory. Long quotations and
political observations speak for the adult rather than the
adolescent. (Germany, NF: 2M)

Borowsky, Peter. Adolf Hitler. Hamburg: Cecilie Dressler,
1978.
    Heavily illustrated biography of Adolf Hitler. Written
in the hope of encouraging readers to form their own
judgments. An objective introduction to the subject that
needs to be accompanied by other books which delve more
deeply into cause and effect. The author concentrates on
the person of Hitler and the events of his life and avoids
comment in such a way that might mislead some young
readers. (Germany, NF: 2A)

Bosch, Martha-Maria. Judith. Stuttgart: Spectrum, 1980.
    Two old friends meet after twenty years: Judith, a
Jew whose family sent her to safety in England and then
perished in Auschwitz, and the narrator, who remembers
the excitement and idealism of the times as well as their
dark underside. A story of what it was like for Jews to
survive the Holocaust from the safety of other countries
and yet feel keenly the guilt, fear, and pain of terrible
loss. The impact is lessened by an overly simplistic
style. (Germany, F: 3E)

Bossman, Dieter. "Was ich über Adolf Hitler gehört habe..."
Folgen eines Tabus: Auszüge aus Schuler-Aufsätzen von
heute. Göttingen: Fischer, 1977. (Fischer)
    Results of a survey made in October 1976-April 1977.
3042 German school children from ages 10 to 23 wrote
themes on what they had heard about Adolf Hitler. The
misconceptions and misinformation they revealed were
viewed by many as a national scandal. (Germany, NF:
1M)

Brand, Sandra. I Dared to Live. New York: Shengold,
1978.
    Autobiography of a Polish Jew who posed as an Aryan
to escape annihilation and used her position as an interpreter to save hundreds of Jews. A simple, evocative
book about a determined suvivor. (Poland, NF: 2M)

Brodman, Aliana. ... und du bist ab. Dortmund: Schaffstein, 1976. (dtv)
    As the child of concentration camp survivors, Gabi is
doubly different. She is Jewish in a Christian country
and the child of parents who are, and always will be,
shadowed by sadness. Sensitively written story of a child
who longs to be like the other children and cannot be, for
anti-Semitism has shattered her family and lives on in her
friends. (Germany, F: 1E)

_____. ... damit die Welt nicht stumm bleibt. Dortmund:
Schaffstein, 1980.
    Follows ... und du bist ab (listed above). Gabi tries
to find roots in a past about which no one will speak and
to which she has no ties yet which colors her present.
(Germany, F: 1A)

Bruckner, Karl. Mann ohne Waffen. Wien: Jugend und
Volk, 1967.
    Fictionalized account of Bruckner's rescue of a pris-
oner of the Gestapo. He is sailing toward Hamburg in
March 1938 when in Santos he sees a man brought on
board in chains. Conflict with the Gestapo agents convinces him that the German occupation of Austria is not
just a rumor. When his plan to help the prisoner succeeds, he becomes a deadly enemy to the Gestapo. (Sea
voyage, F: 2A)

Bruckner, Winfried. Die toten Engel. Das Schicksal jüdischer
Kinder während des 2. Weltkrieges im Warschauer Ghetto.
Ravensburg: Maier, 1976. (Maier)

A group of orphaned children of the Warsaw ghetto
slip over the wall at night to steal food. The author
writes movingly of the incredible will to resist of Jews
who fought the destruction of the ghetto, who clung to
life and hope in the face of overwhelming odds. (Poland,
F: 2A)

Burger, Horst. Vier Fragen an meinen Vater. Reutlingen:
Ensslin & Laiblin, 1976. New title: Warum warst du
in der Hitlerjugend? Reinbeck bei Hamburg: Rowohlt,
1978. (Rowohlt)
A father answers the penetrating questions of his son
about the persecution of the Jews, the complicity of the
Hitler Youth, the eagerness for battle of young boys, and
the refusal of Germans to accept responsibility once the
war was lost. Burger sees a clear connection between
fascism and capitalism and tells which groups profited
and which suffered under the National Socialists. An important feature of the book is his examination of what
happened with the Nazis after the war and of the need
for self-examination today. A book that should be read
by all young people. (Germany, F: 1A)

Burnford, Sheila. Bel Ria. Boston: Little, Brown and Co.,
1978. (Bantam).
_____ . Bel Ria. Tr. from English by René Baldy. Paris:
Presses de la Cité, 1978.
_____ . Bel Ria. Tr. from English by Manfred Ohl.
Frankfurt: Krüger, 1978.
Through the device of a remarkable little dog, the
author explores the effect of war on ordinary people.
In each of the three parts of the book, the love and trust
of Bel Ria work a change in people whose lives are torn
by war. Burnford's book is thought provoking and has a
more mature appeal. It includes some of the most vivid
scenes of war's violence and of the reaffirmation of human love. (Battleship and Great Britain, F: 1M)

Burton, Hester. In Spite of All Terror. Cleveland: World,
1972.
_____ . Auf der anderen Seite. Tr. from English by Grit
Körner. Stuttgart: Union, 1972.
When war threatens, Liz is evacuated from London
along with other children. Even in the country the course
of the war overshadows all, as her guardian's sons volunteer for battle, their grandfather helps with the evacuation of Dunkirk, and Liz braves the dreaded bombing of

London to rescue her cousin.   The author clearly depicts
the "stiff upper lip" that made Britain such a formidable
foe.   (Great Britain, F: 1A)

Cénac, Claude.   Le printemps viendra deux fois.   Paris:
    Hachette, 1970.
        Gil is impatient to join his father in the maquis and
jealous of all the attention his friends are giving Cathérine, a Parisian whose mother has sent her to the
Périgord for safety.   To end the enmity between Gil and
Cathérine, Gil's teacher tells the two of his part in the
resistance and the need for solidarity.   The three throw
their energies into hiding an English parachutist and saving the villagers from the Nazis.   Action without substance.   If all members of the maquis had been as free
with their tongues as those in this book, they would all
have been arrested early in the game, and the French
would have no proud chapter to look back on.   (France,
F: 4A)

Cernaut, Jean.   Comptes à rendre.   Paris: Éditions la Fa-
    randole, 1980.   (Farandole)
        Two French boys resolve to expose a Nazi war crim-
inal living as a successful businessman in Stuttgart.
They are idealistic and scornful of the older generation.
Theirs is the superiority of the young and innocent.   Unfortunately, the too-frequent reiterations of their nobility
become more annoying than convincing, and the book as
a whole is rather flat.   Nevertheless, it is an unusual
book in its use of modern teens to remind young people
of a past that should not be forgotten.   More a condemnation of the failure of the Germans and French to take
concerted action against Nazi war criminals than of the
crimes themselves.   (France and Germany, F: 3A)

Ciravegna, Nicole.   La rue qui descend vers la mer.   Paris:
    Éditions Magnard, 1971.   (Magnard)
        The Germans evacuate and destroy an old quarter of
Marseille with access to the harbor, incarcerating its
inhabitants in Fréjus.   Envisioning himself as the hero
of a western movie, Aldo leads his little band of friends
through the dangers, watching over them like a mother
hen (and with about that much good sense).   The war is
a framework for a superficial, romantic story, whose
characters are more types than people.   Fun to read
but hard to take seriously.   (France, F: 3A)

_____. Aldo et Sarah.   Paris: Éditions Magnard, 1973.
(Magnard)
      Sequel to La rue qui descend vers la mer (listed above).
Aldo brings his little band home, dreams of glory, and
joins the resistance.   The war takes backstage to the
love story of Aldo and Sarah.   Highly romanticized.
(France, F: 3A)

Cohen, Barbara.   Benny.   New York: Lothrop, Lee & Shep-
      ard, 1977.
      Benny Rifkind is good at one thing, baseball, but no
one in his family understands how important it is to him.
His sensitive response to Arnulf, a young German Jew
who is obnoxious and insolent because of his personal
despair, opens his family's eyes.   At last they understand Benny's special character.   Sensitive family story.
The shadow of war touches them through Arnulf.   (U.S.,
F: 3E)

Colman, Hila.   Ellie's Inheritance.   New York: Wm. Mor-
      row, 1979.
      Ellie and her father struggle to make ends meet in
New York in the early 1930's.   The influence of fascism
stretches across the ocean.   Through her involvement
with a committed socialist and then with a German refugee, Ellie becomes engaged in events beyond the confines
of her own life.   The war is foreshadowed, but the book
is primarily a love story.   (U.S., F: 3A)

Cooper, Susan.   Dawn of Fear.   New York: Harcourt Brace
      Jovanovich, 1970.
      In spite of air raids and the sight of London burning
in the distance, life remains happy and uncomplicated for
three friends.   But coming face to face with their parents' fears and the grown-up hatred of two older boys
frees them from the protective shell of childhood and sets
them in a frightening world for which they are not yet
ready.   (Great Britain, F: 2E)

Däs, Nelly.   Wölfe und Sonnenblumen.   Hamburg: Oetinger,
      1978.
      The descendants of German settlers in Russia are
persecuted by the militia in the 1930's and spend years
wandering in the Soviet Union.   Father is arrested, and
Mother comes to hope that the Germans will invade Russia and take them back to the Germany she has long
dreamed of but never seen.   As the tide turns against

the Germans in their aborted attempt to conquer Russia,
the family treks from one refuge to another, living often
in the most primitive conditions yet somehow landing feet
first each time. Däs is a fine storyteller and stays true
to the perspective of a child. Still, she gives the impression that the suffering of the Germans driven from
the eastern lands is comparable with the atrocities suffered
in those lands at the hands of the Germans, a dangerous
implication. (Russia and Poland, NF: 2A)

_____. Der Zug in die Freiheit. Hamburg: Oetinger,
1976.
    Though published before Wölfe und Sonnenblumen, this
book continues the family's story. Driven from their
home in Russia, the family is given shelter in Poland at
the expense of Poles. Nelly is sent to a Hitler Youth
camp. Once again they suffer the nightmare of forced
flight as Russian troops close in. Settling in Germany,
they find that here, too, they are second-class citizens.
That the family's "train to freedom" is toward the Germany of the Third Reich is a disturbing glossing of history. (Poland and Germany, NF: 2A)

Damals war ich vierzehn. Berichte und Erinnerungen von
Winfried Bruckner, Vera Ferra-Mikura, Wolf Harranth,
Nadine Hauer, Hilde Leiter, Lene Mayer-Skumanz, Willi
Meissel, Christine Nöstlinger, Ernst Nöstlinger, Brigitte
Peter, Rudolf Pritz, Käthe Recheis, Renate Welsh.
Wien: Jugend und Volk, 1978.
    The many faces of a terrible time are recalled by
people who experienced them as children and young people.
The remembrances are painful and moving and tell of air
raids, informers, soldiers, concentration camp victims,
Jews, and children struggling to comprehend. A super-
ior collection. (Austria, NF: 1A)

Degens, T. Transport 7-41-R. New York: Viking, 1974.
(Dell)
    A trainload of evacuees from the Russian sector rolls
slowly toward Cologne in 1946. A 13-year-old girl, sent
away by her parents, is contemptuous of all adults but
cannot ignore the plight of an old man who has promised
his dying wife a resting place in Cologne. Through the
terrible ordeal, the disillusioned child gains something
to believe in and a new faith in at least one human being.
Unlike Däs, the author sympathizes with the evacuees
without forgetting what caused them to become refugees.
(Germany, F: 2A)

Del Castillo, Michel. Tanguy. Paris: René Julliard, 1957.
_____. Child of Our Times. Tr. from French by Peter
Green. New York: Dell, 1960. (Dell)
_____. Elegie der Nacht. Tr. from French by Leonharda
Gescher. Reinbeck bei Hamburg: Rowohlt, 1980. (Row-
ohlt)
  Autobiographical novel of a Spanish boy who flees
Franco's troops with his mother, is interned by the
French when his father turns them in, and then deported
to a German concentration camp. When he is finally re-
united with his parents, he has experienced too much pain
to recognize them as part of him. Tanguy's experiences
in the concentration camp are among the most tragic recorded for young people. (France and Germany, F: 1A)

Delstanches, Christian, and Hubert Vierset. Tu n'es pas
mort à Stalingrad. Gembloux, Belgium: Duculot, 1973.
(Duculot)
  A young Berlin archeologist searches for his father,
who was declared missing in Stalingrad. In the course
of his search, he learns of the ghastly fate of the thousands of soldiers Hitler sacrificed in his mad scheme to
conquer Russia. (Germany and Russia, F: 2A)

Demetz, Hanna. Ein Haus in Böhman. Berlin: Ullstein,
1970. (Ullstein)
_____. The House on Prague Street. New York: St.
Martin's Press, 1980.
  One by one a proud, wealthy Jewish family (who feel
more Czech than Jewish) is reduced until at last only
Helenka, a Mischling, remains. It is a story of increasing horror, as the Germans tighten the noose around the
Jews. Even at war's end the hatred continues, for those
once under the thumb of the Nazis now treat those they
suspect of collaborating with the same brutality they have
suffered. (Czechoslovakia, F: 1A)

Des Pres, Terence. The Survivor: an Anatomy of Life in
the Death Camps. New York: Oxford, 1977. (PB)
  Explores the effect of surviving the death camps through
the experiences of those who lived. Those who did survive tell of the need to cooperate and maintain human
dignity in the face of the dehumanizing brutality of the
camp structure. Written for adults, this analysis is
accessible to high school students and is deeply moving.
(Death camps, NF: 1M)

Desroches, Alain. Hitler et les Nazis. Paris: Fernand
Nathan, 1968.
  Brief history of the Third Reich, with emphasis on
the military aspects of World War II. (Europe, NF: 2A)

Deutschkron, Inge. Ich trug den gelben Stern. Köln: Wissenschaft und Politik, 1978.
  With the help of Jewish and non-Jewish friends, Inge
and her mother survive the Nazi era. They are given
work, new identities, and changing shelters by people
who dare defy those who would eliminate all Jews. (Germany, NF: 1M)

Devaney, John. Hitler, Mad Dictator of World War II. New
York: Putnam's, 1978.
  Devaney has borrowed from a number of books about
Hitler to produce a personalized biography for young people. It is filled with quotations, but none is referenced.
The fictionalized style makes the book read like a novel
and gives a picture of a deranged, egocentric man. The
book is indexed, but the only reference to the sources
consulted is in the acknowledgments. (Germany, NF:
2A)

Drouet, Minou. Ouf de la forêt. Paris: Éditions G. P.,
1968.
  In spite of the German occupation, which wreaks havoc
on the normal patterns of life, Ouf retains a touching innocence and trust that extends to all, even if they wear
the uniform of the foe. His decision to help the resistance leads the boy into the dilemma of having to act
against an enemy he loves. A simple book yet one which
explores the impact of inhumanity on innocence. (France,
F: 2A)

Durand, Pierre. Vivre debout, la Résistance. Paris: Éditions la Farandole, 1974.
  Heavily illustrated, somewhat simplistic overview of
the resistance movement in France. Somewhat less than
half of the book actually deals with the resistance itself.
The remainder is a history of the war in France. (France,
NF: 3A)

Ecke, Wolfgang. Flucht. Die Geschichte einer Reise von
Deutschland nach Deutschland. Ravensburg: Maier, 1978.
(Maier)
_____. Flight Toward Home. Tr. from German by Anthony
Knight. New York: Macmillan, 1970.

_____. La fuite. Tr. from French by Jean-Louis Fon-
cine. Paris: Alsatia, 1967.
   A child orphaned by war is kept from joining his only
remaining relative by the restrictions in the Soviet sector
of Germany. Two years later he escapes to the West.
An adventure story in the mold of those which rue the
division of Germany without examining its causes. (Germany, F: 3E)

Ellis, Ella Thorpe. Sleep-walker's Moon. New York:
Atheneum, 1980.
   When Anna's father goes off to war in 1942, he leaves
her with the Raymonds. She has longed to be a part of
the Raymond family but now finds it racked by tensions
she had never seen in their lives. The author explores
the special poignancy of adolescence and the pressures
of war on one family. War casts its shadow but remains
in the background of this book. (U.S. , F: 4A)

Evenhuis, Gertie. What About Me? Tr. from Dutch by Lance
Salway. Harmondsworth, Middlesex, England: Puffin
Books, 1976. (Penguin). Orig. Dutch: En waarom ik
niet?, 1970.
   Eleven-year-old Dirk wants to do his part to resist
the Germans occupying his country, but when the chance
comes, he finds himself longing for the innocence and
security of childhood once again. Though simply written
the book has a surprising wealth of information about
the impact of war on people. (Holland, F: 1E)

Fährmann, Willi. Es geschah im Nachbarhaus. Würzburg:
Arena, 1968. (Arena)
   An instance of persecution of Jews at the end of the
19th century foreshadows the events of Crystal Night and
the rabid anti-Semitism of the Nazis. Though Fährmann's
story occurs long before World War II, it shows the roots
of racial mass psychosis which the Nazis later incorporated
into a political tenet. As such it is an important book,
placing German anti-Semitism in its historical context
and casting more light on the success of the Nazis.
(Germany, F: 1A)

_____. Das Jahr der Wölfe. Würzburg: Arena, 1962.
_____. The Year of the Wolves: the Story of an Exodus.
Tr. from German by Stella Humphries. London: Oxford
Univ. Pr. , 1973.
   In the winter of 1944-45 the Germans of East Prussia

flee their homes to avoid the sure revenge of the Russian
army.   The Bienmann family is caught in the dread flight.
Fellow travelers starve, freeze, fall through the ice.
They are caught in the path of first one army and then
another.   Fährmann portrays well the plight of the refugees without losing sight of its historical context.   (Germany, F: 1A)

Fénelon, Fania (pseud.).   Sursis pour l'orchestre.   Témoin-
age recueilli par Marcelle Routier.   Paris: Stock, 1976.
(Stock)
_____, with Marcelle Routier.   Playing for Time.   Tr.
from French by Judith Landry.   New York: Berkley
Books, 1979.   (Berkley)
_____.   Das Mädchenorchester in Auschwitz.   Tr. from
French by Sigi Loritz.   Frankfurt: Röderberg, 1980.
Interned in Auschwitz, the French cabaret singer survived as part of the women's orchestra, a bizarre musical group in the middle of hell.   Fénelon's recollections
are vivid and horrifying yet contain humor and humanity
as well.   (Auschwitz, NF: 1M)

Finckh, Renate.   Mit uns zieht die neue Zeit.   Baden-Baden:
Signal, 1979.
Cornelia Keller's lack of empathy for her fellow human
beings makes her a perfect candidate for leadership roles
in the Hitler Youth.   Stirred by the new ideals, bursting
with zealous enthusiasm for "Volk, Vaterland, und Führer,"
Nela refuses to believe all evidence of the rotten core of
National Socialism.   She stubbornly clings to her loyalty
until well after the war.   Though Nela is appalling, her
beliefs abhorrent, the book deserves an audience, for
there were many Nelas in the Third Reich.   (Germany,
F: 2A)

Foncine, Jean-Louis.   Le glaive de Cologne.   Paris: Alsatia,
1976.   (Epi)
Eight years after the war a group of French Scouts
is summoned to the Black Forest by an unusual request.
There Olivier at last solves the mystery surrounding the
death of his father in World War II.   A good story but
only minimally interesting for a study of the war.   (France
and Germany, F: 3A)

Fonvilliers, Georges.   L'enfant, le soldat et la mer.   Paris:
Éditions Magnard, 1968.   (Magnard)
Pierre and his school friends long to perform heroic

deeds to destroy the hated Germans yet Pierre cannot
keep himself from learning to love a German soldier who
has offered his friendship. The story has become something of a youth classic in France, the age-old confronta-
tion between loyalty to country and to humanity. (France,
F: 2A)

Forman, James. Ceremony of Innocence. New York: Haw-
    thorn, 1970. (Dell)
    Novel based on the resistance activities and execution
of Hans and Sophie Scholl. More romanticized than the
account by Vinke but one of the few accounts available
in English. (Germany, NF: 2A)

_____. Horses of Anger. New York: Farrar, Straus &
Giroux, 1967.
    Hans's fervent support of Hitler is tested when the
Hitler Youth member becomes a 15-year-old warrior and
faces a dichotomy in his loyalty: between the disillusionment and growing resistance of his beloved uncle and the
fanaticism of his long-time friend.

_____. My Enemy, My Brother. New York: Meredith
Press, 1979. (Schol. Bk. Serv.)
_____. La route d'Israël. Tr. from English by Gene-
viève Hurel. Paris: R. Laffont, 1971.
    Six teenagers who have survived the Holocaust emi-
grate to Palestine at a time when such a decision is
illegal and dangerous. While telling the story of their
new commitments and problems on a kibbutz, the author
uses flashbacks to describe their fates at the hands of
the Nazis. (Poland and Israel, F: 2A)

_____. The Survivor. New York: Farrar, Straus &
Giroux, 1976.
    A family of Dutch Jews is hounded by the Germans.
They go into hiding, but the Germans are relentless.
Flushed out of their refuge, they are interned in Ausch-
witz. Only David survives the war. (Holland/Westerbork/
Auschwitz, F: 2A)

_____. The Traitors. New York: Farrar, Straus &
Giroux, 1968.
    Two brothers choose different paths: Karl, that of
the Hitler Youth, and Paul, that of resistance. The clash
of beliefs comes to its head when Paul and his father
form a group to prevent the SS from destroying the town

in the path of the Americans and Karl leads the children
in his Hitler Youth group in a fanatic attempt to save the
town from the enemy. (Germany, F: 2A)

Francke, Gunhild. Last Train West. Sydney, Australia:
     Hodder and Stoughton, 1977.
     In Silesia, Francke's family is largely untouched by
war until Germans are evacuated from the east as German soldiers retreat. Cold, hunger, and primitive conditions take their toll as the refugees trudge west. The
Americans who occupy the town in which the family finds
refuge are insensitive and impose severe restrictions.
Only when Father finds a teaching position in Lübeck, and
the rest of the family joins relatives in Sweden do their
fortunes improve. Francke blames all of their problems
on the Russians and Americans without ever asking what
brought them to battle with Germany. (Germany, NF:
3E)

Frevert, Hans, and Marieluise Christadler. Masken des
     Krieges: ein Lesebuch. 2. Ausgabe. Baden-Baden:
     Signal, 1979.
     The faces of war from early times through the pres-
ent. Under the heading, "Imperialistische Krieg II," pp.
70-116, the editors have brought together letters, stories,
and firsthand accounts by both perpetrators and victims
to form a mosaic which damns war. A good book to
counter the textbook approach to the history of wars,
which too often makes them seem like mere chess problems, with no relation to human suffering. (NF: 1A)

Friedländer, Saul. Quand vient le souvenir.... Paris:
     Éditions du Seuil, 1978.
          . When Memory Comes. Tr. from French by Helen
     R. Lane. New York: Farrar, Straus & Giroux, 1979.
     (Avon)
          . Wenn die Erinnerung kommt. Tr. from French
     by Helgard Oestreich. Stuttgart: Deutsche Verlags-
     Anstalt, 1979.
     Fine memoirs of a Jewish boy whose family flees
Prague only to find themselves in danger later in Paris.
His parents leave him in a boarding school and try to
flee but are turned over to the French militia by the
Swiss border guards (because they are neither old nor
sick--nor accompanied by children). In the ultra-con-
servative school he attends, the boy leaves the camp of
the persecuted for that of the persecutors. By the end

of the war he has become a supporter of Pétain and has
decided to become a priest. A perceptive priest talks
to him of Auschwitz and of the long history of the Jews,
wanting him to be free to choose. An older, more pro-
found loyalty re-establishes itself. The boy returns to
Judaism and immigrates to Palestine. Mature students
should be encouraged to read this memoir, which shows
the terrible shock it was for assimilated Jews to realize
they had been chosen for destruction and the psychological
toll on those who changed their identities and survived.
(Czechoslovakia, France, and Israel, NF: 1M)

Fuchs, Ursula. Emma oder Die unruhige Zeit. Neunkirchen:
   Anrich, 1979.
        Julie is six when the war breaks out. With Emma,
   the doll she receives for her birthday, she lives all of
   the dislocations of the war--air raids, children's evacu-
   ations, and liberation by the Americans. Only when the
   family flees the Russians to enter the British zone is
   Emma left behind. The author holds to her child heroine's perspective throughout the book and has little to
   say about the fate of the Jews or the activities of the
   Nazis. One of the few books on the subject written for
   the very young, around ages 8 to 10. (Germany, F:
   1E)

Gardam, Jane. A Long Way from Verona. London: Hamish
   Hamilton, 1971.
        Because of her ruthless honesty, Jessica finds that
   people often like her less the longer they know her. Her
   outspokenness is a part of her determination to become
   a writer and to record life exactly. She also has a pen-
   chant for trouble and earns enough demerits to be expelled from school, but other concerns (such as an escaped Italian POW) keep the headmistress from tallying
   the marks of her bad conduct. The Communist son of
   a rich family decides Jessica must see the slums of London to understand life, but when they are caught there
   in a hellish air raid, it is he who is most ready to abandon the victims. Jessica's self-confidence and her belief
   in her writing sink to their lowest point for lack of nur-
   turing. Then her poem wins the Times' poetry competition. In the glow of success, Jessica's confidence is
   restored. (Great Britain, F: 3A)

Gehrts, Barbara. Nie wieder ein Wort davon? München:
   Deutscher Taschenbuch Verlag, 1978. (dtv)

The experience of two families of friends during the
Third Reich is related by 13-year-old Hanna. Though
opposed to Hitler, they appear to outsiders to be supporters of the regime. The children must join the Hitler
Youth and fight in a war they oppose. Nevertheless,
Hanna's father is arrested and sentenced to death. The
book takes place from 1940-1943 and portrays the terrible
price a repressive regime exacts from its citizens. (Germany, F: 2A)

Gervasi, Frank. Adolf Hitler. New York: Hawthorn Books,
1974.
Gervasi begins with Hitler's fanatic militarism in
World War I and builds a picture of his greed for power
and the frenzy with which he carried out his borrowed
ideas. A political history written specifically for adolescents. Thoroughly indexed. (Germany, NF: 2A)

Gray, Martin. Au nom de tous les miens (récit recueilli
par Max Gallo). Paris: Laffont, 1977. (L. G. F.)
_____. For Those I Loved. Tr. from French by Anthony
White. Boston: Little, Brown, 1972. (NAL)
_____. Der Schrei nach Leben. Die Geschichte eines
Mannes, der die Unmenschlichkeit besiegte, weil er an
die Menschen glaubte. Tr. from French by Roland Fleiss-
ner and Arno Aeby. München: Scherz, 1980.
Wrenching autobiography of a young Jewish man whose
grim determination to survive to tell of the treachery of
the Nazis carries him through the destruction of the Warsaw ghetto, Gestapo interrogations, and concentration
camps. After the war he builds a new life only to have
his wife and four children destroyed by a forest fire in
southern France. The French edition has been abridged
for younger readers. (Poland, NF: 1A; M for English
and German editions)

Green, Gerald. The Artists of Terezin. New York: Hawthorn Books, 1969. (Schocken)
Green writes with poetic anguish of the establishment
of Terezin, the model Jewish ghetto where the elite were
to die. Within its walls many of the best Jewish artists
of their time painted and sketched the wretched reality
behind the facade with which the Nazis fooled the outside
world. Green reproduces some of the works which survived to tell the tale. A troubling, moving attempt to
come to grips with the question of why the Holocaust
could happen. (Terezin, NF: 1M)

Greene, Bette. Summer of My German Soldier. New York:
    Dial Press, 1973. (Bantam)
        Patty Bergen, a 12-year-old Jewish girl who is as
    much of an outsider in her own family as she is in Jen-
    kinsville, Arkansas, hides a young German soldier who
    has escaped from the nearby prisoner-of-war camp. An-
    ton's loving acceptance of Patty gives her a core of se-
    curity she will need in the troubled years ahead, for he
    is caught and killed. Her father treats her as a slut,
    the town as a traitor, when they learn Patty hid an en-
    emy. The book is emotionally powerful. In the midst
    of small-minded, bigoted people, Patty, Anton, and Ruth
    (the family's black helper) stand tall, for their weapon
    against injustice is love. (U.S., F: 1A)

            . Morning Is a Long Time Coming. London: Ham-
    ish Hamilton, 1978. (Archway)
        Sequel to Summer of My German Soldier (listed above).
    Patty uses her grandparents' graduation gift to sail to
    Europe and try to come to grips with her loss of Anton,
    her years as an outcast, and her need to find her own
    identity. (U.S. and France, F: 4A)

Grosman, Ladislav. The Shop on Main Street. Tr. from
    Czech by Iris Urwin. Garden City, New York: Double-
    day, 1970. Orig. Czech: Obchod na korze, n.d.
            . Der Laden auf dem Korso. Tr. from Czech by
    Rudolf Iltis and Günter Deicke. München: Kindler, 1970.
        Tender yet shattering story of a decent man forced to
    violate his conscience until he is at last destroyed. An
    honest carpenter is told to Aryanize the notions shop of
    an old Jewish woman. Despised by both the Jewish com-
    munity which actually supports the shop and the fascists
    who have put him in charge of it, Tono finds refuge with
    old Mrs. Lautman, who regards him as just a kindly
    helper and companion. Events roll over both of them.
    Tono accidentally causes her death and hangs himself,
    a victim of events too large and too evil for him to con-
    trol. An intense, moving little book. (Czechoslovakia,
    F: 1A)

Grün, Max von der. Wie war das eigentlich? Kindheit und
    Jugend im Dritten Reich. Darmstadt: Luchterhand,
    1979.
            . Howl Like the Wolves: Growing Up in Nazi Ger-
    many. Tr. from German by Jan van Huerck. New York:
    Wm. Morrow, 1980.

Born in 1926, Max von der Grün experienced firsthand
the cruel efficiency with which the Nazis stifled all opposition to carry out Hitler's mad ambitions. He combines
personal narration with documents, letters, and testimony
to produce a damning portrait of the Third Reich and a
record of resistance to it. The placement of the documentary material sometimes interrupts the text without
enhancing it, a problem which could have been solved
by reorganization and smoother transitions. However,
it is a highly effective book, an interesting combination
of personal and political history. The translation has
been well done. Its layout is actually an improvement
over the original. (Germany, NF: 1A)

Grund, Josef Carl. <u>Flakhelfer Briel</u>. Ravensburg: Maier,
1973. (Maier)
In August 1944 school boys born in 1928 are drafted
and placed in units around military centers and in cities.
The young anti-aircraft assistants are full of loyalty and
enthusiasm until they learn how they are being used.
Stripped of belief, they become bitter and disillusioned.
(Germany, F: 3A)

_____. <u>Nachruff auf Harald N</u>. Konstanz: Bahn, 1973.
From his home in what later becomes part of the
Soviet Union, Harald's father is called into service by
the Germans and soon killed. Forced to be a man at
nine and to help run the family business, Harald exper-
iences the full horrors of air raids, senseless deaths,
and flight. After difficult years under the Russians,
Harald N. is able to reach West Germany and a new life.
Religious faith sustains the family through terrible times.
(Russia and Germany, F: 3A)

Guillot, René. <u>L'homme de la 377</u>. Paris: Librairie Hachette, 1967.
Fifteen-year-old François and a French-speaking English agent parachuted from London derail four trains
within their first month of working together as alleged
uncle and nephew. Then Pascal demands a cruel sacrifice of François--to plant explosives along a length of
track over which his real uncle and his uncle's friend,
the conductor and mechanic of Engine 377, will be traveling with cargo destined for the German war industry.
François carries out his duty, and both men are wounded.
Blood from an old German railroad guard saves the life
of one of them. Another parachute/resistance story.

This one is mostly heroics without substance. (France,
F: 4E)

Haar, Jaap ter. Boris. Tr. from Dutch by Jürgen Hillner.
Braunschweig: Westermann, 1968. Orig. Dutch: Boris,
1966.
_____. Boris. Tr. from Dutch by Martha Means. New
York: Dell, 1971. (Dell)
_____. Boris. Tr. from Dutch by Joan Verspoor. Paris:
Éditions G.P., 1969.
    The siege of Leningrad is already 500 days old when
Boris and Nadja decide to risk gathering potatoes from
the fields that lie between the two armies. Both are
weak from hunger. Nadja's strength gives out far short
of their goal. Boris looks around in despair and sees
a German soldier standing over them. The soldier and
his comrades bring the children to safety and change forever Boris's ideas about enemies, hatred, and war. The
book is important for its conveying of the terrible suffering of the Russians. The author gives no easy answer to
the ambiguous questions posed by war. (Russia, F: 1A)

Hannam, Charles. A Boy in That Situation. New York:
Harper & Row, 1978. Orig. title: A Boy in Your Situation, 1977.
_____. ... und dann musste ich gehen. Tr. from Eng-
lish by Charles Hannam and Eva-Maria Spaetn. Würzburg:
Arena, 1979.
    Despised as Jews and outsiders in their own land,
Karl Hartland and his sister are sent to safety in England in 1939, there to be considered enemy aliens. After a year in a hostel for refugee boys and training as
a farm worker, Karl is able to enter a boarding school
and recover his interrupted schooling. The book is a
bit tedious, Karl an unlikable hero, but his childhood
memories are honest. He stole, lied, deceived, pulled
practical jokes, talked dirty, and was fascinated by his
bodily functions. That he was a Jew never occurred to
him until it became a reason for others to heap scorn
upon him. (Germany and England, NF: 2M)

Hardey, Evelyn. ... damals war ich fünfzehn. Reutlingen:
Ensslin & Laiblin, 1979.
    Wartime journal of an adolescent girl. In spite of
air raids, burning houses, blocked streets, and nights
spent in bomb shelters, Evelyn is most interested in the
things that interest every teenager--friends, flirtations,

the beginnings of independence. Hardey remembers what
it was like to be a teenager in troubled times. Her autobiographical novel is thus more convincing than Borkowski's reconstructed journal, for she has remained true
to her adolescent narrator while at the same time opening the window for young readers on the deceptions and
brutality of the times. (Germany, F: 1A)

Hartman, Evert. War Without Friends. Tr. from Dutch by
Jan Michael. N. p. , n. d. (typed manuscript from the
publisher of the original: Rotterdam: Lemniscaat) Orig.
Dutch: Oorlog zonder Frieden, 1979.
    This is an unusual book, included here because the
English translation has been made and may become available. It is the story of one of a hated and isolated minority in Holland in World War II, a member of the
Jeugdsturm, the Dutch National Socialist (NSB) youth organization. His father is a small-minded zealot whom
people loathe and fear. His mother is torn between loyalty to her husband and antipathy for his beliefs and
deeds. The book shows Arnold's evolution from unquestioning allegiance through doubt and discomfort and finally
to rejection. Arnold is not a particularly sympathetic
character. No intellectual process brings him to reject
his father's fanaticism but rather his longing to be accepted and his growing distaste at seeing people who
could be his friends hounded by the Gestapo. Not out-
standing but one of a kind and, therefore, interesting.
(Holland, F: 2A)

Haugaard, Erik Christian. Chase Me, Catch Nobody! Boston: Houghton Mifflin, 1980.
    On a field trip in Germany in 1937 a 14-year-old
Danish boy helps a man hunted by the Gestapo to deliver
fake passports. His involvement is unintentional but
deepens when he sees men in black uniforms questioning
his teacher. Afraid he has been found out, Erik runs.
The people who hide him use him to get rid of their secret burden, a young Jewish girl, and then put the Gestapo on the trail of the two fleeing teenagers. (Denmark
and Germany, F: 2A)

_____. The Little Fishes. Boston: Houghton Mifflin,
1967.
_____. Kinder der Strasse: 3 neapolitanische Bettelkinder
versuchen zu überleben. Tr. from English by Christa
L. Cordes. Würzburg: Arena, 1972.

The beggar children of Naples bear a double burden
in war, the extreme poverty that sharpens their wits if
they are to survive and traps them in a circle of hopelessness and the bombings that destroy even the meager
shelter and tenuous ties they are able to arrange in their
lives. They are used and discarded by adults. Peace
will make little difference in their lives other than a release from one kind of fear. Eleven-year-old Guido has
an eloquence, sensitivity, and maturity beyond his years.
A very poetic book about the soul-numbing reality of poverty and war. (Italy, F: 1A)

Hautzig, Esther. The Endless Steppe: Growing Up in Si-
    beria. New York: Thomas Y. Crowell Co. , 1968.
    (Schol. Bk. Serv.)
    Hautzig's family is exiled to Siberia after the Russians
occupy Poland in 1940 and accuse her father of being a
capitalist and an enemy of the people. In spite of their
bitterly hard life in the wastes of Siberia, the family is
fortunate, for they are Jews. Had they not been exiled,
they would have fallen victim to the Germans. Though
her parents suffer in their exile, Esther adapts with the
resilience of youth. She comes to love the steppes and
leaves them with reluctance when the family is repatriated. Hautzig is a fine storyteller. Hers is the only
one of these books to tell of the fate of those whom the
Russians evacuated from Poland. Their fate was grueling, but, ironically, they were lucky, for they had at
least a chance for survival. (Poland and Siberia, NF:
2A)

Held, Jacqueline. La part du vent. Gembloux, Belgium:
    Duculot, 1974. (Duculot)
    In her fictionalized autobiography the author records
her and her mother's war experiences for her own three
children. The narrator is six years old in 1940 when
her father is declared missing in Germany. Except for
the talk she overhears from adults and the temporary
psychosis bombings cause her, she lives the normal life
of a child. In spite of her missing father and an uncle
in the resistance, she is little affected by the war. The
story is episodic rather than linear. Its existential style
would require a mature reader to appreciate it. (France,
F: 4A)

Holman, Felice. The Murderer. New York: Scribner's,
    1978.

The few Jewish families of a mining town in Pennsylvania are despised by the Polish miners, for they are
the merchants who supply the miners and Jews besides.
Hershy longs both to be a part of the Poles and at the
same time to be unique. He is puzzled by the Poles'
scorn and accusation that he killed Christ and saddened
to learn of the cycle of poverty that traps the miners in
debts. In Hershy, Colman has created a delightfully
well-rounded character. Hitler's shadow begins to reach
across the ocean, while at home the Depression nearly
ruins both merchants and miners. A fine, sensitive
book. (U.S., F: 2E)

Jacot, Michael. The Last Butterfly. New York: Ballantine,
     1974. (Ball.)
_____ . Les enfants de Terezin. Tr. from English by
     W. Morganes. Paris: Flammarion, 1974. (Flammarion)
     A washed-up clown finds new joy and purpose in life
when he is forced to perform for the children of Terezin.
Rather than concentrating on the horrors of Terezin,
though he describes them as well, Jacot celebrates the
spark of love and human dignity which even the worst
horrors cannot extinguish. Antonin's pettiness, his pa-
thetic pride dissolve when he takes on the task of bringing some measure of joy to abused children. His training as a clown suddenly takes on deep significance. The
children become the most important audience in the world.
A novel filled with humanity and love in the middle of
squalor. (Czechoslovakia and Terezin, F: 1M)

Janssen, Pierre. A Moment of Silence. Tr. from Dutch
     by William R. Tyler, with photographs by Hans Samson.
     New York: Atheneum, 1970. Orig. Dutch: Een Paar
     minuten is het stil, n. d.
     Simple, moving portrayal of the Dutch response to the
occupation. Janssen chose war memorials throughout
Holland to tell the story of those who fell victim to oppression, those who suffered and died, and those who
stood firm and were killed. His purpose is to show
children the importance of valuing and guarding freedom.
(Holland, NF: 1E)

Joffo, Joseph. Un sac de billes. Paris: J. C. Lattès,
     1973. (Lattès)
_____ . A Bag of Marbles. Tr. from French by Martin
     Sokolinsky. Boston: G. K. Hall, 1975.
_____ . Ein Sack voll Murmeln. Tr. from French by

Lothar von Versen. Berlin: Ullstein, 1975. (Ullstein)
At the end of 1941 two Jewish boys set out from Paris
with fifty francs in their pockets; their goal is the free
zone. They are on their own in a land filled with guns,
prisons, and people in uniforms. At an age when most
children play marbles, they will do anything necessary
to survive. The hostile adult world they view with mock-
ing eyes. (France, NF: 1M)

Karau, Gisela. Janusz K. oder viele Worte haben einen dop-
pelten Sinn. Starnberg: Weismann, 1974. (Weismann).
Originally published in the DDR under the title, Der gute
Stern des Janusz K., n.d.
Interspersed with the story of solidarity and resistance
among the Communist prisoners of Buchenwald are documents typifying the cold, sordid efficiency with which the
Nazis selected and annihilated their victims. Unfortunately, the reproduction is poor, the print tiny, so that
their impact is too often lost. In contrast with most
books for young people, which emphasize that survival
in a concentration camp meant focusing on one's own
needs and which show little organized resistance or co-
hesiveness among the inmates, Janusz K. places its emphasis on the solidarity of the anti-fascist network which
gave strength and hope to its members. The broken
spirits of most accounts are here replaced with effective
moral opposition. The hunger, torture, SS cruelty, and
informers are all here but softened by unity among the
Communists, so much so that the book's credibility suffers. (Buchenwald, F: 2A)

Kerr, Judith. When Hitler Stole Pink Rabbit. New York:
Coward, McCann & Geoghegan, 1972. (Dell)
_____ . Trois pays pour la petite Anna. Tr. from English by Huguette Perrin. Paris: Éditions G. P., 1977.
_____ . Als Hitler das rosa Kaninchen stahl. Tr. from
English by Annemarie Böll. Ravensburg: Maier, 1974.
(Maier)
Because of his outspokenness, Anna's father is a tar-
get for the Nazis as soon as Hitler takes over. Suddenly
and for the first time, the family's Jewishness looms
large in their lives, and they flee to Switzerland. To
protect their neutrality, the Swiss refuse to print Father's writings, and once again the family moves on.
The promise of support in Paris proves illusory, and
after struggling for two years, he moves the family to
England to start once again. Simple story of a privileged

family which recognized the danger in time to flee and
of the difficulties of starting over in a new country. It
has little to say about the horrors which followed Hitler's
rise to power. (Germany, Switzerland, and France, F:
1E)

_____. The Other Way Around. New York: Coward,
McCann & Geoghegan, 1975. (Dell)
_____. Warten bis der Frieden kommt. Tr. from Eng-
lish by Annemarie Böll. Ravensburg: Maier, 1975.
(Maier)
    Sequel to When Hitler Stole Pink Rabbit (listed above).
The family has left France for London. Once again they
leave a life pattern and language for new uncertainties.
While Anna and Max adjust and mature in their new en-
vironment, their parents struggle with loneliness and dis-
couragement. As Germans in a land at war with Germany,
they are viewed as enemies in spite of their having been
hounded from their home. (England, F: 2A)

_____. A Small Person Far Away. London: Collins,
1978.
_____. Eine Art Familientreffen. Tr. from English by
Annemarie Böll. Ravensburg: Maier, 1979. (Maier)
    Final book in the trilogy. Anna's mother attempts
suicide long after the war. Anna must drop her happy,
comfortable life in London to return to Berlin, there to
deal with her mother's anguish and to confront all the
ghosts of her childhood. (Germany, F: 3A)

Kerr, M. E. Gentlehands. New York: Harper & Row,
    1978. (Bantam)
    A refined, wealthy animal lover living quietly in Mon-
tauk, New York, is revealed as a notoriously vicious ex-
SS guard. The story is more about his grandson's growth
than the grandfather's crimes but one of the few novels
for young people to touch on the issue of the many like
"Gentlehands" who were never punished for their crimes
against humanity. (U.S., F: 3A)

Kirchner, Wolfgang. Wir durften nichts davon wissen. Rein-
    beck bei Hamburg: Rowohlt, 1980. (Rowohlt)
    Father's blind obedience, Mother's stubborn naïveté,
and Diti's bitterness against the Poles become maddening
in the course of the book. The Germans of Danzig turned
on their Polish neighbors in 1939 and now in 1945 cannot
understand why they are suffering at the hands of the

Poles. They expect the Poles to forgive and forget and
seem to believe that their own losses and trials now that
the tide has turned make them martyrs. The narrator
is empathetic with his family, relating their wrenching
fate at war's end and at the same time revealing the
German atrocities which led them to this point. (Poland,
F: 1A)

Klaussner, Wolf. Jüppa und der Zigeuner. Aarau: Sauer-
    lander, 1979.
        The inn has been in the Rost family for generations,
but times are hard now that Jüppa's father has refused
to support Hitler in an overwhelmingly pro-National Socialist village. To Jüppa the family's exclusion is not
so important because of his strong bond with his father
and because he enjoys school. Then in August 1944 the
Gestapo knock on the door. They assault Jüppa, checking his penis for circumcision, and take away his sister.
Three of them rape her. After four village Nazis get
drunk in the inn and call Jüppa, "Itzig" ("kike"), his
father tells the boy that his mother was half Jewish. In
the abandoned quarry where Jüppa memorizes his lessons
(so as not to be thrown out of school for being one-quarter
Jewish), Jüppa finds a gypsy boy who has escaped from
a concentration camp. With concern and loving care,
Jüppa shelters the boy, who is even more of an outsider
than he. The end of the war changes little. Jüppa's
school remains authoritarian. He and his father have to
work for the Americans, giving the villagers a new reason to hate them. The Americans are sometimes as vicious as the fascists. When Jüppa can stand the school
no longer, he drops out. Psomi, deeply disappointed by
the Americans, leaves Germany forever. A fine book
in both literary and historical terms. (Germany, F:
2M)

Klein, Mina C., and H. Arthur Klein. Hitler's Hang-ups:
    an Adventure in Insight. New York: Dutton, 1976.
        In spite of the kitschy title and an organization which
sometimes confuses more than clarifies, the Kleins' book
is an interesting correction for young people tempted to
see Hitler as a hero. The authors concentrate on Hitler's
social, sexual, intellectual, and psychological abnormal-
ities. A serious criticism is the lack of footnotes. The
authors cite none of their sources. (Germany, NF: 3E)

Klingler, Maria. Nimm den Diktator und geh: ein Mädchen
    1945. Reutlingen: Ensslin & Laiblin, 1976.

In the last days of the war Uncle Felix's home in the
Tirol becomes a haven for refugees from the east.
Klingler leaves political events largely in the background
and concentrates on the escapades of her young heroine,
Bibi, whose memories have more to do with childhood
adventures than war, though these adventures are shaped
by refugees, food shortages, enemy bombing and rowdy
American soldiers. (Austria, F: 2A)

Kluger, Ruth, and Peggy Mann. The Secret Ship. Garden
City, N.Y.: Doubleday, 1978. (Adapted from The Last
Escape: the Launching of the Largest Secret Rescue
Movement of All Time.) Garden City, N.Y.: Doubleday,
1973.)
An account of one of the daring ship rescues of European Jews arranged by the small but highly organized
Mossad, whose mission was to save Jews. The account
itself is not well written, but three sections are particularly interesting: the introduction, the account of the
Evian Conference (pp. 75-92), and the conclusion. These
three sections are worthy of being read by themselves as
a brief record of the fate of Jews under Hitler. (Romania and Israel, NF: 2E)

Koehn, Ilse. Mischling, Second Degree: My Childhood in
Nazi Germany. New York: Greenwillow Books, 1977.
(Bantam)
_____. Mischling zweiten Grades. Kindheit in der Nazi-
zeit. Reinbeck bei Hamburg: Rowohlt, 1979. (Rowohlt)
Vivid account of a girl whose grandparents are so determined that their daughter and granddaughter survive
that they force Ilse's mother and father to divorce. Not
until after the war does Ilse learn that her father had
one Jewish parent. Ilse does all the right things--Hitler
Youth, children's camp in Czechoslovakia, leadership
training--but only out of necessity and not out of conviction. Because Ilse was not aware of her Jewish heritage,
her story is representative of the many young people who
worked neither for nor against the Nazis, the ordinary
people who just wanted to survive. (Germany, NF: 1A)

Korschunow, Irina. Er hiess Jan. Köln: Benziger, 1979.
A young German girl falls in love with a Polish forced
laborer. Someone informs on them, and they are caught
together by the Gestapo. She escapes with the help of
a sympathetic guard but never learns what happened to
Jan. In telling her story to the farmers who hide her,

Regine speaks for those who believed in their Führer
until signs of Nazi inhumanity reached them on a personal level. (Germany, F: 1A)

Lacq, Gil. Les enfants de la guerre. Paris: Hachette,
    1979. (Hachette)
    Six years old when the Germans occupy Belgium, Gil
adjusts to rationing, air raids, black marketeers, and
resistance fighters as though they were a normal part
of life. The adult author intrudes on the child's-eye
view at times. These passages are always thought provoking but detract from the story and are less accessible
for younger readers. Lacq tells his story with rollicking
good humor, showing that not only does laughter survive
in war, but it is probably even more essential then. An
anti-war book combined with the hilarious memories of
a mischievous child in war. (Belgium, NF: 1A)

Lafitte, Jean. Nous retournerons cueillir les jonquilles.
    Paris: Éditions la Farandole, 1980. (Farandole)
    Fictionalized account of the sabotage of a Nazi mili-
tary base in Saint-Assise, summer 1942. The daring
plan is carried out in broad daylight. All members of
the resistance group are arrested and interned at Mauthausen. The dry style and all-adult cast limit its appeal
to young adults. Originally published in 1959 and abridged
for the new edition. (France, F: 3A)

Larsen-Ledet, Dorte. Zwei Kaffee und ein Berliner. Tr.
    from Danish by Gerda Neumann. Köln: Benziger, 1979.
    Orig. Danish: To kaffe og en berliner, n. d.
    When his son brings home the daughter of the man who
informed on his father in World War II, Mr. Lassen is
incensed. His father had been head of a resistance group
and died in a concentration camp. Grethe's father is
equally concerned, but in his case it is because he wants
to explain himself. As part of a German minority in
Denmark, he had built up a small business making products for the Wehrmacht. Jens's grandfather's group
bombed it. Grethe's father recognized one of the bombers
and reported him. Coming from a Nazi family, her father knew nothing of concentration camps or other atrocities and considered it his patriotic duty to turn in the
criminal. Knowing the story, Jens and Grethe must decide if their friendship is worth the pain it causes their
families. (Denmark, F: 2A)

Lazar, Auguste. Die Brücke von Weissensand. E. Berlin:
Kinderbuchverlag, 1965.
    Unpretentious little book about simple people who act
heroically. When the SS march a column of Auschwitz
prisoners through Weissensand, Frau Kupferschmidt and
two forced laborers hide two of the young women. In
the time they are hiding and in the letters they write
later, they tell of the bestiality of their SS guards, the
horrors of Auschwitz, and their fears of discovery when
they leave Frau Kupferschmidt. The events speak for
themselves, with no need for the author to further glo-
rify or condemn the protagonists. Both horrifying and inspiring. One of the best from the DDR. (Germany,
NF: 1M)

Leitner, Isabella. Fragments of Isabella: a Memoir of
Auschwitz. Edited and with an epilogue by Irving A.
Leitner. New York: Crowell, 1978. (Dell)
    Spare, searing memoir of an Auschwitz survivor. In
few other books are the atrocities described with such
intensity and relentlessness. The shadow of Auschwitz
on the author's life never fades, the pain never dies.
The whole book is a cry of anguish. (Auschwitz, NF:
1M)

Levitin, Sonia. Journey to America. New York: Atheneum,
1970. (Atheneum)
_____. Flucht über den Ozean. Tr. from English by
Hannelore Placzek. Olten u. Freiburg i. Br.: Walter,
1973.
    Though they must leave everything behind, the Platts
are grateful to escape from Germany in 1938. The new
race laws and constant fear of the Gestapo have made
life for the Jews of Berlin a nightmare. While Mr. Platt
travels to America to prepare the way for his family,
Mrs. Platt and the girls become victims of bureaucracy
and indifference in Switzerland. Nearly a year later the
family is reunited in America. (Germany and Switzerland, F: 1E)

Levoy, Myron. Alan and Naomi. New York: Harper & Row,
1977. (Dell).
_____. Der gelbe Vogel. Tr. from English by Fred
Schmitz. Köln: Benziger, 1980.
    Alan risks becoming more of an outsider to help re-
construct the shattered life of a young French refugee.
Having watched the Gestapo club her father to death,

Naomi has retreated into the protection of madness.
With love and patience, Alan covers her scars, but he
cannot heal her nor shield her from a final blow to her
fragile peace. A tender, sensitive story. (U.S., F:
3E)

Limpert, Richard. Über Erich. 1933-1953. Mühlheim a.d.
Ruhr: Anrich, 1972. (Anrich)
In a style similar to Richter's, with a series of short
episodes, the author traces Erich from childhood to sol-
diering to desertion, through years in a Russian POW
camp, and then back home, where he finds the war and
its victims have been forgotten. He is a young man com-
pelled to be a part of something he neither likes nor supports but without the firm conviction that would push him
to resist. He is Everyman in war. A brief, compelling
work. (Germany and Russia, NF: 2A)

Little, Jean. From Anna. New York: Harper & Row, 1972.
(Har-Row)
_____. Alles liebe, deine Anna. Tr. from English by
Karl Hepfer. München: Bertelsmann, 1980.
Beautifully sensitive story of a Jewish family which
immigrates to Canada when Hitler takes over the government in Germany. Anna is the youngest child. All her
life she has felt awkward, inept, stupid. Only her father truly sees the love locked inside her, for her clumsiness and prickliness hide her pain and specialness from
others. In her new home a perceptive doctor and her
new teacher see beyond her protective shell and unlock
her love. (Germany and Canada, F: 3E)

Marder, Eva. Und das war erst der Anfang. Hamburg:
Oetinger, 1981.
Eve is a child who cannot march in step. From her
parents and her grandmother she has learned to be skep-
tical, questioning, and to distrust Hitler and his minions.
One by one her friends abandon her, leaving Eve alone
to swim against the stream. A very fine book about the
gathering storm and the difficulty of following one's conscience. (Germany, F: 1A)

Marignac, Jeannine. Têtu, agent de liaison. Paris: Éditions la Farandole, 1965. (Farandole)
A novel of the resistance in France with flat characters and little adventure. Alain, whose father is a POW,
joins the movement. When he has to go into hiding, his

mother and 9-year-old sister volunteer to help the underground as well. As the Allies march through France,
Alain and his mother take to the barricades to fight for
the liberation of Paris. (France, F: 4A)

Maschmann, Melita. Fazit. Mein Weg in der Hitler-Jugend.
München: Deutscher Taschenbuch Verlag, 1979. (dtv)
Originally published in 1963 under the title, Fazit. Kein
Rechtfertigungsversuch.
_____. Account Rendered; a Dossier on My Former Self.
Tr. from German by Geoffrey Strachan. New York:
Abelard-Schuman, 1965.
_____. Ma jeunesse au service du nazisme. Tr. from
German by Anny Rouffet. Paris: A. Michel, 1963.
     The author, in a letter written after the war to the
Jewish friend she had rejected, tries to clarify her involvement in the Hitler Youth and the process by which
she gradually distanced herself after the war. She explains what sparked the enthusiasm of herself and her
peers but does not examine the monstrous results of their
actions. Her fascination and complete identification with
the Hitler Youth are frightening, for she seems never to
have come to grips with the political and historical reality of the Third Reich. Nevertheless, hers is a point
of view worth examining. (Germany, NF: 2M)

Meltzer, Milton. Never to Forget: the Jews of the Holocaust. New York: Harper & Row, 1976. (Dell)
     Six million Jews were killed, a number too great to
grasp. Meltzer tells the story behind those numbers--
the roots of anti-Semitism, Hitler's campaign against the
Jews, ghettos, Nazi labor and death camps, Jewish resistance. He lets the victims speak for themselves
through songs, poems, letters, diaries, and memoirs.
Perhaps the best book young people can read for an overview of the Holocaust. (Germany, NF: 1A)

Meynier, Yvonne. Un lycée pas comme les autres. Paris:
Presses de la Cité, 1965.
_____. The School with a Difference. Tr. from French by
Patricia Crampton. New York: Abelard-Schuman, 1965.
     Through an exchange of letters between two girls
evacuated to the countryside with their school and their
parents in Rennes, the author gives a humorous and ul-
timately painful picture of a family's experiences during
the last days of the war in France. Paralleling the destruction, suspicion, and hated occupation of the city is

the story of the country school isolated from much of the war yet a place of moral resistance. (France, F: 2A)

_____. Le bonheur est pour demain. Paris: Éditions
G. P. , 1965.
That peace after war is not restored overnight is the theme of this sequel to the book above. Although Rennes has been liberated, blackout curtains are still required, rations are still short, and water is not always available. Collaborators suddenly act like enraged patriots. Looters are common. But families are reunited. People swap resistance stories. Deportees and prisoners return. Odette keeps a journal of all the events from 1944 to 1946. (France, F: 2A)

Moskin, Marietta. I Am Rosemarie. New York: John Day, 1972. (Schol. Bk. Serv.)
Two years of increasing restrictions have made life miserable for the Brenners. Then in August 1942 the Gestapo round them up as part of the plan to make Holland free of Jews. Throughout the years in concentration camps, Rosemarie retains a firm grip on her humanity, helped by the grim determination of her mother and the calm detachment of her father. Humanity, life, and hope triumph in the face of the Nazis' perversity. (Holland and concentration camps, F: 1A)

Mühlenhaupt, Curt. Ringelblumen. Bayreuth: Loewes, 1974.
Humorous memories of a childhood in Berlin in the 1920's. Unemployment, family hard times, fights between Nazis and Communists are all here but seen through a child's eyes. (Germany, F: 3E)

Murray, Michele. The Crystal Nights. New York: Seabury, 1973. (Dell)
In 1938, 15-year-old Elly is tired of the same old talk about the Depression and Hitler. She has her own adolescent interests to pursue and is resentful when the events of Crystal Night intrude on her world. With the arrival of her cousin and aunt, Jews fleeing Germany, and evidence of anti-Semitism in her own hometown, she is forced to face adult reality, but it is primarily Elly's growing sense of responsibility for others that makes the book special. An interesting contrast with books set in Germany in the period 1938-39. (U.S. , F: 2A)

Neumann, Robert. Children of Vienna. New York: Dutton, 1947.

_____. Les enfants de Vienne. Tr. from English by
Marcel Duhamel. Paris: Gallimard, 1968. (Gallimard)
_____. Die Kinder von Wien. Weinheim: Beltz und Gel-
berg, 1979. (Beltz)
    Shattering story of six children who are the flotsam of
war. Though their immediate past histories vary--con-
centration camp, Nazi brothel, Werewolf unit, BDM camp
--they share a common and uniting goal, survival. In
the wreckage of Vienna they conspire to live. A black
American chaplain, overwhelmed by their need, tries to
rescue them but is tangled in a web of soulless bureaucracy. This well-written, shocking book is intended for
a mature audience and is one of the most condemnatory
of war. (Austria, F: 1M)

Noack, Hans-Georg. Die Webers: eine deutsche Familie
1932-45. New ed. Ravensburg: Maier, 1980. (Maier)
Originally published in 1962 under the title, Stern über
Mauer. Zwangsherrschaft und Widerstand, Aufzeichnung-
en aus den Jahren 1932-1961.
_____. Hier à Berlin. Tr. from German (of original
work) by Edith Vincent. Paris: Éditions de l'Amitié,
1976. (Amitié)
    In telling the story of one family, in which one son
chooses the path of zealous nationalism and the other of
resistance, Noack has given the flavor of an era. While
the book is brief, it includes the major elements that convinced most people to either support Hitler or remain silent and others to resist--rise of the National Socialists,
propaganda and censorship, easy victories, persecution
of the Jews, informers, Hitler Youth, and the disastrous
Russian campaign. Chapter headings and sometimes whole
chapters depart from the story to fill in the history of
those years, always with emphasis on the human rather
than the military face of the war.
    A clear distinction must be made between Die Webers
and the first version, Stern über Mauer. The earlier
book begins by drawing a parallel between the DDR in
1961 and Germany under Hitler. The story of the Webers
is framed by the escape to the West of Karl-Heinz's son
and the political oppression under the Soviet system.
The horror of Nazism is diminished by the comparison
with the DDR and the implication that both systems are
equally bad. In the new edition all reference to events
after the war has been omitted. The book ends in 1945
when Russian tanks roll into Berlin. (Germany, F: 1A)

Nöstlinger, Christine. Maikäfer, flieg! Mein Vater, das
    Kriegsende, Cohn und ich. Weinheim: Beltz und Gelberg,
    1973. (dtv)
_____. Fly Away Home. Tr. from German by Anthea
    Bell. New York: Watts, 1975.
        Christel and her family, including her deserter father,
    are living in a Vienna suburb when the Russians take
    over. Lusty, swaggering, and sometimes dangerous, the
    Russian soldiers move into their lives and become part
    of the family to Christel, but it is the dwarf-like, grimy
    cook she loves. An interesting contrast to books by Däs
    and Francke in terms of Nöstlinger's view of the Russian
    occupiers. She sees the Russians not as barbarians but
    simply as men reacting to the war with the whole range
    of emotions common to all soldiers. (Austria, F: 1A)

Oker, Eugen. ... und ich der Fahnenträger. Eine wahre
    Satire. München: Nymphenburger, 1980.
        Satire of a young boy so committed to the National
    Socialist cause that he finds an excuse for every atrocity
    he witnesses or learns of, a 150 percenter. He has no
    doubts and no conscience beyond what he perceives as the
    will of the Führer. He is the sort of child who could be
    expected to turn in his own parents. (Germany, F: 2M)

Orgel, Doris. The Devil in Vienna. New York: Dial Press,
    1978.
_____. Ein blauer und ein grüner Luftballon. Tr. from
    English by Inge M. Artl. München: Bertelsmann, 1980.
        Autobiographical novel of a Jewish family which watches
    the Devil in the form of Hitler take over Austria and
    escapes to Yugoslavia just before the tide breaks over
    them. The story is told through entries in a diary and
    explores the deep and troubled friendship between a Jew-
    ish girl and the daughter of National Socialists. (Aus-
    tria, F: 1A)

Ossowski, Leonie. Stern ohne Himmel. Weinheim: Beltz
    und Gelberg, 1978.
        Five friends, four boys and a girl, find a Jewish boy,
    escaped from a concentration camp, in the cellar which
    houses their secret supply of food. If they hide him they
    are traitors; if they turn him in, he may reveal their
    food cache. In facing moral ambiguity and personal ex-
    pediencey, the young people come to grapple with ques-
    tions of justice and injustice and with what they have be-
    come under the National Socialists. They come to realize

that Abiram is a human being like any of them and that
they owe allegiance to a higher good.   The cast of characters is varied and believable, including the boy who is
willing to betray his friends for a false ideal.   In dealing
with the conflict between questioning patriotism and treason based on justice, the author has raised questions
which it is important for young people to consider.   Published first in the DDR in 1958.   (Germany, F: 1A)

Pausewang, Gudrun. Auf einem langen Weg. Was die Ada-
    mek-Kinder erlebten, als der Krieg zu Ende ging.   Ra-
    vensburg: Maier, 1978.
        Two young refugee children become separated from
    their mother and must make their way alone.   By claim-
    ing that the Russians won the war, Pausewang seems to
    imply that they were and still are the only enemy of
    Germany, that Germany was the victim of their aggres-
    sion.   She has her protagonists show no sympathy for
    the suffering of concentration camp victims.   The om-
    niscient author excuses the atrocities of her countrymen
    by equating them with the hardships of German refugees
    and by her lack of sympathy for victims of the Nazis.
    (Germany, F: 4A)

Pelgrom, Els.   The Winter When Time Was Frozen.   Tr.
    from Dutch by Maryka and Raphael Rudnik.   New York:
    Wm. Morrow, 1980.   Orig. Dutch: De Kinderen von
    het Achtste Woud, 1977.
        On their farm in Holland the Everingen family shelters
    refugees from the battle of Arnhem, a resistance fighter,
    and a Jewish family.   Except when the war intrudes, life
    on the farm is idyllic.   The Everingens are unfailingly
    selfless but somehow less convincing than the Oostervelds
    of Reiss's The Upstairs Room.   The book is simply writ-
    ten and does show some of the problems of survival in
    wartime but suffers from a mechanical translation.   (Hol-
    land, F: 3A)

Pleticha, Heinrich.   Geschichte aus erster Hand: von den
    Entdeckungsreisen bis zum zweiten Weltkrieg.   Würzburg:
    Arena, 1979.
        Pages 176-243 deal with World War II through the first-
    hand reports of eyewitnesses.   Particularly interesting
    are chapters on the Munich Putsch and Hitler's success-
    ful threatening of Schuschnigg.   (Germany, NF: 2A)

Procházka, Jan.   Es lebe die Republik.   Ich, Julina und das

Kriegsende. Tr. from Czech by Peter Vilimek. Recklinghausen: Bitter, 1968. (Maier) Orig. Czech: At'žije
republika. Já a Julina a konec velké války, n. d.
_____. Long Live the Republic (All about Me, and Julie,
and the End of the Great War). Tr. by Peter Kussi.
Garden City, N. Y.: Doubleday, 1973.
       To 12-year-old Olin the end of the great war seems
less important than his own daily struggles with a brutal
father, a gang of older boys who beat him up, and with
the confusion of injustices he witnesses among people he
has always known. He brushes close to death time and
again in the final skirmishes that mark the liberation of
Czechoslovakia from the Nazis. Though the book is
grimly frank, it is lightened by Olin's ability to see the
potential for humor in unlikely situations. An exceptional
novel and one of the best for showing the various ways
people react to war. (Czechoslovakia, F: 1A)

Ray, Hélène. Ionel, la musique et la guerre. Paris: Fantasia Magnard, 1972.
       A Romanian violin prodigy is sent by his parents to
the Paris Conservatory, where they think his being a
Jew will not matter. When the Germans march into
Paris he goes into hiding, protected and encouraged by
people who love him and believe in him as a musician.
Romanticized but very readable story of a young man for
whom music is life, even in wartime. (Romania and
France, F: 2A)

Rees, David. The Exeter Blitz. London: Hamish Hamilton,
1978.
       On the day in 1942 when their town is destroyed in
an air raid, the members of Colin's family are dispersed.
By following each through the course of the bombing and
its aftermath, Rees builds a picture of the nightmare of
a town under fire. The rather dry style is reminiscent
of the British reputation for understatement. (Great
Britain, F: 2A)

_____. The Missing German. London: Dennis Dobson,
1976.
       An 18-year-old German escapes from a submarine
accident off the coast of North Devon. By hiding him,
two boys confront the question of humanity versus country, a moral dilemma which marks them even after the
boy turns himself in. Because the characters are rather
superficially handled, their story is less convincing than

that of Patty and Anton in <u>Summer of My German Soldier</u>
by Bette Greene. (Great Britain, F: 3A)

Reiss, Johanna. <u>The Upstairs Room</u>. New York: Crowell,
    1972. (Bantam)
_____. <u>Und im Fenster der Himmel</u>. Tr. from English
by Inge M. Artl. Köln, Benziger, 1975. (dtv)
    Fictionalized autobiography of two Jewish girls who are
hidden by a peasant couple. The Oostervelds are salt of
the earth, no-nonsense and full of love. Their helping
hand is offered as matter-of-factly as they milk the cows
and feed the chickens. As might be expected, the girls
are bored and restless, longing to live normally. They
learn of concentration camps and the annihilation of the
Jews through resistance newspapers and secretly heard
radio broadcasts, thus giving the reader some background
of the war to accompany the personal story. (Holland,
F: 1A)

_____. <u>The Journey Back</u>. London: Oxford Univ. Pr.,
    1977.
_____. <u>Wie wird es morgen sein?</u> Tr. from English by
Inge M. Artl. München. Deutscher Taschenbuch Verlag
    1980. (dtv)
    Sequel to the title above. Sini, Annie, and their rela-
tives relate the difficulties faced after the war by survivors of Nazi persecution. (Holland, F: 2A)

Renoy, Georges. <u>Hitler</u>. Gembloux, Belgium: Duculot,
    1980. (Duculot)
    The author spent his youth under the occupation in
France and learned to hate Hitler passionately. His
biography of the archfiend is subjective, emotional, and
effective. In evocative prose the author gives not only
a history of the Third Reich but also its ambience.
(Germany, NF: 1A)

Richter, Hans Peter. <u>Damals war es Friedrich</u>. Nürnberg:
    Sebaldus-Verlag, 1961. (dtv)
_____. <u>Friedrich</u>. Tr. from German by Edite Kroll.
    Harmondsworth, Middlesex, England: Kestrel Books,
    1971. (Dell)
_____. <u>Mon ami Frédéric</u>. Tr. and adapted from Ger-
man by Christiane Prélet. Paris: Desclée de Brouwer,
    1963. (Apparently La Farandole has published a new and
better translation in French. I have not seen it, but it
would be worth checking, as this translation leaves something to be desired.)

Slowly, relentlessly, the rabid anti-Semitism of the
Nazis crushes Friedrich, from his birth in 1925 until
his death outside an air raid shelter in 1942. Richter
does not explore his characters or make extraneous judgments. He has a dark tale to tell, a tale of human degradation. He does so through episodes, each fitting
into the others like pieces of a whole. His books remain
some of the most powerful and cautionary. In the hands
of a good teacher, they are the springboard for intensive
discussions. (Germany, F: 1A)

_____. Wir waren dabei. Freiburg i. Breisgau: Herder,
1962. (Arena)
_____. I Was There. Tr. from German by Edite Kroll.
Harmondsworth, Middlesex, England: Kestrel Books,
1972. (Dell)
_____. J'avais deux camarades ...: dix années dans les
Jeunesses hitlériennes. Tr. from German by Alain Royer.
Paris: Éditions Mazarine, 1980.
The narrator goes along with the times, joining the
Jungvolk and marching in step. Along with his best
friends, he is a mirror of the era, for Heinz is the son
of an important Nazi official and Günther of a Communist.
Through their varying perspectives, Richter condemns
the Third Reich without being didactic or judgmental. He
never tries to apologize for or excuse the narrator's
complicity or participation in the Hitler Youth nor for
his moral cowardice. Nor does he try to depict his
characters as victims without will. What he does do is
to explore how it happened that so many were an active
if unwitting part of the Nazi machinery. (Germany, F:
1A)

_____. Die Zeit der Jungen Soldaten. Stuttgart: Thiene-
mann, 1980.
_____. The Time of the Young Soldiers. Tr. from Ger-
man by Anthea Bell. Harmondsworth, Middlesex, England: Kestrel Books, 1976.
As a Hitler Youth the narrator cannot wait to become
a soldier and play heroes' games. The reality is crushing. War is ugly, dehumanizing, grotesque, terrifying.
A good companion piece to Richter's two previous works.
(Germany, F: 1A)
Note concerning the English translation: Anthea Bell
has made some curious cuts, omitting, for example, the
chapter in which a young soldier watches concentration
camp inmates being herded away from the approaching

Russians and observes that it is only fair they should
starve when soldiers are on short rations. She made
cuts in her translation of Nöstlinger's book as well.
The nature of and reason for the cuts will be the subject of a later article.

Rinaldo, C. L. <u>Dark Dreams</u>. New York: Harper & Row,
1974.
_____ . Dunkle Träume. Tr. from German by Hans-
Georg Noack. Baden-Baden: Signal, 1977.
      When his father goes off to war in 1943, Carlo goes
to live with his grandmother in a shabby clapboard house
on an alley way. Physically fragile, he has to cope with
his own fears and with the neighborhood bullies. The
man-child, retarded Joey J., takes Carlo under his wing,
offering him protection from his tormentors and unquestioning friendship. Their simple love leads to unavoid-
able tragedy in a world where innocence is suspect. The
war is far away for Carlo and Joey J., intruding only
in the games they invent and the shattered leg that sends
Carlo's father home. Interesting contrast with the memories of authors living in Europe in 1943-44. (U.S., F:
4A)

Rose, Anne. <u>Refugee</u>. New York: Dial Press, 1977.
      The threat of a Nazi takeover in Belgium spurs Elleke's
parents to send her to relatives in America. As a Jew
she will be safe there. Just six days before Hitler invades, her parents are able to flee to Rio de Janeiro.
Only occasional news reaches her from her best friends
in Antwerp. Lara's letters sound increasingly desperate
in spite of the censors' cuts, and she learns that Ginna
has become a prostitute to survive. Elleke avoids other
refugees in her school, shunning the painful reminder of
the comfortable life she left, but she is frustrated by the
American students' casualness about events in Europe.
After a four-year separation, Elleke and her parents
have grown apart. Her free, confident ways are hard
for them to accept. Only after the end of the war, when
they visit Antwerp and receive letters from survivors
scattered around the globe, do they learn of the Nazi
death camps and the terrible suffering of friends and relatives. (Belgium and U.S., F: 3E)

Rubin, Arnold P. <u>The Evil That Men Do: the Story of the</u>
<u>Nazis</u>. New York: Messner, 1977.
      Overview of the evil deeds of the Third Reich and the

complicity of people in Germany and in the other nations
of the world that stood by and let it happen. The best
and most original chapter is the tenth, in which Rubin
discusses the question of guilt. The chapter would make
an excellent text for classroom discussion. (NF: 1A)

Ruck-Pauquet, Gina. Kralle. München: Lentz, 1979.
     By picturing the war through the eyes of a cat, the
author has told only as much about war as a child could
understand. Kralle's happy world is shattered by air
raids. She becomes part of the refugee tide, is com-
forted by a male cat, suffers the death of her kittens,
learns the soothing security of peace restored. Because
of its simplicity, it is appropriate for children by age
10. (Germany, F: 3E)

Rydberg, Lou and Ernie. The Shadow Army. New York:
     Thomas Nelson, 1976.
     Story of the Greek resistance to the German occupa-
tion. As an adventure story it works in spite of the
Rydbergs' need to interject explanations in such a way
that they interrupt the story. However, had all resistance fighters been as indiscreet as these, they would
have had no success to look back on. Zei's books are
better. (Crete, F: 3E)

Ryss, Yevgeny. Search Behind the Lines. Tr. from Rus-
     sian by Bonnie Carey. New York: Wm. Morrow,
     1974. Orig. Russian: Devočka Iščet otcsa, 1946.
     When the war begins Kolya and his grandfather hide
deep in the forest with the daughter of a colonel. For
three years the old man and the two children live like
Robinson Crusoe. Then a stranger frightens them, and
Kolya, 12, and Lena, 7, set out to search for her father. Their adventures show their ingenuity in the face
of danger and despair. With liberation comes the re-
uniting of families. The characters are believable, the
depiction of the countryside in Russia during wartime
realistic. (Russia, F: 2A)

Sachs, Marilyn. A Pocket Full of Seeds. Garden City,
     N. Y. : Doubleday, 1973.
     _____. Du soleil sur la joue. Tr. from English by
     Rose-Marie Vassallo. Paris: Flammarion, 1980.
     (Flammarion)
     The warning signs are there, but Nicole's father ig-

nores them and his wife's pleading until it is too late.
In November 1943, while Nicole is saying goodbye to a
friend, they and other Jews of Aix-les-Bains are rounded
up. Taken in by a teacher some students call a collaborator, Nicole constructs the events which led to her losing her family. Simple vocabulary and style. (France,
F: 1E)

Samuels, Gertrude. Mottele. New York: Harper & Row,
1976. (NAL)
A 12-year-old orphan joins a band of Jewish partisans
and vows to avenge his murdered family. He manages
to infiltrate a German officers' club by playing his violin, takes his revenge, and finds a new sense of purpose
and loving acceptance among the partisans. Based on the
same incident which inspired Suhl's book Uncle Misha's
Partisans. (Ukraine, F: 2A)

Schönfeldt, Sybil Grafin. Sonderappell: 1945, ein Mädchen
berichtet. Wien: Überreuter, 1979.
In the last months of the war, 17-year-old Charlotte
is sent to do labor service in Oberschlesien. There
military-type discipline precludes discussion. The girls
are controlled body and soul by their National Socialist
leaders, propagandized to make them unquestioningly
obedient. Through the experience of a friend whose
father is arrested, Charlotte begins the painful process
of questioning the foundations of her belief. (Germany,
F: 1M)

Scholl, Inge. Die weisse Rose. Frankfurt: Fischer, 1977.
(Fischer)
_____. Students Against Tyranny: the Resistance of the
White Rose, Munich 1942-1943, rev. ed. Tr. from Ger-
man by Arthur R. Schultz. Middletown, Conn.: Wes-
leyan Univ. Pr., 1970.
_____. La rose blanche. Six Allemands contre le naz-
isme. Tr. from German by Jacques Delpeyrou. Paris:
Éditions de Minuit, 1979.
Scholl's brief book is a eulogy to her brother and sister,
who were executed in 1943 for distributing resistance
flyers at the University of Munich. (Germany, NF: 1M)

Seiffert, Dietrich. Einer war Kisselbach. Reinbeck bei
Hamburg: Rowohlt, 1980. (Rowohlt)
Hans-Joachim Kisselbach patterns himself after Shat-
terhand, the Karl May hero, and blindly and wholeheart-

edly follows that other admirer of Karl May, Adolf Hitler.
On occasion he worries, as when he learns of the defeats
in Russia, but he suppresses his questions with belief in
the Führer and remains loyal to the end, through Hitler
Youth, an elite Nazi school, and service in the Navy. It
is hard to feel empathy for Shatterhand, an average boy
who shelves his mind and falls into the party line. The
book seems almost to excuse rather than expose. (Germany, F: 3M)

Selber, Martin. Geheimkurier A. Reinbeck bei Hamburg:
     Rowohlt, 1976. (Rowohlt) Originally published in 1968
     under the title, Die Grashütte.
     A young boy who dares not to conform is condemned
and rejected in what has always been his vacation paradise. The Hitler Youth he refuses to join and the parents to whom they carry tales cast him in the role of
scapegoat. He follows his conscience and reaps his reward. After he hides a Communist who is on the run,
he discovers that there are others standing aside from
the Nazis and who accept and respect him. Marder's
book on a similar theme is better, but this is still a
good example of both the price and reward of marching
to one's own drummer. First published in the DDR.
(Germany, F: 2E)

Selve, Francine de. La maison du Batiou. Paris: Éditions
     Magnard, 1969.
     A crusty old recluse takes in a refugee boy the other
villagers have turned away. Though it was to have been
for one night, the relationship grows and deepens as the
two find acceptance and love in each other. Bébel becomes a favorite of the villagers, who, through his eyes,
come to view old Batiou differently. As the Germans'
fortunes turn sour, Batiou's open contempt for them becomes dangerous, and Bébel takes on a protective role.
The old man and the young boy are believable and touching. In spite of the war, they are happier together than
ever before in their lives. (France, F: 2A)

Solet, Bertrand. Les jours sombres. Paris: Éditions la
     Farandole, 1974.
     An adventure story about the resistance in France.
Pierre escapes from a German POW camp and goes into
hiding in unoccupied France. When the Germans invade
the rest of the country and arrest the leader of his re-

sistance group, Pierre joins the <u>maquis</u> and becomes head of a band. In the second half of the book he is joined by a 15-year-old fugitive from the SS. Through this device the author is able to describe not only the activities of the <u>maquis</u> but also of the liberation of Paris, for Pierre sends Jean back to Paris to see to his family. A simple book, full of action. No attempt to deal with motivations or ideologies or ambivalences. The good guys are French, the bad guys German. (France, F: 3A)

Spiraux, Alain. <u>Hitler, ta maman t'appelle!</u> Paris: Pierre Belfond, 1976. (Belfond)
_____. <u>Time Out.</u> Tr. from French by Frances Keene. New York: Times Books, 1978.
  In a rundown Jewish quarter of Paris in the late 1930's, a Polish mother begins calling her 9-year-old son Hitler whenever he misbehaves. The epithet becomes an obsession with the small boy and becomes the fantasy he acts out, first in private and then in public. Only the shoemaker, Leibich, understands the grip Moïché's fearful fascination has on the boy, for he secretly shares the preoccupation. He insists that Hitler is in all of us, but only a few recognize it. While Moïché is able to grow out of his obsession, the demon takes over Leibich and drives him to his death. A very sophisticated book. Only a mature young adult could comprehend the psychological intensity and philosophical questions it raises. (France, F: 3M)

Staden, Wendelgard von. <u>Nacht über dem Tal: ein Jugend in Deutschland.</u> Düsseldorf: Diederichs, 1980.
_____. <u>Darkness Over the Valley.</u> Tr. from German by Mollie C. Peters. New Haven, Conn.: Ticknor and Fields, 1981.
  When war sweeps over her family's upper-class farm in Württemberg, 14-year-old Wendelgard comes strongly under the influence of her mother, who had once supported and now opposes the Nazis. A concentration camp is erected nearby, and mother and daughter focus their energies on a dangerous and hopeless task, easing the lot of the prisoners. Only a few of the 2000 men can they actually help. Still, their acts of defiance encourage those they touch and show the possibility of effective resistance. A believable, straightforward account of heroism. (Germany, NF: 1M)

Stokis, Claude. Réseau clandestin. Paris: Hachette, 1967.
    Two schoolmates respond to the call to action they
    read on a flyer dropped by an English plane and form
    their own resistance group. Roland ends up trying to
    hide three Jews, a downed English pilot, and a resistance
    fighter, using the latter's contacts to keep them fed and
    gradually bringing them to safety. Adventure, humor,
    and fairly believable characters make this one of the bet-
    ter French resistance novels. (France, F: 2A)

Suhl, Yuri. On the Other Side of the Gate. New York:
    Watts, 1975.
    In a Jewish ghetto, ringed by barbed wire and guarded
    like a prison, a young couple defy their oppressors by
    bearing and hiding a child. As people are deported from
    the ghetto, the father devises a daring scheme. Through
    contacts with the Polish underground, he smuggles the
    child out in a water barrel. Through this child the com-
    munity will live on. (Poland, F: 1E)

_____. Uncle Misha's Partisans. London: Hamish Ham-
    ilton, 1975.
    A 12-year-old Jewish violinist whose family was killed
    by the Nazis joins a band of Jewish partisans and uses
    his musical talent to take revenge for their deaths. Based
    on an actual episode. Suhl is a fine storyteller, and the
    novel is well written and stirring. (Ukraine, F: 1A)

Szabó, Magda. Abigail. Tr. from Hungarian by Henrietta
    and Géza Engl. Kassel: Corvina, 1970.
    So that he can organize military resistance against the
    fascists, Gina's father puts her in a strict boarding
    school. So hidden and severe is it that he feels sure
    she will not be found and taken hostage. Until she learns
    the reason for his sending her away, she is angry and
    hurt and becomes an outsider in the school. Once she
    holds a new and dangerous secret, she loses her resent-
    ment of the school and learns to think of the girls as
    family. A treacherous young lieutenant she has fallen in
    love with tries to lure her from the school, but she is
    saved by the teacher she has despised and mocked and
    who is now revealed as an important link in the resis-
    tance. Gina's growth is well portrayed by the author.
    With the background of the growing resistance movement
    in Hungary and the treachery of the fascists, the book is
    well worth reading, albeit less from the standpoint of the
    war than that of the characters. (Hungary, F: 3A)

Terlouw, Jan. Michel. Tr. from Dutch by Robert Petit.
  Paris: Éditions G. P. , 1976. Orig. Dutch: Oorlogs-
  winter, 1972.
  _____. Winter in Wartime. New York: McGraw-Hill,
  1976.
      All through the occupation of the Netherlands, Michel,
  16, has held his peace, following his conscience but not
  becoming a part of the resistance. In the winter of 1944-
  45 he takes a stand when he moves to help a friend who
  is caught by the Germans. From then on he is deeply
  involved, unaware that the uncle he trusts is a German
  agent. Rather than making Michel a noble hero, Terlouw
  shows him full of self-doubts. He misjudges people,
  makes mistakes, but tries to act with integrity. (Holland, F: 2A)

Tetzner, Lisa. Erlebnisse und Abenteuer der Kinder aus
  Nummer 67. 9 vol. Aarau: Sauerländer, 1956. (Sauerländer)
      Through the fates and interactions of children of a
  Berlin apartment building, the social history of the period
  between the Weimar Republic and the end of the Second
  World War is brought to life. The simple relationships
  of the children become complicated by political considera-
  tions. One boy's father is interned in a concentration
  camp; some families immigrate to America; one girl is
  of Jewish descent. After the war the survivors meet
  to form a foundation for peace. Each volume can be
  read alone. The nine volumes are now being reissued
  in paperback by Sauerländer Verlag. (Germany, F: 1A)

Toporski, Werner. Mädchen mit Stern. Reutlingen: Ensslin
  & Laiblin, 1980.
      Jonas is a proud member of the Hitler Youth until he
  sees a group of younger boys taunting a Jewish girl and
  instinctively comes to her rescue. From then on he
  must maintain a facade of loyalty to protect Agnes while
  becoming increasingly disillusioned because of her experience. The book shows the dangers and fear faced by
  those who dared care for their fellow human beings under
  the Third Reich. (Germany, F: 1A)

Uhlman, Fred. Reunion. Harmondsworth, Middlesex, Eng-
  land: Penguin Books, 1978. (Penguin)
  _____. L'ami retrouvé. Tr. from English by Léo Lack.
  Paris: Gallimard, 1978.
  _____. Reunion (Versöhnt). Tr. from English and ed. by

Franz Tanzer, Eugen Stamm, and Thomas Stamm.   Köln:
Interorga, 1978.
   Poignant story of a Jewish boy who in 1932 becomes
the close friend and confidant of the son of aristocrats,
only to learn that Konradin's mother is adamantly anti-
Semitic, his father a Nazi supporter, and Konradin himself is convinced that Hitler is the man of the hour.
Though Konradin still loves Hans and wants him to accept him as he is rather than as an impossible ideal,
Hans is too hurt, and the boys drift apart.   Anti-Semitism
makes school impossible for Hans.   In January 1933 he
immigrates to America.   His parents stay behind but
commit suicide when the persecution of the Jews becomes
too terrible.   Years later Hans receives an appeal for
funds from his old school.   Among the list of 26 of the
46 boys in his class who died in the war is Konradin's
name, executed for his part in the plot to kill Hitler.
Uhlman writes poetically and movingly.   So skilled is
his writing that the reader often experiences a shock of
recognition when a character or incident is so right that
the reader feels a part of the story.   (Germany, F: 1M)

Uris, Leon.   Mila 18.   Garden City, New York: Doubleday,
   1961.   (Bantam)
_____ .   Mila 18.   Tr. from English by Jean Nioux.
   Paris: R. Laffont, 1962.   (Laffont)
_____ .   Mila 18.   Tr. from English by Evelyn Linke.
   München: Heyne, 1976.   (Heyne)
      Tragedy of the Jews of the Warsaw ghetto and their
   desperate revolt against death.   (Poland, F: 1M)

_____ .   QB VII.   Garden City, N.Y.: Doubleday, 1972.
   (Bantam)
_____ .   Q.B. 7.   Tr. from English by Jacques Brécard.
   Paris: Le Club français du livre, 1971.   (Laffont)
_____ .   QB VII: Ein Prozess erregt die Welt.   Tr. from
   English by Evelyn Linke.   Zürich: Kindler, 1970.
   (Heyne)
      A doctor sues a New York writer for claiming that he
   performed barbarous experiments on his patients in a
   concentration camp.   During the course of the trial, the
   full story of the atrocities in the camps is revealed
   through the testimony of eyewitnesses. (U.S. , F: 1M)

Vinke, Hermann.   Carl von Ossietzky.   Hamburg: Cecilie
   Dressler, 1978.
      Biography of the journalist and radical democrat who

from 1927-33 edited the Weltbühne, the most well-known
political journal of the Weimar Republic. The paper un-
covered numerous scandals, making Ossietzky a target
of the Nazis. He was among the first to be arrested by
the Nazis. In a concentration camp when he was awarded
the 1935 Nobel Peace Prize, he was released in 1936 due
to public pressure. In 1938 he died as the result of barbarous mistreatment. For its clarification of a dark
time as well as the example of Ossietzky, the book is
an excellent resource. (Germany, NF: 1A)

_____. Das kurze Leben der Sophie Scholl. Ravensburg:
Maier, 1980. (Maier)
Vinke uses the words of peers, family, friends, and
officials to bring Sophie to life. Excerpts from her many
letters and her diary show a serious, clear-eyed, thoughtful young woman, extremely perceptive and concerned
with finding and giving meaning to life. In 1943 she was
executed for distributing anti-Nazi flyers. No attempt is
made to fill in where written and oral records are lacking. Sophie is a quiet heroine whose tragic death continues to stir people. (Germany, NF: 1M)

Vries, Anke de. The Secret of Belledonne Room 16. Tr.
not given. New York: McGraw-Hill, 1979. Orig. Dutch:
Belledonne Kamer 16, 1977.
A half-Dutch, half-French boy finds a bullet and an
intriguing notebook among his grandfather's effects and
decides to investigate. In a village in the French Alps,
he learns of the events his grandfather had witnessed
during the war. A young Jew who had escaped from a
concentration camp fell in love with the daughter of a
wealthy resistance fighter. Girauld killed the young man
because he could not bear to see his daughter involved
with a Jew. The book is similar to Kerr's Gentlehands
in terms of its theme. (France, F: 4A)

Vytrisal, Franz L. Licht in dunkler Nacht. Recklinghausen:
Bitter, 1979.
When the Sudetenland once again becomes Czechoslovakia, the Germans still living there become targets for
revenge. Men and young people are forced to labor for
the Czechs in work camps, industries, and on farms.
In the iron mine at the foot of the Altvatergebirge German laborers toil in a mine made dangerous by reckless
mining during the war. To meet their quota, the workers must face the threat of cave-ins or drowning. Friend-

ship and fraternity eventually conquer the hate and mistrust between the Germans and the Czechs.   Interesting
from the point of view of people on whom the tables were
turned after the war and who considered themselves innocent victims.   (Czechoslovakia, F: 3A)

Walsh, Jill Paton.   Fireweed.   New York: Farrar, Straus
& Giroux, 1969.   (Avon)
     Two teenage refugees from misunderstandings with adults
combine forces in war-torn London.   They set up house
in the abandoned, bombed-out shell of Julie's aunt's
home and revel in their independence.   But theirs is a
fantasy world that is interrupted by the intrusion of a
small child, homesickness, and a punishing air raid.
Both Julie and Bill are young and egocentric, but in each
other they find joy in the middle of destruction.   (Great
Britain, F: 2A)

Werstein, Irving.   The Uprising of the Warsaw Ghetto, November 1940-May 1943.   New York: Norton, 1968.
     Account of the occupation of Poland, the construction
of the Warsaw ghetto, and the brave resistance of the
last 60,000 Jews there.   Werstein has drawn from eyewitness accounts to illustrate the incredible brutality of
the Nazis and the inspiring example of those who resisted.
(Poland, NF: 1A)

Westall, Robert.   Fathom Five.   New York: Greenwillow
Books, 1979.
     A ring of spies in an English harbor town is passing
important military information to the Germans.   A group
of teenagers becomes suspicious and through a series of
dangerous escapades cracks the ring.   As a book about
the war it is minimally interesting, but as a spy story
for teenagers it is first-rate.   (Great Britain, F: 4A)

_____.   The Machine Gunners.   New York: Grosset &
Dunlap, 1975.   (G & D)
_____.   Chassy s'en va t'en guerre.   Tr. from English
by Jean-Marie Léger.   Paris: Éditions Stock, 1978.
     With a live machine gun stolen from a German plane,
a group of children sets up a fortress in the backyard
of a bombed house.   They consider all adults to be cow-
ardly enemies, incapable of fighting the Germans.   A
downed German pilot stumbles into their fortress and
becomes first their prisoner and then their friend.   An
invasion alarm proves to be false, but it brings the group
into a state of battle readiness, an edginess that nearly

ends in their killing the Polish soldiers who are searching
for the missing children and does lead to Rudi's death
(the pilot). The violence of the children's encounters
with those outside their band are reminiscent of Lord of
the Flies. Their dreams and fantasies are of war. The
ugly reality of air raids and sudden death have destroyed
any innocence they once had. (Great Britain, F: 2A)

Wuorio, Eva-Lis. To Fight in Silence. New York: Holt,
Rinehart and Winston, 1973.
     Story of the brave resistance of the Danes to the Nazi
occupiers. Through the device of an extended family,
the author also tells a little about the Norwegian resistance as well. The family's struggle to throw off the
Nazi shackles culminates in their taking part in the evacuation of the Danish Jews. Afterwards they must flee
themselves. (Norway and Denmark, F: 1A)

Yelnik, Odile. "V" comme victoire. Paris: Laffont, 1968.
     A group of school friends practices petty acts of sab-
otage against the Germans until they take on something
larger, hiding a Jewish classmate. Bringing him to
safety puts them in contact with a resistance network,
and the boys devise ingenious schemes to be useful.
(France, F: 2A)

Zassenhaus, Hiltgunt. Walls: Resisting the Third Reich--
One Woman's Story. Boston: Beacon Press, 1974.
(Beacon Pr.)
          . Murs: une femme seule face au 3e Reich.   Tr.
from English by Martine Carré-Bellissant and Nicole
Moreau de Balasy. Paris: Lavauzelle, 1975. (Lavauzelle)
          . Ein Baum blüht im November. Bericht aus den
Jahren des Zweiten Weltkriegs. Hamburg: Hoffmann
und Campe, 1974. (Lübbe)
     Using her knowledge of Scandinavian languages and her
job as a censor, Zassenhaus is able to forward requests
for food to families of Jews in Polish ghettos and to
smuggle vitamins, food, and hope to Norwegian prisoners
of war. Religious faith was important to Zassenhaus, and
at times she sounds rather preachy. However, she showed
a great deal of ingenuity, courage, and determination, and
her story is an important one. (Germany, NF: 2M)

Zei, Alki. Petros' War. Tr. from Greek by Edward Fenton. New York: Dutton, 1972. Orig. Greek: O Mega-
los peripatos tou Petrou, 1971.

_____. La guerre de Petros. Tr. from Greek by Gisèle
Jeanperin. Paris: Éditions G. P., 1976.
_____. Mit dreizehn ein Mann. Tr. from Greek by
Thomas Nicolaou. E. Berlin: Kinderbuchverlag, 1977.
    In German-occupied Greece people are starving, but
a strong resistance movement forms. Petros' involvement begins when he sees the neighbor's German lover
beating the dog her English lover had given her. Zei
writes skillfully. Her story is engaging. In spite of
their age, children are not allowed to be innocent bystanders but are caught up in the struggle against the
occupiers. (Greece, F: 1A)

_____. Wildcat Under Glass. Tr. from Greek by Edward
Fenton. New York: Holt, Rinehart and Winston, 1968.
Orig. Greek: To Kaplani tis vitrinas, 1963.
_____. Le tigre dans la vitrine. Tr. from Greek by
Gisèle Jeanperin. Paris: Éditions la Farandole, 1973.
    Splendid story of children who are called upon to do
their part in the struggle against fascism and who, for
the most part, behave heroically. The exceptions are
the child of a Greek fascist and a young girl who is
swayed by flattery to join a fascist youth group. The
story takes place before the German occupation. (Greece,
F: 1A)

Ziemian, Joseph. Sag bloss nicht Mosche zu mir, ich heisse
Stasiek. Tr. from Polish by Eckard Birnstiel. Berlin:
Basis, 1979. (Basis)
    Straightforward, moving report on the Jewish children
who survived the destruction of the Warsaw ghetto and
went into hiding under the very nose of the Nazis. (Poland, NF: 1A)

ABBREVIATIONS FOR PAPERBACK PUBLISHERS

American

Archway	Archway Paperbacks
Atheneum	Atheneum Publishers
Avon	Avon Books
Ball.	Ballantine Books
Bantam	Bantam Books, Inc.
Beacon	Beacon Press, Inc.
Berkley	Berkley Publishing Corp.

Dell	Dell Publishing Co. , Inc.
G & D	Grosset & Dunlap, Inc.
Har-Row	Harper & Row Publishers, Inc.
NAL	New American Library
PB	Pocket Books, Inc.
Penguin	Penguin Books, Inc.
Schocken	Schocken Books, Inc.

French

Amitié	Éditions de l'Amitié
Belfond	Éditions Pierre Belfond
Duculot	Éditions J. Duculot (Belgium)
Epi	Éditions de l'Epi
Farandole	Éditions la Farandole
Flammarion	Librairie E. Flammarion et Cie.
Gallimard	Éditions Gallimard
Hachette	Hachette
Laffont	Éditions Robert Laffont
Lattès	Éditions J. C. Lattès
Lavauzelle	Éditions Charles Lavauzelle
L. G. F.	Librairie Générale Française
Magnard	Éditions Magnard
Stock	Éditions Stock

German

Arena	Arena-Verlag Georg Popp
dtv	Deutscher Taschenbuch Verlag
Lübbe	Gustav Lübbe Verlag
Maier	Otto Maier Verlag
Neithard	Neithard Anrich Verlag
Rowohlt	Rowohlt Taschenbuch Verlag
Sauerländer	Sauerländer Verlag
Ullstein	Ullstein Taschenbuch-Verlag

U.S. DISTRIBUTORS OF EUROPEAN BOOKS

Adco International Co.
80-00 Cooper Ave., Bldg. 3
Glendale, New York 11385

The Baker & Taylor Co.
Div. of W. R. Grace & Co.
1515 Broadway
New York, New York 10036

Booksmith Inc.
225 Park Ave. S.
New York, New York 10003

Iaconi Book Importers
300 Pennsylvania Avenue
San Francisco, California 94107

Key Book Service Inc.
425 Asylum St.
Bridgeport, Connecticut 06610

World Books Import & Export Inc.
51 E. 73 St.
New York, New York 10021

DIRECTORY OF FOREIGN PUBLISHERS

Abelard-Schuman: Abelard-Schuman, Ltd., Furnival House, 14-18 High Holborn, London, W. C. 1, England.

Alsatia: Alsatia SA, 10 rue Bartholdi, F-68001 Colmar, France.

Editions de l'Amitié: Editions de l'Amitié, G-T Rageot, 21 rue Cassette, F-75006 Paris, France.

Anrich: Neithard Anrich Verlag, Neunkirchen 5, D-6101 Modautal 3, West Germany.

Arena: Arena-Verlag Georg Popp, Talavera 7-11, D-8700 Würzburg 1, West Germany.

Bahn: Friedrich Bahn Verlag GmbH, Zasiusstr. 8, Postfach 1186, D-7550 Konstanz, West Germany.

Basis: Basis-Verlag, Postfach 645, D-6100 Berlin 15, West Germany.

Pierre Belfond: Editions Pierre Belfond, 3 bis passage de la Petite-Boucherie, F-75006 Paris, France.

Beltz und Gelberg: Beltz Verlag, Am Hauptbahnhof 10a, Werderstr., Postfach 1120, D-6940 Weinheim, West Germany.

Benziger: Benziger Verlag, Martinstr. 16, D-5000 Köln, West Germany.

Bertelsmann: C. Bertelsmann GmbH, Neumarktstr. 18, D-8000 München, West Germany.

Bitter: Georg Bitter Verlag, Herner Str. 62, Postfach 248, D-4350 Recklinghausen, West Germany.

Le Club Français du Livre: Le Club Français du Livre, 7
& 9 rue Armand-Moisant, F-75015 Paris, France.

Collins: William Collins Sons & Co. Ltd. , 14 St. James's
Pl. , London SW1A 1PS, England.

Corvina: Corvinaverlag, Korbacher Str. 235, D-3500 Kassel,
West Germany.

dtv: Deutscher Taschenbuch Verlag, Friedrichstr. 1a, Postfach 400422, D-8000 Munchen 40, West Germany.

Desclée de Brouwer: Desclée de Brouwer SA, 76 bis rue du
Saint-Pierre, F-75007 Paris, France.

Deutsche Verlags-Anstalt: Deutsche Verlags-Anstalt GmbH,
Neckarstr. 121-125, Postfach 209, D-7000 Stuttgart, West
Germany.

Diederichs: Eugen Diederichs Verlag, Brehmpl. 1, Postfach
140163, D-4000 Düsseldorf 14, West Germany.

Dennis Dobson: Dennis Dobson, 80 Kensington Church St. ,
London W8 4BZ, England.

Cecilie Dressler: Cecilie Dressler Verlag, Poppenbütteler
Chaussee 55, Postfach 220, D-2000 Hamburg 65, West
Germany.

Duculot: Editions et Imprimerie J. Duculot SA, rue de la
Posterie, Parc industriel, B-5800 Gembloux, Belgium.

EPI: Epi SA Editeurs see Desclée

Ensslin & Laiblin: Ensslin und Laiblin Verlag GmbH & Co. ,
Harretstr. 6, Postfach 754, D-7412 Eningen, West Germany.

Fantasia Magnard see Magnard

Farandole: Editions La Farandole, 146 rue du Faubourg
Poissonnière, F-75010 Paris, France.

Fischer (Frankfurt):   S. Fischer Verlag, Geleitsstr. 25,
Postfach 700480, D-6000 Frankfurt am Main 70, West
Germany.

Fischer (Göttingen): W. Fischer Verlag, Stresemannstr. 30, Postfach 621, D-3400 Göttingen, West Germany.

Flammarion: Flammarion et Cie., 26 rue Racine, F-75278 Paris, France.

Editions G. P.: Editions G. P., 8 rue Garancière, 75006 Paris, France.

Gallimard: Editions Gallimard, 5 rue Sébastian-Bottin, F-75007 Paris, France.

Hachette: Librairie Hachette, 79 blvd. St-Germain, F-75006 Paris, France.

Hamish Hamilton: Hamish Hamilton Ltd., Garden Ho, 57-59 Long Acre, London WC2E 9JL, England.

Herder: Verlag Herder GmbH & Co., Hermann-Herder-Str. 4, D-7800 Freiburg im Breisgau, West Germany.

Heyne: Wilhelm Heyne Verlag, Türkenstr. 5-7, Postfach 201204, D-8000 München 2, West Germany.

Hodder and Stoughton: Hodder and Stoughton Ltd., Mill Rd., P. O. Box 700, Dunton Green, Sevenoaks, Kent TN13 2YA, England.

Hoffmann und Campe: Hoffmann und Campe Verlag, Harvestehuder Weg 45, D-2000 Hamburg 13, West Germany.

Interorga: Eduard Hermansen (Interorga), Belvederestr. 59, Postfach 450324, D-5000 Köln 41, West Germany.

Jugend und Volk: Jugend und Volk Verlagsgesellschaft mbH, Tiefer Graben 7-9, A-1014 Wien, Austria.

René Julliard: Editions René Julliard, 8 rue Garancière, F-75006 Paris, France.

Kestrel Books see Penguin

Kinderbuchverlag: Der Kinderbuchverlag Berlin, Behrenstr. 40-41, Postfach 1225, DDR-108 Berlin.

Kindler: Kindler Verlag GmbH, Leopoldstr. 54, Postfach 401043, D-8000 München 40, West Germany.

Albrecht Knaus: Albrecht Knaus Verlag, Postfach 520455,
D-2000 Hamburg 52, West Germany.

Krüger: Wolfgang Kruger Verlag, Geleitsstrasse 25, Postfach
700480, D-6000 Frankfurt am Main 70, West Germany.

L. G. F.: Librairie Générale Française, 12 rue François 1er,
75008 Paris.

R. Laffont: Les Editions Robert Laffont, 6 pl. St-Sulpice,
F-75006 Paris, France.

J. C. Lattès: Editions Jean-Claude Lattès, 91 rue du Cherche-
Midi, F-75006 Paris, France.

Lavauzelle: Charles Lavauzelle, B. P. 8, F-87350 Panazol,
France.

Lentz: Georg Lentz Verlag, Romanstr. 16, D-8000 München,
West Germany.

Loewes: Loewes Verlag KG, Bahnhofstr. 15, Postfach 2606,
D-8580 Bayreuth, West Germany.

Lübbe: Gustav Lübbe Verlag GmbH, Scheidtbachstr. 29-31,
Postfach 200127, D-5060 Bergisch Gladbach 2, West Germany.

Luchterhand: Hermann Luchterhand Verlag, Heddesdorfer
Str. 31, Postfach 1780, D-5450 Neuwied 1, West Germany.

Magnard: Les Editions Magnard Sàrl, 122 blvd. St-Germain,
F-75279 Paris, France.

Maier: Otto Maier Verlag, Marktstr. 22-26 & Robert Bosch
Str. 1, Postfach 1860, D-7980 Ravensburg, West Germany.

Editions Mazarine: Editions Mazarine, 34 ave. Marceau,
F-75008 Paris, France.

A. Michel: Albin Michel, 22 rue Huyghens, 75014 Paris,
France.

Editions de Minuit: Les Editions de Minuit SA, 7 rue
Bernard-Palissy, F-75006 Paris, France.

Fernand Nathan: Fernand Nathan Editeur, 9 rue Méchain,
F-75014 Paris, France.

Nymphenburger: Nymphenburger Verlagshandlung, Romanstr. 16, D-8000 München 19, West Germany.

Oetinger: Verlag Friedrich Oetinger, Poppenbütteler Chaussee 55, Postfach 220, D-2000 Hamburg, West Germany.

Oxford Univ. Pr.: Oxford University Press, Walton St., Oxford OX62 6DP, England.

Penguin: Penguin Books Ltd., 536 King's Rd., London SW10 OUH, England.

Presses de la Cité: Les Presses de la Cité, 8 rue Garancière, F-75006 Paris, France.

Roderberg: Roderberg-Verlag GmbH, Schumannstr. 56, Postfach 4129, D-6000 Frankfurt am Main 1, West Germany.

Rowohlt: Rowohlt Taschenbuch Verlag GmbH, Hamburger Str. 17, Postfach 1349, D-2057 Reinbeck bei Hamburg, West Germany.

Sauerländer: H.R. Sauerländer und Co., Finkenhofstr. 21, D-6000 Frankfurt am Main 1, West Germany.

Schaffstein: Hermann Schaffstein Verlag, Postfach 1283, D-4600 Dortmund 1, West Germany.

Scherz: Scherz Verlag GmbH, Stievestr. 9, D-8000 München 19, West Germany.

Schwabenverlag: Schwabenverlag AG, Senefelderstr. 12, Postfach 4280, D-7302 Ostfildern 1, West Germany.

Editions du Seuil: Editions du Seuil, 27 rue Jacob, F-75261 Paris, France.

Signal: Signal-Verlag Hans Frevert, Balger Hauptstr. 8, Postfach 813, D-7570 Baden-Baden, West Germany.

Spectrum: Spectrum Verlag Stuttgart Gmbh, Friedrichstr. 16-18, Postfach 1940, D-7012 Fellbach 4, West Germany.

Stock: Editions Stock, 14 rue de l'Ancienne Comédie, F-75006 Paris, France.

Thienemann: K. Thienemanns Verlag, Blumenstr. 36, D-7000 Stuttgart 1, West Germany.

Überreuter: Verlag Carl Überreuter, Alserstr. 24, Postfach
60, A-1095 Wien, Austria.

Ullstein: Verlag Ullstein GmbH, P.O. Box 110303, D-1000
Berlin 11, West Germany.

Union: Union Verlag Stuttgart, Alexanderstr. 51, Postfach
326, D-7000 Stuttgart 1, West Germany.

Walter: Walter-Verlag GmbH, Erwinstr. 58-60, D-7800
Freiburg-im-Breisgau, West Germany.

Weismann: Weismann Verlag-Frauenbuchverlag GmbH, Kreitt-
mayrstr. 26, D-8000 München, West Germany.

Westermann: Georg Westermann Verlag, Druckerei und Kar-
tographische Anstalt, Georg-Westermann-Allee 66, D-3300
Brunswick, West Germany.

Wissenschaft und Politik: Verlag Wissenschaft und Politik,
Berend von Nottbeck, Salierring 14-16, D-5000 Köln,
West Germany.

CURRICULUM SOURCES

CHAPTER 1: HITLER AND HIS CREW

"The Anatomy of Nazism," by Earl Raab. The Anti-Defamation League of B'nai B'rith, 823 United Nations Plaza, New York, New York 10017.
>Booklet examining the roots of Nazism, life under the Nazis, and propaganda techniques. A filmstrip based on the booklet (50 frames, color) is also available.

"Hitler's Executioners" (78 min., b & w). Macmillan Audio Brandon, 34 MacQuesten Parkway, South, Mount Vernon, New York 10550.
>Documentary film on the rise and fall of the Third Reich, using film clips from the era.

"Nazi Germany." Great Britain: Longman, 1972. Social Studies School Service, 10,000 Culver Blvd., Dept. T1, P.O. Box 802, Culver City, California 90230
>Nine study units to help teachers explain Nazi Germany. The units include Hitler Youth, Nazi Education Factors in the Rise of Hitler, Hitler--Contemporary View, Hitler--Retrospective View, The SS, Nazi Philosophy--General Views, Nazi Philosophy--Anti-Semitism, and Anti-Semitism in Practice.

"The Rise of the Nazi Horror: Who Was Responsible?" by Bernard Feder. (Excerpted from Viewpoints in World History. Litton Educational Publishing, 1974.) American Book Company, 7625 Empire Dr., Florence, Kentucky 41042.
>Booklet using primary sources to examine the rise of Nazism, the complicity of ordinary people, and finally the massacre at My Lai. The author poses probing questions for discussion.

"The Third Reich in Perspective: A Resource Unit on Nazism," by Gertrude Noar. Anti-Defamation League of B'nai

B'rith, 823 United Nations Plaza, New York, New York
10017.
>Suggestions for teaching activities, lists of audio-
visual materials, and an extensive bibliography.

"The Wave." ABC Theater for Young Americans, October
4, 1981. ABC Television Network, 1330 Ave. of the Amer-
icas, New York, New York 10019, Attn: ABC Theater for
Young Americans (The Wave).
>TV drama based on the experience of a high school
teacher in California who decided in 1969 to show his
class how easily people can fall under the sway of a
charismatic tyrant. His students very quickly began
acting like the Hitler Youth they had criticized. Prime
Time School Television, 40 E. Huron, Chicago, Illi-
nois 60611, has published a guide to the program.

CHAPTER 2: THE HOME FRONT, CIVILIAN VICTIMS OF WAR

"The Anatomy of Nazism" (see entry under Chapter 1 sources).

"Nazi Germany" (see entry under Chapter 1 sources).

"Nazi Germany: Years of Triumph" (Part II of "The Rise
and Fall of the Third Reich," 58 min., 1968). Films Inc.,
165 W. 46th St., Room 1105, New York, New York 10036.
>Based on William Shirer's book. This segment of the
film concentrates on the years between 1933 and 1939
when the Third Reich was showing its true face yet
encountering little opposition.

CHAPTER 3: CONTROLLING OPPOSITION

"The Anatomy of Nazism" (see entry under Chapter 1 sources).

"The Arrival of Hitler" (12 min., b & w). Macmillan Audio
Brandon, 34 MacQuesten Parkway, South, Mount Vernon,
New York 10550.
>The first part of the propaganda film, "Triumph of
Will." Shows the adulation of the crowd for Hitler
and was used as a propaganda film during World War
II.

"But Never Forget" (30 min., kinescope). Jewish Welfare
Board, 15 E. 26th St., New York, New York 10010.

CBS television documentary showing the concentration camps in Buchenwald, Dachau, and Mauthausen.

"The Rise of Hitler" (Part I of "The Rise and Fall of the Third Reich"--see entry under Chapter 2 sources).

CHAPTER 4: THE FATE OF THE JEWS

"The Eighty-first Blow (120 min.; shorter version, 90 min., b & w). Alden Films, 7820 20th Ave., Brooklyn, New York 11204.
> Uses the Nazis' own documentation to show their atrocities against the Jews. Explicit footage makes the film painful to watch. For a mature audience. In Hebrew, with English subtitles.

"Genocide" (52 min., color). Canadian Jewish Congress, National Holocaust Remembrance Committee, 1590 Ave. Dr. Penfield, Montreal, Quebec H3G 1C5.
> Part of the "World At War" series produced by Thames Television of London. This segment shows the Nazi persecution of the Jews and includes interviews with survivors of Auschwitz, colleagues of Adolf Eichmann and Heinrich Himmler, a camp guard, and Lord Avon. Appropriate for high school.

"The Holocaust: A Study of Genocide." New York: Board of Education of the City of New York, Division of Curriculum and Instruction, 1979.
> An entire teaching unit on the Holocaust, with suggested lesson plans for social studies and literature, reading selections, learning activities, annotated bibliography, filmography, sources of additional support materials, and an index.

"Human Rights and the Holocaust," by Lillian Dubsky. Educational Activities, Inc., P.O. Box 392, Freeport, New York 11520.
> Eight stories of Holocaust survivors. Four of the stories are on cassette, four in a booklet. Six transparencies and a teacher's guide complete the set.

CHAPTER 5: TO THE VICTOR
BELONG THE SPOILS

"The Song and the Silence" (80 min.). American Jewish

Congress, 15 E. 84th St., New York, New York   10028.
>The ruthlessness of the Nazis in Eastern Europe is
>shown through this film about a small Hassidic com-
>munity destroyed by the Nazis.

CHAPTER 6:   FIGHTING BACK, RESISTANCE
TO THE NAZIS

"Act of Faith" (28 min., b & w).   Canadian Jewish Congress,
National Holocaust Remembrance Committee, 1590 Ave. Dr.
Penfield, Montreal, Quebec H3G 1C5.
>CBS television film showing the activities of the Dan-
>ish resistance movement and the rescue of the Jews
>of Denmark.

"Resistance: Jewish Ghetto Fighters and Partisans" (85-
frame filmstrip, 18-min. cassette, b & w).   Jewish Media
Service, 15 E. 26th St., New York, New York   10010.
>Resistance in Eastern Europe.   A "Teacher's Guide
>for Pupil Activities" includes activities, discussion
>ideas, and a list of books and films for further study.

CHAPTER 7:   THE CANNON FODDER

"Joseph Schultz" (14 min., color).   Anti-Defamation League
of B'nai B'rith, 823 United Nations Plaza, New York, New
York   10017.
>Based on an actual incident during World War II when
>a German soldier refused to participate in the execu-
>tion of innocent villagers and was killed by his com-
>rades.